ML

REA

ACPL ITEM
DIS

D0622710

The Atom Bomb Spies

By the same Author

The Rise of Castlereagh · The Russian Journals of Martha and Catherine Wilmot (with the Marchioness of Londonderry) · More Letters from Martha Wilmot: Impressions of Vienna (with the Marchioness of Londonderry) · The Empress Catherine and Princess Dashkov · Air Defence and the Civil Population (with G. R. Falkiner Nuttall) · Londonderry House and its Pictures · Princess Lieven · Judge Jeffreys · Mexican Empire · A Victorian Historian: Letters of W. E. H. Lecky · Privacy and the Press · John Law · The Trials of Oscar Wilde · Mr and Mrs Beeton · Cases that Changed the Law · Carson · The Trial of Craig and Bentley · United in Crime · The Strange Death of Lord Castlereagh · The Trial of Sir Roger Casement · Sir Patrick Hastings: His Life and Cases · Recent Developments in Historical Method and Interpretation · Simla and the Simla Hill States Under British Protection · An International Case Book of Crime · The Quiet Canadian · Oscar Wilde: The Aftermath · A History of Pornography · Norman Birkett · Cynthia · The Story of Lamb House · Lord Reading · Henry James at Home · Strong for Service: The Life of Lord Nathan of Churt · The Other Love · Their Good Names · Stalin: The History of a Dictator · Baldwin: The Unexpected Prime Minister · Oscar Wilde: A Biography · British Air Policy between the Wars 1918–1939 · Crime Has Its Heroes · Solitary in the Ranks: Lawrence of Arabia as Airman and Private Soldier · The Londonderrys: A Family Portrait

The Atom Bomb Spies

BY

H. MONTGOMERY HYDE

HAMISH HAMILTON

LONDON

ALLEN COUNTY PUBLIC LIBRARY
EORT WAYNE, INDIANA

First published in Great Britain 1980
by Hamish Hamilton Ltd
Garden House 57–59 Long Acre London WC2E 9JZ

Published in Canada by Nelson Canada
81 Curlew Drive, Don Mills, Ontario M3A 2R1

Copyright © 1980 by Harford Productions Ltd

British Library Cataloguing in Publication Data

Hyde, Harford Montgomery
    The atom bomb spies.
    1. Espionage, Russian – History – 20th century
    2. Atomic weapons – History
    I. Title
    327'.12'0947   UB271.R9
    ISBN 0-241-10271-5

Text set in 10/12 pt Linotron 202 Plantin,
printed and bound in Great Britain
at The Pitman Press, Bath

2141678

To Sir William Stephenson, D.F.C., M.C., Order of Canada,
who inspired the writing of this book

Contents

Illustrations

Acknowledgements

First, I wish to express my sincere thanks to my old friend and war-time chief Sir William Stephenson ("Intrepid"), whose timely presence in Ottawa in 1945 largely contributed to saving the life of the Russian defector Igor Gouzenko, who might otherwise have beeen "liquidated" by his Soviet masters. Sir William, recently invested with the Order of Canada at his home in Bermuda by the Canadian Governor-General for his war-time services to allied security intelligence and "Special Operations", has kindly given me the benefit of his extensive knowledge and experience in the fields of espionage and counter-espionage.

His help has been invaluable to me in writing this book, which was initially undertaken at his suggestion. I had originally intended to confine it to the story of Gouzenko's defection and the immediate aftermath under the title of *Intrepid's Last Case;* but as the writing proceeded the narrative came to include the activities of all the alleged atom bomb spies both in North America and Britain and consequently required a more comprehensive title.

For permission to quote from letters and other documents in copyright, I am indebted to the following: Mr Robert and Mr Michael Meeropol (the letters of Julius and Ethel Rosenberg), the Canadian National Archives (the diaries of William Mackenzie King), the U.S. Department of Justice (papers concerning Harry Gold, Klaus Fuchs, Benjamin and Ruth Greenglass, and the Rosenbergs in the FBI archives in Washington, D.C.), and the Public Record Office of England (Commonwealth departmental correspondence).

Of the many printed sources which I have used I wish particularly to mention the information I have received from *The Traitors* (1952) by Alan Moorehead and *The Unquiet Death of Julius and Ethel Rosenberg* (1975) by Alvin H. Goldstein.

I would also like to thank the following for their assistance in various ways: Mr Cedric Belfrage, Mrs A. Colombini, Mr Ernest Cuneo, Mr Richard Deacon, Professor J.L. Granastein, Dr Norman Hillmer, Mr Robert Lamphere, Miss Hannah Longrigg, The Rt. Hon. Malcolm MacDonald, Sir Rudolf Peierls, Mr Marshal Perlin, Sir Michael Perrin, Mrs Peter Roberts and Professor Allen Weinstein.

Acknowledgements

Finally, I have to thank my wife for her painstaking help at every stage, which has included the typing of the original draft and for making many useful criticisms and suggestions of which I have gladly taken advantage.

H.M.H.

April, 1980

CHAPTER ONE

The Defector

[1]

About eight o'clock in the evening of 5 September 1945, a grave-eyed, serious young man of twenty-five left the Soviet Embassy in Ottawa, as it happened, for the last time. His name was Igor Sergeievitch Gouzenko and he worked for the Military Attaché, Colonel Nikolai Zabotin, as principal cypher clerk. The embassy building, situated at 285 Charlotte Street, was a three-storey structure of red brick with a sloping slate roof and white porches, of a type favoured by well-to-do citizens in the late nineteenth century, when large homes housed large families. Early in 1942 it had become the diplomatic headquarters of the Soviet Ambassador, Georgei N. Zarubin. The main portion of the house was used by the Ambassador and his diplomatic and personal staff, while the rear wing, formerly the kitchen and servants' quarters, was protected by iron bars and steel shutters across the windows and was closed off from the rest of the embassy by double steel doors. This was the secret cypher department, where the technical work of encyphering and decyphering the secret and confidential cables and des-patches which passed between Ottawa and Moscow was carried on. The Embassy's secret files were also located in this wing, to which access was gained by pressing a bell concealed under the banister of the main staircase, when the steel doors would be opened by the door-keeper, who first looked through a spy hole to approve members of the embassy staff, of whom Gouzenko was one and who had a small office in Room 12 in this wing. Here he did most of his work, and every night the code and cypher books which he used would be placed in a sealed bag. The bag was then handed over to the duty officer who would lock it in a large steel safe along with the daily cables to and from the Directorate of Military Intelligence in Moscow and also Colonel Zabotin's duty diaries and reports, to all of which Gouzenko had access, as well as other documents kept in the secret registry.[1]

The Military Attaché worked mostly from his house, 14 Range Road, in another part of the town, where there was a camera and other equipment for photographing documents. Gouzenko would call there, often several times a day, with decyphered cables from the Embassy and he would get from Colonel Zabotin his cables for encyphering and despatch to Moscow. In fact, Colonel Zabotin's duties went far beyond the normal role of a Military Attaché in so far as he directed his country's complex and far-reaching espionage network in Canada in addition to his overt military functions. Although Zarubin was aware of these under-cover operations, the ambassador was not personally concerned with them, although he had an overall responsibility for his mission's secret intelligence work. According to Gouzenko, Zarubin had no right of access to the secret rooms in the special wing of the Embassy, but it is more likely that he deliberately kept away from them so as to avoid any risk of compromising himself. Incidentally, among others they accommodated was the local NKVD (secret police) chief Vitali Pavlov, who was nominally Second Secretary in the Embassy. It may be added that Georgei Zarubin was a man of outstanding ability, since he began his career as a factory hand at the age of thirteen and was to end up as a Deputy Foreign Minister twenty-seven years later. He was also to serve as his country's ambassador in London and Washington.

It is a cardinal rule of secret intelligence that sources of information must be carefully protected, and on one occasion Colonel Zabotin was rebuked by the Director in Moscow for indicating the source of a report on credits to finance post-war trade between Great Britain and the Soviet Union, which on the face of it must have come from an employee in the British High Commission in Ottawa. Although young Gouzenko was ignorant of the identity of most of the secret agents mentioned in Zabotin's cables, since they were always referred to by different code names, he had soon gained a very clear idea from the nature of his work of the details of the espionage system which his immediate chief was carrying on against a people whose way of life he had come to respect and admire, although Colonel Zabotin had done his best to disabuse him of any such ideas at a recent staff conference. 'Yesterday they were allies, today neighbours', said the Military Attaché. 'Tomorrow they will be our enemies.' But Gouzenko remained unconvinced.

A graduate in engineering, Igor Gouzenko had been carefully screened and trained in the Soviet Military Intelligence Academy in Moscow before being sent to Ottawa in the summer of 1943, being listed as a 'civilian employee', although he held the rank of Lieutenant in the Soviet army. He had wished to take his wife and mother with him, but so far as his mother was concerned he was told that this was impossible. ('Wives yes, but mothers no.') The reason was soon apparent, namely that Gouzenko's mother must remain behind as a hostage or insurance against his possible defection while serving abroad. But it was a great consolation that his wife Svetlana, whom he called Anna, and who was pregnant with her first child at this time, could be with him in Ottawa, although she had to follow on by sea while Igor flew to Canada by the arctic route accompanied by Colonel Zabotin, who was taking up his appointment at the same time.

Igor was waiting for his wife when she arrived and shortly before their first child Andrei was born, they settled into a small apartment in a suburb of the capital. They were very happy in their new life and as time passed became less and less reconciled to the idea of giving it up and returning to their drab and cramped home in Moscow, where living conditions, according to Soviet propaganda, were the best in the world. In fact they were nothing compared with what the Gouzenkos observed and experienced in Ottawa. The sense of personal security, freedom to speak as they liked and to look at what and where they liked, the surplus of food and consumer goods in the shops and supermarkets, the workers driving round in their own cars—this was the lot of the ordinary Canadian citizen and the lesson was not lost upon Igor and Anna Gouzenko, particularly when Igor realised the significance of the covert operations which were going on in Colonel Zabotin's office. 'For the first time this spying on Canadians was beginning to make me feel uncomfortable', Igor afterwards recalled. 'The arrival of Anna, the subsequent birth of my son Andrei, and the supreme contentment of our home at 511 Somerset Street, had altered my outlook. Candidly, everything about this democratic living seemed good. I had been in Canada long enough to appreciate that free elections were really free, that the press was really free, that the worker was not only free to speak but to strike.'

Igor Gouzenko had been in Ottawa for about fifteen months when the blow fell which he had come to dread, although he had not expected it so soon. One afternoon in September 1944, Colonel Zabotin called him into his office. The Military Attaché was staring at a letter which Gouzenko could see from the envelope lying open on his desk had just arrived in the diplomatic bag from Moscow. 'For reasons unstated', said Zabotin, 'the immediate recall of you and your family has been ordered by the Director'.[2]

When he had recovered from his initial shock, Gouzenko racked his brains as to any possible reason for his recall, and he could find none. 'Poor Andrei!' Anna exclaimed when he broke the news to her. 'I thought our child would grow up in this country. Now we have to take him back to misery and starvation and hopeless living. It is awful . . . awful!'

Next morning Gouzenko went straight to Range Road and tackled his chief, pointing out that the military section was very undermanned, that he was leading his class in English studies at the Embassy school, and that perhaps he could be shifted to work as an interpreter.

'Yes, that's right', Zabotin agreed, 'but Moscow decides these things'. However, he added that he would ask the Director to reconsider his recall until further additions to the Embassy staff made his departure 'more practical'.

Moscow's reply came three days later in a form which greatly relieved

Gouzenko. It was to the effect that he should remain at cypher work 'for the time being'. Since codes and cyphers called for implicit trust on the part of the Military Intelligence Directorate, Gouzenko realised that he was still regarded by the authorities in Moscow as a loyal Soviet citizen. But Anna was not so impressed when Igor told her. 'Let's face facts', she said. 'It's only a reprieve. We shall still have to face the crisis one day. What then?'

Igor thought carefully for a few moments. Then he spoke. 'We won't go back, Anna', he said. 'Andrei deserves his opportunities in this country. You are entitled to live like these Canadian wives.' They would pack up and disappear somewhere in Canada or even the United States and would change their names, while Igor took other work.

Anna sobbed in gratitude, and they began to work out their plans for the future. On no account, they agreed, must they let drop any hint that, in the event of their recall, which could only be a matter of time, they contemplated any other course than to obey it without question.

In fact their recall was accelerated by an incident, the full significance of which Igor did not appreciate at the time. One evening, by mistake, he forgot to lock up a top secret document, probably a cable, which he left among a number of unimportant papers on his desk. When he found it there next morning, he was understandably upset, although it appeared to have passed unnoticed since it was in exactly the same place as he had left it. However, to be on the safe side, he reported his omission to Colonel Zabotin. The Military Attaché, who was a kindly and genial officer, realised that if he reported it to Moscow Gouzenko might get into serious trouble, so he contented himself with giving Gouzenko a little lecture on the importance of safeguarding security in the cypher office and saying nothing about it. Unfortunately the document had been noticed by the Russian cleaner, who was an NKVD agent, and she told Vitali Pavlov who in turn passed on the information to Moscow. This resulted in a sharp rebuke to the Military Attaché and Gouzenko's definite recall. For similar offences a negligent cypher officer had been known to face a firing squad.

It was in August 1945 that orders came from Moscow that Gouzenko's successor Lieutenant Koulakov was on his way, and after Gouzenko had instructed him in his cyphering duties he was to hand over to him and return immediately with his family to Moscow. By this time Anna was again pregnant.

'This is your chance to do something big for this country and yourself, and most of all for Andrei and the new baby', Anna insisted. 'Canada is to be our home. Let us not take everything and give nothing.'

What Igor Gouzenko now determined to give was complete documentary proof of the Soviet spy system in Canada as it operated and had been operating for the past few years. But time was short, and he realised that he would have to work at top speed and at some personal risk to himself if he was to achieve his purpose within the time available. Secret documents marked 'Burn after reading', which he was ordered to put in the large embassy incinerator, he would deliberately keep back. Others he would carefully abstract from the files, taking them home with him and hiding them in various places in his apartment, in pots and pans and under dishes. Two telegrams, which he judged so important that they might be missed, he copied and placed the copies in the files, taking the originals home with him. One from Moscow asked for information about the atomic bomb; the other from Zabotin, whose code name was 'Grant', informed the Director of the recent election of Fred Rose, a Communist, as a member of the Canadian Federal Parliament. Thus Gouzenko went through all the secret and confidential files, turning down the corners of the telegrams and other top secret documents which he intended to take away with him when he left the Embassy for the last time.

He went home a littler earlier for supper on that particular evening, which he had chosen because Lieutenant Koulakov, who was likely to be the first to notice his absence, was duty officer at Zabotin's house that night and would not be expected to reappear for work before noon on the following day. Also Zabotin himself was going to a party and would almost certainly not turn up until at least midday.

After he had returned to the Military Attaché's house to check that Lieutenant Koulakov was at his post and declining an invitation to go to a cinema with some other members of the staff on the pretext that he had already seen the film being shown there, Gouzenko went on to the Embassy in Charlotte Street. As he was signing the attendance book, he noticed to his dismay that Pavlov, the head of the NKVD in Canada, was in the reception room. But Pavlov did not appear to notice him as he pressed the secret button under the banister. Fortunately the steel doors were opened by the Commercial Attaché's cypher clerk, a man named Ryazanov, who happened to be a friend of Gouzenko. When Ryazanov asked him if he was working late, Gouzenko replied, 'No. There are just a couple of telegrams to do and then I'll catch an 8.30 show.' Ryazanov observed that this was a good idea and was sorry he could not come along too, but he was duty officer that night.

Gouzenko went into his office and after closing the door carefully he went to his desk and removed Zabotin's confidential code and cypher bag with the documents he had left there in the afternoon. He then settled down to encypher the two telegrams. At first sight they did not seem to be very important, but on scrutinising them more carefully he recognised that they fitted in with other intelligence data and that they originated with an agent whose code name was 'Nora' and who Gouzenko knew worked in the Canadian Department of External Affairs. Her real name was Emma Woikin. So he decided to add the copies to the other material he had collected instead of leaving the telegrams to be dealt with by Lieutenant Koulakov next day as he might have done. 'It was too bad for Emma that I stopped to reconsider them', he recalled later. 'Those telegrams cost her a two-year prison sentence.' Next he removed all the papers from the secret files which he had marked, over a hundred in all, stuffing some of them into his pockets and others into his shirt. Finally he walked across the corridor and handed the two telegrams to Ryazanov for despatch to Moscow. He also handed over Zabotin's sealed bag containing the Military Attaché's codes and cyphers to be put in the safe. He thought that Ryazanov might notice his bulging pockets and shirt, but he did not. Nor did the attendant on the main door after Gouzenko signed out in the attendance book. The doorman was an NKVD man named Gouzev, who let him pass with a cursory nod. Fortunately his boss Pavlov had already left.

Once outside the Embassy, Gouzenko caught a street-car in the downtown direction and after getting off went straight to Queen Street and the offices of the *Ottawa Journal* with his precious burden.

[2]

It was getting on for nine o'clock when Igor Gouzenko reached the newspaper offices, and the presses were already printing the early edition of the paper. On being told the editor's office was on the sixth floor, he went up in the elevator, but as he reached the door marked 'Editor' and was about to knock he hesitated and doubts began to assail his mind. Surely, he thought to himself naïvely, there must be a NKVD agent working on the paper. He decided to think it over and went down in the elevator, which stopped at the lower floors to let in others. One of them was a girl who smiled at him and asked, 'What are you doing here? Is there some news breaking at the Embassy?' Gouzenko was too petrified to reply, but when the elevator reached the ground floor he muttered a few words of apology to the effect that he was in a hurry and then dashed into the street, where he caught another street-car and went home.[3]

'Don't worry about her', his wife reassured him when he had told her of his encounter. 'She must be a journalist. Many journalists have been to receptions at the Embassy and that is where she probably met you. They have good memories.' Even if there was a NKVD agent on the *Ottawa Journal*, Anna argued, it did not matter and he couldn't do anything to stop him. 'Go right back to the newspaper office and see the editor', she added. 'You still have several hours at least before the Embassy learns what has happened.'

Igor took the documents out of his shirt. They were soaked in sweat since it had been an extremely hot and humid day. After drying them Anna wrapped them up in a clean sheet of paper and gave them back to her husband.

By the time Igor got back to the newspaper offices, it was past ten o'clock and the editor had gone for the night. He walked down the corridor until he reached the news room, which was filled with reporters and sub-editors. He went to the nearest desk and told a man working at a typewriter there that he wished to see whoever was in charge. 'It is extremely important', he added.

The man got up and took him over to the other side of the room, where an older man wearing a green eye-shade told him to sit down. Gouzenko then produced the documents and spread them out on the desk before him, explaining who he was and that these were proof that Soviet agents in Canada were collecting data on nuclear secrets and the atom bomb.

The man with the eye-shade stared at him with amazement and picked up some of the documents. They were written in Russian, a language he did not understand. Nor did he think it worthwhile trying to find someone who did. 'I'm sorry', he said. 'This is out of our field.' He went on to suggest that he should go and see the Royal Canadian Mounted Police or else come back in the morning to see the editor.

Gouzenko explained hastily that by next morning the NKVD might be on his trail and might even have killed him. But he saw from the newspaperman's expression that he thought he was crazy.

'Sorry', he said. 'I'm busy.' The man then got up and walked away, leaving the unfortunate Gouzenko sitting there helpless and confused. Out again in the street, Gouzenko realised that he must now try to contact a high official, and the Minister of Justice seemed the logical person. So he walked to the Justice Ministry in Wellington Street, where a tall man in RCMP uniform stopped him at the door. When he heard what he wanted, the policeman answered politely but firmly: 'It's after midnight. You can see nobody till morning. Sorry.'

The word 'Sorry' was beginning to get on Gouzenko's nerves. 'It's desperately necessary that I reach the Minister right away', he persisted. 'By telephone, at least.'

The RCMP man shook his head. 'It can't be done.'

Gouzenko returned home depressed and not a little frightened. 'Don't worry', said Anna cheerfully. 'You've got the whole morning to reach the Minister. Have a good sleep and you'll feel better.'

But he still worried and slept fitfully. Next morning he and Anna agreed that they should go together to the Justice Ministry and that Anna, in spite of the fact that she was seven months pregnant, should take Andrei with her. She also said she would take the papers in her bag, since if the NKVD did succeed in catching up with them, they would go for him, and Anna might have time to slip away.

They reached the Ministry around nine o'clock, shortly after it had opened, and Gouzenko explained to the man at the reception desk that he had to see the Minister on a matter of absolute urgency. The man looked at him doubtfully, then spoke for a few minutes to someone on the telephone. They were then escorted to the Minister's private office, where a courteous male secretary inquired the nature of their business. After Gouzenko had explained that the matter was of such importance that he dared not speak to anyone but the Minister himself, the secretary disappeared into an inner office where Gouzenko could hear him speaking on the telephone. He returned a few minutes later. 'The Minister is in his other office over in the Parliament Buildings', he said. 'I will take you there.'

They went over to Parliament Hill and through the picturesque halls to the office of the Minister, the Rt. Hon. Louis St Laurent. There Gouzenko had to see another secretary, whom he appears to have told that he had documents of importance which he could only show the Minister himself. However, he did add some details indicating espionage and mentioning individuals. The secretary then picked up the telephone and spoke to someone in French, which Gouzenko could not understand, although he knew that it was about him since he heard his name mentioned. When the secretary eventually put down the receiver, he told the other secretary to take the Gouzenkos back to the Justice building and wait there for the Minister.

Reaching any federal minister and for that matter senior officials on the morning of 6 September could not have been more difficult or unfortunate for the Gouzenkos, for it was the day of the opening of the new parliamentary session when the Prime Minister, Mr Mackenzie King, and the other ministers had to be in their places in the chamber for the traditional ceremony.

When the seventy-year-old bachelor Prime Minister and Liberal Party Leader, who was also Secretary of State for External Affairs, arrived at his office in the Parliament Buildings at 10.45 a.m., he found Mr Norman Robertson, the Permanent Under-Secretary of the External Affairs Department, waiting for him with Mr Hume Wrong, another senior officer of the department. They did not have much time to tell the Prime Minister what they had learned about Gouzenko from Mr St Laurent. But both were looking very serious. The same night Mackenzie King wrote in his diary:

> Robertson said to me that a most terrible thing had happened. It was like a bomb on top of everything and one could not say how serious it might be or to what it might lead. He then told me that this morning, just half an hour ago, a man had turned up, with his wife at the office of the Minister of Justice. He said he was from the Russian Embassy. That he was threatened with deportation and that once he was deported, that would mean certain death. That the Russian democracy was different from ours.

He went on to say that he had in his possession documents that he had taken from the Embassy and was prepared to give to the Government. They would be seen to disclose that Russia had her spies and secret service in Canada and in the US and was practising a species of espionage. That some of these men were around [Edward] Stettinius [US Secretary of State] in the States, and that one was in our own Research Laboratories here (assumedly seeking to get secret information with regard to the atomic bomb). He indicated that he had to do with the cyphering of messages . . . At any rate he said that he had enough evidence to prove that instead of being friends, the Russians were really enemies . . .

The secretary had talked with Mr St Laurent who thought it best not to see him. Robertson and Wrong were asking my advice, whether they should not have the mounted police take him in hand and secure the documents which he had. The man, when he was told the Minister would not see him, then said that he would have to commit suicide right there. There could be no hope for him because when the vault was opened at the Embassy, they would discover there that the papers had gone and would know that he had taken them.

I said to both Robertson and Wrong that I thought we should be extremely careful in becoming a party to any course of action which would link the Government of Canada up with this matter in a manner which might cause Russia to feel that we had performed an unfriendly act. That to seek to gather information in any underhand way would make clear that we did not trust the Embassy. The man might be only a crank trying to preserve his own life . . .

Robertson seemed to feel that the information might be so important both to the States and to ourselves and to Britain that it would be in their interests for us to seize it no matter how it was obtained. He did not say this but asked my opinion. I was strongly against any step of the kind as certain to create an issue between Russia and Canada, this leading to severance of diplomatic relations . . .[4]

The Prime Minister now had to leave to take his place in the chamber, but he asked Robertson to keep in touch and arranged to see him with Mr St Laurent after the House adjourned in the afternoon.

Meanwhile the Minister of Justice had told his secretary, as he subsequently admitted when the matter was raised in the House of Commons, that he 'could not receive an official from a friendly Embassy bearing tales of the kind he had described to my secretary'. This message was relayed by telephone to his secretary in the ministry after the Gouzenkos had waited there for two hours. 'Very well, sir', said the secretary, adding, as he turned to the Gouzenkos, 'I am very sorry. The Minister is unable to see you.'

Igor looked frightened, and muttered something about going home to his flat and suicide being now his only course. But Anna said to him quietly in Russian, 'Let's go to the newspaper office'. This they eventually decided to do.

The editor was not available when they got to the *Ottawa Journal*, but a nice woman reporter came out, patted little Andrei on the head, and invited them to sit down. After Igor had repeated his story and produced the documents, she looked at them and took them into the editor's office. After a short time she re-emerged. 'I'm terribly sorry', she said, handing back the documents. 'Your story just doesn't seem to register here. Nobody wants to say anything but nice things about Stalin these days.'

In response to Anna's question as to what they should do next, the kindly woman reporter said, after a few moments' thought: 'Why not go to see the RCMP about taking out naturalisation papers? That should prevent the Reds from taking you back.'

So back they went to the Justice building, only to be told that the RCMP did not deal with naturalisation applications and that they should go to the Crown Attorney's office in Nicholas Street. This office turned out to be some distance away, it was getting hot, and by the time they got there they were all very tired, particularly Andrei who began to cry. To add to their troubles they were told that the woman who dealt with naturalisation applications had gone to lunch. By this time it was 1.45 p.m. and the Gouzenkos also went off to have some food, after which Anna decided to take Andrei, who had fallen asleep at the table, back to Somerset Street and leave him with a friendly neighbour, which she did.

When Anna returned, they both went back to the Crown Attorney's office where they were given forms to fill in and told to come back next day with photographs. Asked how long naturalisation would take, the girl attending to them replied she could not say for sure, possibly several months. On hearing this disquieting news, Anna burst into tears.

When she had dried her eyes she noticed a woman in a red dress seated on the other side of the room. She was Mrs Fernande Joubarne, secretary to the Crown Attorney, Mr Raoul Mercier. On an impulse Anna went over to her and poured out her story. 'Everything is here', she concluded, opening her handbag with the documents, 'including secret information on the atomic bomb. You must tell your government about this'.

'The Crown Attorney is in court at the moment', replied Mrs Joubarne, 'but I will try to put you in touch with the proper people'.

Eventually she succeeded in getting through to the office of Mr Norman Robertson, who, as we have seen, had already been apprised of some of the facts of the Gouzenko story. He promised to call back shortly.

[3]

Norman Robertson was apparently about to get into touch with the Prime Minister when he got a message from him, asking him to come over to his office in the House of Commons since Parliament had risen for the day and St Laurent had remained behind to tell the Prime Minister what had taken place with the Gouzenkos in the Justice Ministry. 'We learned later', the Prime Minister wrote in his diary, 'that the Russian man had left saying he was going to his own flat; that there was nothing but suicide ahead of him'. He continued:

Again, Robertson thought of getting the police to seize the papers. I suggested that a Secret Service man in plain clothes watch the premises. If suicide took place let the city police take charge and this man to follow in and secure what there was in the way of documents, but on no account for us to take the initiative. Robertson then thought of himself going to the Embassy and stating what this man had said. Both St Laurent and I counselled against that course. We felt it was better to let things come out wholly apart from the Government itself . . .

Robertson at one stage expressed the situation as that of the possibility of our being a party to suicide on the one hand if we did not get the papers and protect the man, and murder on the other if we allowed him to fall into the hands of the Embassy which would send him back to Russia where he would be executed. There was this aspect to consider, but it was clear that we could not save the individual situation by any course we could take, but we might involve the countries in an open breach . . .

My own feeling is that the individual has incurred the displeasure of the Embassy and is really seeking to shield himself. I do not believe his story about their avowed treachery.[5]

'I thought this was a case where we could not be too careful or too cautious', the Prime Minister was later to tell the House of Commons, defending his handling of the matter: 'that this man represented that he had come from the Russian Embassy; that we could not say whether the documents he had in his possession were fabrications or not; that we did not know what his own state of mind might be or how responsible he was; that we knew nothing of the circumstances which had caused him to leave the Embassy and come to the Government and that I thought he should be told to go back to the Embassy with the papers that he had in his possession'. All this was now embodied in a brief message from Robertson to the Crown Attorney's office: 'The Prime Minister has advised to get rid of these people at once'.

Mrs Joubarne was a loyal public servant. But she was also a human being, and she realised what would inevitably happen if Gouzenko went back to the Soviet Embassy. So with the Crown Attorney's permission, she made a last attempt to help by enlisting the interest of the press. But everywhere the reply was the same, even when a reporter who knew Mrs Joubarne turned up and heard what the Gouzenkos had to say. 'It's too big for us to handle—much too big', said the reporter. 'Its a matter for the police or the government.' Mrs Joubarne sighed. 'There's nothing more I can do', she said. And turning to Anna, she added: 'Good luck to you. Let me know if it's a boy or a girl.'

'You have been so kind', said Igor, thanking her. 'You were the only one who would talk to us. We will never forget you.'

As they walked out into the blazing afternoon sun, Anna took Igor by the arm. She was dog-tired. 'Let's go home', she said. Igor, who was also pretty well exhausted, agreed.

As they neared Somerset Street, Igor told Anna to go in by the back entrance and fetch Andrei from the friendly neighbours who had been looking after him. Igor would enter their own apartment, No. 4, on the second floor by the back way, and if all was well he would wave to Anna across the rear area. When he listened outside his door all was quiet, so he unlocked it and went inside where everything seemed in order. He then went out to the back and signalled to Anna to come over with their child, which she did. Afterwards Igor lay down on the bed and tried to sleep, but without any success. After a little while he got up and looked out of one of the front windows, which faced a park. To his horror he saw two strange men sitting on a park bench and looking up at the window. They must be NKVD men, he thought, and the impression was confirmed when there was a knock on the front door, repeated several times. 'Gouzenko!' a harsh voice shouted in Russian. *'Otcroite dwer!'* (Open the door.)—Igor recognised the voice as that of the Military Attaché's driver Sub-Lieutenant Lavrentiev. He held his breath, though he knew that the caller must have known that someone was at home since little Andrei had dashed across the room and fallen down, hitting the back of the door.

Gouzenko then picked up the child and went out of the back door which led to the rear balcony shared with his immediate neighbours, a Canadian air-force sergeant and his wife who occupied Apartment 5. Sergeant Harold Maine was smoking a pipe and reading the evening paper while Mrs Maine was sewing. 'Excuse me', Gouzenko interrupted. 'May I speak with you?' The sergeant looked up in surprise, as he gathered from Gouzenko's appearance that this was no ordinary social call. What happened then may best be related in the sergeant's own words:

I told him sure he could speak with me, if he had something to say; so he asked if the wife and I would look after their little boy if anything should happen to him and his wife. So about that time I figured maybe we should go inside, so we went in to our apartment, and while in there he said he wanted to be sure that somebody would look after his little boy if anything should happen to them.

So after a bit of a conference my wife and I decided we would look after him, because we didn't want to see him stuck with nobody to look after him should anything happen to them.[6]

Igor Gouzenko left by the back entrance to return to his own apartment, and as he did so both he and the RCAF sergeant could see Lavrentiev walking along the lane at the back of the apartment building. At this Gouzenko became so apprehensive that he asked if he and Anna could also be taken in by the Maines, and to this the sergeant agreed. At this moment, another neighbour, Mrs Frances Elliot who lived in the adjoining Apartment 6 on the same floor, appeared, and when she heard the Gouzenkos' story she said she would be glad to take in all three since she was alone, her husband and son being away. This offer was gratefully accepted. Meanwhile Sergeant Maine said he would fetch the local police and he went off on his bicycle to do so.

Two constables, Tom Walsh and John McCullough, duly arrived, and Igor Gouzenko asked them for protection since he had information of extreme importance to the Canadian Government. Without committing themselves the policemen said they would keep the block of flats under observation. 'Keep the light on in the bathroom. We can see it from the park. If you need us, put out the light.'

About 11.30 p.m. footsteps were heard on the front stairs, and Sergeant Maine opened his door to see four men, three in plain clothes and one in uniform with the Red Star insignia, standing outside the Gouzenkos' apartment. 'Where is Gouzenko?' asked the leader, who turned out to be the NKVD chief Vitali Pavlov. Sergeant Maine replied that he had no idea and shut his door. The four men then made as if to leave but were soon back outside Apartment 4 where they broke open the front door and went inside. By this time, Mrs Elliot, who had heard the commotion, turned off the light in the bathroom.

Constables Walsh and McCullough were quickly on the scene. They went into Apartment 4, which they saw was being systematically ransacked by the marauding party. 'What are you people doing here?' asked Walsh.

Pavlov immediately produced a card identifying himself as Second Secretary of the Soviet Embassy. The others were all members of the embassy staff, he went on. In fact, the officer in uniform was Lieutenant-Colonel Rogov, Assistant Military Attaché (Air). The two in civilian clothes besides Pavlov were Lieutenant Pavel Angelov, a member of the Military Attaché's staff, and Pavlov's confidential cypher clerk Alexander Farafontov.

Pavlov, who did most of the talking, explained that they were looking for certain official papers. 'The man who owns this flat has left town and is in Toronto', he said, 'but we have his permission to go into his apartment and get what we need'.

Walsh pointed out the broken lock, part of which was lying on the floor. 'For people who have permission to enter a flat you certainly chose a funny way to get in', he said. He picked up the piece on the floor. 'This doesn't look as if it had been done with a key', he went on. 'You must have used a bit of pressure to get in and from the marks on the door you did not put them there with your fingers.' Pavlov looked at the constable and shrugged his shoulders. 'We lost the key', he replied. 'There is something here which we have to get. This is Soviet property, and we can do as we wish. You will please leave.'

The constables shook their heads. 'Not until an inspector arrives', they said. One of them went out and put a call through to municipal police headquarters. A quarter of an hour later Detective Inspector Duncan Macdonald arrived and quickly sized up the situation. But when he asked Pavlov and the others to accompany him to the police station, Pavlov claimed diplomatic immunity for himself and his companions and they refused to budge. The inspector then went off to verify their diplomatic status. When he returned the Russians had gone, the constables having made no attempt to detain them.

The Gouzenkos remained in Apartment 6 under the care of the city police. Around four o'clock in the morning, there was a gentle tap on the door of Apartment 4, but as the police had now padlocked it the caller, who was accompanied by another man, made no attempt to enter and they went away. It was to this caller, as it transpired, that Gouzenko primarily owed his life, besides being able to put his revealing documents to the best possible use.

After breakfast another Inspector of police arrived and told Gouzenko that the RCMP would like to have a talk with him in the Justice Ministry.

'At last, Igor, at last!' Anna spoke with obvious relief. 'They are going to listen to you. I am so glad.'

[4]

The person who had tapped on the door of the Gouzenkos' apartment in Somerset Street in the middle of the night was a forty-nine-year-old Canadian, Sir William Stephenson, MC, DFC, who directed the British secret intelligence and security organisation in the Western Hemisphere from an inconspicuous office on the thirty-sixth floor of a New York skyscraper in Rockefeller Plaza.[7] His code name in the service was 'Intreprid', which reflected his gallantry and enterprise since as a pilot in the Royal Flying Corps in the First World War he had shot down twenty-seven enemy aircraft before being himself shot down, taken prisoner and escaped to rejoin the RFC, while after the war his scientific inventions as an industrialist in England had made him a millionaire by the time he was thirty. On the occasion of his nocturnal visit he was accompanied by Mr Thomas Archibald Stone, Counsellor in the Canadian Embassy in Washington. Both men were on a routine visit to Ottawa. Stephenson had arrived late the previous afternoon about the time Gouzenko and his wife, after vainly trudging round the city with their child and priceless cache of documents, had returned to their apartment. As was his habit when staying overnight in Ottawa or Toronto, the British Intelligence chief put up at the Seignory Club near the Federal capital. From there he telephoned Norman Robertson at his private residence and invited him over for a drink. However, Robertson, apparently at Mackenzie King's instance, asked Stephenson to come to his house instead. There Stephenson found Tommy Stone closeted with the Under-Secretary and talking about Gouzenko, to whom Robertson had sent a message through the Crown Attorney's office that he should return to the Russian Embassy with his documents. Stephenson, Mackenzie King noted in an aide-memoire which he dictated next morning, 'came up and saw Robertson last night. Robertson will a little later tell me of his talks with him . . . I am glad I insisted on Robertson not going down [to the Seignory Club] but having him [Stephenson] come up. Robertson obviously is greatly fatigued. I will get further developments later.'[8]

When he heard the bare facts of the case, Stephenson felt strongly that Igor Gouzenko might conceivably have information of great importance to impart, also that his life might well be in immediate danger unless he were given police protection at once. Stephenson consequently urged Robertson to 'take him'. Robertson said he had already detailed two RCMP men in plain clothes to keep the Gouzenkos' apartment under observation and it was these two men on their bench in the park that Gouzenko mistook for NKVD agents. Some time after the break-in, and the local police inspector had arrived, Gouzenko repeated his request that he wished to make a statement to the RCMP, and word to this effect had been telephoned to Robertson, who apparently was still sitting up and talking over drinks with Stephenson and Stone. 'This was arranged for', to quote Mackenzie King's aide-memoire, 'and this morning at an early hour his statement was taken and the whole matter has been brought officially by the police to the attention of the Minister of Justice'.

When Robertson 'phoned me no word had been sent to the Embassy by our Government but once the Minister of Justice has concluded the review—I am dictating this at 11 a.m.—the Ambassador will be asked to come over or to send someone and he will be told of the information given the government.

I asked about the documents. Robertson said they were still in the man's possession. They might be turned over by him to the police. If they were they would be given back to the Embassy and possibly the police, meanwhile, might photostat copies.[9]

The same afternoon, bearing in mind that it was exactly a month before, on 6 August, that the Americans had dropped their atom bomb on Hiroshima, which at the first reckoning killed over 78,000 human beings, Mr Malcolm MacDonald, the British High Commissioner in Ottawa, gave a garden party at his official residence Earnscliffe to celebrate the end of hostilities. It was attended by a large gathering including Mr Mackenzie King and all the Ministers of his government, the other Commonwealth High Commissioners and the foreign ambassadors including Mr Zarubin, head of the Russian mission, as well as Members of Parliament and other prominent Canadian citizens. Georgei Zarubin, who spoke only Russian, was accompanied by Vitali Pavlov who acted as interpreter as well as keeping an eye on his ambassador for the NKVD. The official guests filed past the High Commissioner, who had a few words with each. When it came to Zarubin's turn, the Russian, knowing Malcolm MacDonald's interest in bird-watching, jokingly asked him: 'Has any little bird whispered any important secret to you lately?'

'No', answered the High Commissioner. 'Have you caught any big fish in the last few days?'

After this had been translated, the ambassador smiled and shook his head.

MacDonald noticed that he seemed rather weary about the eyes. 'Too bad!' he quipped. 'You look as if you had been out fishing all night. The fish can't have been biting.'

This remark clearly startled the interpreter Pavlov. But before he had time to translate it into Russian, the next guest pressed forward to shake hands with the High Commissioner, and the Soviet ambassador and his companion moved on to join the crowd gossiping and sipping tea on the lawns.[10]

Little did he know it at the time, but the British High Commissioner's last remark was a strikingly accurate shot in the dark. After Pavlov had reported to Zarubin that Gouzenko was missing, the two men concluded that in the circumstances he might have committed suicide by drowning himself. Accordingly they poked about in the Ottawa river near the Embassy early in the morning, hoping that in this event they might recover the cypher clerk's body.

Mackenzie King was at the garden party for a short time, but he left to return to his office on receiving a telephone message from Robertson that he wished to see him urgently as soon as he got back. Before he left Earnscliffe, the Prime Minister chatted informally with the Soviet ambassador and his wife, and in the course of their conversation Zarubin intimated that Stalin wished to confer a high honour on General Crerar, the Commander-in-Chief of the Canadian Army, for his war-time services in Europe, an honour to which Mackenzie King saw no objection. At the same time the Prime Minister thought the ambassador looked 'quite concerned' and that 'indeed, he had a very anxious look on his face'.

Immediately after the Prime Minister returned to his office he saw Robertson, who brought him up-to-date on the Gouzenko affair, which had developed in the most alarming manner. Robertson's voice trembled as he spoke, and (as Mackenzie King noted in his diary) 'betrayed a tremendous concern'.

He said he had got particulars of what the police had and that everything was much worse than what we would have believed. First of all he mentioned that all the documents had been photostated. The originals were with the Police but still we would have records now, and knew what was in them. They disclose an espionage system on a large scale. Not only had [Edward] Stettinius been surrounded by spies, etc., and the Russian Government been kept informed of all that was being done from that source, but that things came right into our own country to a degree we could not have believed possible. He then told me that they went into our own Department of External Affairs, that in the cypher room there was an agent of the Russians who had seen and knew all our cyphers and had known what they contained. The same was true of Earnscliffe.

In the cypher room at Earnscliffe Mr MacDonald's despatches were all seen, read and known. In our Research Laboratories here at Ottawa, where we had been working on the atomic bomb, there is a scientist who is a Russian agent. In the Research Laboratories in Montreal there is an English scientist who is pro-Russian and acting as a Russian agent.[11]

According to Robertson, Gouzenko had said that there was the freest talk among the embassy staff about the next war. He also said that it was Zabotin, the Military Attaché, who had been directing the espionage, a man whom Robertson told King was one of the pleasantest men he had had to deal with. Robertson added that he thought he would get into touch with Stephenson in New York, along with FBI men from the United States. 'He felt that what we had discovered might affect the whole meeting of the Council of Foreign Ministers;* that if publicity were given to this it might necessarily lead to a break in diplomatic relations between Canada and

---

* The Council was meeting in London at this time to discuss peace settlements with the defeated countries in the War.

Russia and might also lead to that in regard to other nations as well, the US and UK. All this might occasion a complete break-up of the relations that we have been counting on to make the peace. There was no saying to what terrible lengths this whole thing might go.'

The Prime Minister thereupon authorised Robertson to inform the British High Commissioner and the United States Ambassador Mr Ray Atherton of the situation, but at the same time advised very strongly 'against taking any quick steps, any public disclosures at an early moment. We must get the whole case as fully worked out as we possibly can. Avoid arrests, etc., keeping an eye on everything and everyone.'

Robertson said he had never been suspicious in his life. He felt now there was something real which had to be faced. What he felt most of all was that the people who were helping in this kind of thing were people supposed to be of the highest types of character. He doubted in some cases if it was at all for money. There was a sort of idealism of the Russian revolution which sought to get human rights for the masses of the people and this became a religion with some persons and they were prepared to do anything to further the movement.

I think myself it is all part of a world revolution—a world communist movement to get on the part of the workers a control of the Government completely out of the hands of those who have privilege, power, etc. But, he, Robertson, says that democracy in Russia is not understood by our people. It is really a Russian imperialism—an autocracy of the most desperate and wicked kind, but they are using the language of idealism and words and symbols which, while being used and understood by us in one way, have a different meaning to them and have become symbols for this power of the world-controlled business.[12]

Immediately after he had left the Prime Minister, Robertson telephoned Earnscliffe, conveying his apologies to the High Commissioner for not being able to come to the garden party and explaining that he was detained in his office by urgent business which had suddenly arisen. Indeed, he added, he wished for Mr MacDonald's help and asked whether he would come and see him as soon as the party was over. The High Commissioner promised to do so, and as soon as the last guest had departed he drove to Robertson's office. He found him conferring with two high-ranking officers of the RCMP.

'Come in, Malcolm', said Norman Robertson when the High Commissioner was shown into his office. 'I've got something interesting that the Prime Minister wants me to tell you. He'd be grateful if you would report it by top-secret telegram to your PM, Mr Attlee.'[13]

Robertson proceeded to outline the salient facts of the Gouzenko story, and added that what Gouzenko had begun to disclose at his interrogation by the RCMP that morning was of such importance that it had been decided to remove him with his wife and son to a secret place of safety several hundred miles away from Ottawa, where he would be safely out of reach of his recent Soviet masters. Meanwhile the documents which Gouzenko had handed over were being translated from their original Russian, and it appeared from one of them that there were upwards of twenty Soviet agents working in Canada, among whom was a member of the High Commissioner's staff, Miss Kathleen Willsher, who worked in the confidential registry at Earnscliffe. Robertson went on to tell MacDonald that the authorities had not yet decided what to do about these apparently treacherous individuals, some of whom held important posts in Canadian Government departments, in the Bank of Canada and in other similar institutions. A decision would be reached shortly after consultation with their allies in London and Washington. In the meantime Robertson would be grateful if the British High Commissioner would keep a discreet eye on Miss Willsher to ensure that, without arousing her suspicion, she had no access to fresh confidential information which they did not wish the Russians to pursue.[14]

Kathleen Mary Willsher, known to her friends as Kay, had come to Canada to work in the High Commission as a shorthand-typist fifteen years previously and she was now about forty. She was a graduate of the London School of Economics where no doubt she had imbibed some of the left-wing political views of the notorious Professor Harold Laski, and she spoke French, German and some Russian, in addition to English. According to Malcolm MacDonald she was a pleasant, bespectacled woman who suffered from a double sense of frustration. First, she was a spinster and had no boy-friend or immediate prospect of getting married. Secondly, she considered her academic qualifications entitled her to more rapid promotion in the British Government service than she had received, having after fifteen years in the British High Commission only reached the position of assistant registrar in the registry. For several years she had been a keen member of the Canadian Communist Party, which later became known as the Labour Progressive Party. In this she appears to have found some outlet for her emotional and intellectual needs. Although she had a code-name ('Elli' or 'Ellie') in Colonel Zabotin's files, she did not report directly to the Russians but through a 'cut-out'. At first this was Fred Rose, a Communist Member of the Federal House of Commons (code-name 'Fred' or 'Debouz'), and latterly an official of the Bank of Canada named Eric Adams (code-name 'Ernst'), whom she would meet from time to time, and pass on information from the registry on subjects in which they had expressed interest. Although Rose and Adams, like her, belonged to the Communist Party, her chief the British High Commissioner thought that she may have been unaware that they were spying for the Russians and that her information would be passed on to Zabotin. According to Malcolm MacDonald, she may well have thought what she was doing was merely designed to further the Marxist-Leninist cause in Canada. On the other hand she had by her actions knowingly infringed the Official Secrets Act, and when she subscribed to it shortly before the outbreak of the war she was fully aware of the penalties to which she might be liable should she commit a breach of it.

To Robertson's request to watch Kay Willsher, Malcolm MacDonald naturally agreed, as well as to the Canadian Prime Minister's invitation conveyed to him through Robertson to serve on a small informal committee consisting of himself and Robertson, together with their two deputies, and two senior intelligence officers in the RCMP. As the Russian documents were translated, Robertson pointed out, they would no doubt reveal many unexpected and perhaps dangerous circumstances. He added that, in addition to other assistance which he could give, MacDonald's membership of the committee would enable him to report promptly to Attlee in London every aspect of developments in the Gouzenko affair, since Mackenzie King 'wished to share all the secrets with his colleagues in London'. Needless to say, MacDonald accepted the invitation.

[5]

Next day, Friday, 7 September, the Prime Minister went off for the weekend to Kingsmere, his farm in the country. The following morning he telephoned Robertson, who told him that the Russian Embassy was demanding to know the whereabouts of Gouzenko as they wished to get hold of him. Mackenzie King's reaction was to direct Robertson 'to make sure that the embassy did not issue some writ of habeas corpus which might compel the RCMP officers to deliver him up'.

> He [Robertson] did not tell me where the man and his family were secreted, but I said that at all costs we must not let him come into the hands of the Embassy people. He said there is no doubt that the police feel that the man would have been killed or would allegedly have committed suicide, had the two men from the Embassy and the two others [of the NKVD] that had been with them been able to get hold of him the night before last. He said this man is telling them everything and we will have a very full and complete story.
>
> Robertson said that Stephenson and FBI representatives would be here tonight. I told him I would be able to come in from Kingsmere at any moment.[15]

The same evening Mackenzie King telephoned Robertson again. Robertson said he was on the point of calling Dr C. J. Mackenzie, President of the National Research Council, to let him know what information had been obtained which directly implicated the Research Council. In fact there were four agents working in the Council, although only three had been identified at that moment. The three who had been identified were, with their code-names, Durnford Smith ('Badeau), E. W. Mazerall ('Bagley') and Dr Raymond Boyer ('The Professor'). All that was originally known of the fourth agent was that his code-name was 'Alek' and his work was closely concerned with the manufacture of the atom bomb. Smith and Mazerall, both Canadians, were concerned respectively with the development of radio communications and radar equipment. Along with Israel Halperin (code-name 'Bacon'), an artillery major in the Canadian army dealing with explosives, the group was known as the 'B' group since their code-names began with that initial, and they were immediately 'controlled' by another agent, David Lunan (code-name 'Back'), a Scotsman who edited the Canadian journal of the armed forces *Canadian Affairs*, and reported directly to Major Rogov, the Air Attaché in Zabotin's office. On the other hand, Boyer, who was stationed in Montreal, reported to Fred Rose. The Professor was a well-off, French-speaking Canadian, with a Ph.D. degree in chemistry at McGill University where he subsequently worked on the development of the explosive known as RDX (Research Department Explosive), in a way that had never been attempted before. According to Zabotin, he was also the best of the specialists on the V.T. fuse in the American continent. This was the fuse which annihilated the Japanese air force, and although it was first developed in Canada in 1943, the details of its manufacture and wiring were known only to the United States. It was referred to in some of the Soviet documents as the 'electro bomb', and a diagram of its wiring had been obtained from Boyer.

It should perhaps be mentioned at this point that all the agents had code-names which were invariably used by Colonel Zabotin (whose own code-name was 'Grant') in his communications with the Directorate of Military Intelligence in Moscow. Some of them were quickly identified from their context or from Gouzenko's personal knowledge, but others took considerably longer to elucidate. On one occasion, for example, during a discussion about the atomic bomb in the Military Attaché's office, the real name of 'The Professor' slipped out. According to Gouzenko, 'Colonel Zabotin mentioned Professor Boyer of McGill University'. The identity of 'Alek' was eventually established through a telegram from Zabotin to the effect that 'Alek' was shortly due to take up an appointment as a lecturer in the University of London. 'We have worked out the conditions of a meeting with Alek in London', Zabotin cabled Moscow on 31 July 1945.

Alek will work in King's College, Strand. It will be possible to find him there through the telephone book. Meetings: October 7, 17 and 27 on the Street in front of the British Museum. The time, 11 o'clock in the evening . . . At the beginning of September he must fly to London. Before his departure he will go to the uranium plant in the Petawawa district where he will be found for about two weeks. He promised, if possible, to meet us before his departure.[16]

Inquiries revealed that 'Alek' was a British nuclear physicist, Dr Allan Nunn May, who was already known to the Russians as a Communist sympathiser, although he was never a party member. On his arrival in Canada in January 1945, Nunn May had joined the Anglo-Canadian research team working under Professor Cockcroft, Director of the Atomic Energy Division of the Canadian National Research Council in Montreal. Here, some months later, he had been 'contacted' by Lieutenant Pavel Angelov of the Soviet Military Attaché's office and recruited to 'the net', as the Russian espionage system was known.

After speaking to Robertson on Saturday evening, 8 September, Mackenzie King made the following entry in his diary:

> R told me he saw Malcolm MacDonald this morning and gave him the facts regarding his code room. He said he was calling Mackenzie of the Research [Department] this moment to let him know what relates to our own Research Department.
>
> Two on the British side* will be coming up tonight and FBI men will be here in Ottawa on Monday morning. Meanwhile a letter had come today from the Russian Embassy asking for the man [Gouzenko], claiming that he had stolen money from the Embassy, and I think Robertson said should be held for capital punishment. He says the man is out in the country. We have him secure.
>
> Robertson suggested we send no answer to the Russian note until Monday. I have asked him to see if, meanwhile, some steps cannot be taken whereby this man can be held by the Crown in a way that will prevent the Russians getting near him at all. Robertson said of course the man is clinging to us, would not leave on any account. To do so would mean certain death for him.
>
> Robertson feels, with the background of what we know, the letter from the Embassy is impudent.[17]

In the letter, which was in Russian, it was stated that, as a result of Gouzenko's failure to report for work on 7 September, Pavlov and 'two other colleagues of the Embassy'—in fact, as we have seen, there were three and not two—after receiving no answer to their knock on the door of the

---

* Peter Dwyer of MI6, then working under Stephenson, and Roger Hollis of MI5, a counter-espionage expert, later Sir Roger and head of MI5 in 1964, when the self-confessed Russian spy Sir Anthony Blunt was first unmasked.

Gouzenkos' apartment, opened the door 'with Gouzenko's duplicate key'; this again was incorrect, since the visitors actually forced the lock and broke into the apartment. 'It was later established', the Russian note continued, 'that I. Gouzenko had robbed some money [sic] belonging to the Embassy'. The note also complained of the 'rude treatment' accorded Pavlov and his companions by the local police who had violated the Russians' diplomatic immunity by detaining them on Russian property. The note concluded:

> The Embassy of the USSR asks the Department of External Affairs to take urgent measures to seek and arrest I. Gouzenko and hand him over for deportation as a capital criminal who has stolen money belonging to the Embassy . . .
>
> The Embassy asks the Department that it should be informed of action taken in relation to the above.[18]

Immediately after breakfast on Sunday, 9 September, Mackenzie King again spoke to Robertson and learned that the Soviet Embassy was still pressing the Department of External Affairs for help in finding Gouzenko. Later in the day the Prime Minister returned to Laurier House, his official residence, in Ottawa, where he learned that Robertson had seen Malcolm MacDonald and told him that the most dangerous spy which the Gouzenko documents had so far revealed was Dr Allan Nunn May. 'They had agreed on a communication to the British Foreign Office', Mackenzie King noted, 'giving an outline of what we knew and suggesting that at my instance, Byrnes, the US Secretary of State, should be advised, so as to have this knowledge before the Council of Ministers met in London. Robertson and I both agreed that great caution must be used from now on in the matter of avoiding any kind of publicity, hoping that matters can be straightened out without the public ever becoming aware of what took place.'[19]

Professor (later Sir) John Cockcroft, Jackson Professor of Natural Philosophy in Cambridge and a future Nobel prizewinner in physics, was an English scientist of international repute, who had been seconded to take charge of the atomic laboratories in Montreal. Robertson and MacDonald decided that he must be apprised at once of his assistant's treachery. MacDonald accordingly telephoned Cockcroft in Montreal and asked him to come and see him in Ottawa on a matter of great importance and utmost secrecy, that he should tell no one of his journey, that he should make it by driving himself in his own car the whole distance each way, and that he must start from Montreal about the time of night when everyone else in the city normally went to bed, and that he must return before the citizens of Montreal woke up in the morning.

As a result, Cockcroft reached Earnscliffe about two a.m. After apologising for summoning him at such an unconscionable hour, the High Commissioner poured him an extra strong whisky and soda and they sat down to talk. MacDonald began by saying that his visit must remain unknown to anyone else in his Montreal team. Cockcroft nodded his head sagely. Then MacDonald told him that he had received secret intelligence that Nunn May was a spy for the Russians.[20]

'To this day I can see the jump of astonishment he gave', Malcolm MacDonald told me long afterwards. 'For a moment he stared at me incredulously, but then he accepted the statement as one of fact.' In reply to MacDonald's questions, Cockroft informed him how much and how little Nunn May knew about the scope of their work in Montreal, so that the High Commissioner could report it to the top authorities concerned in Ottawa, London and Washington. In fact, it amounted to a great deal. According to Mackenzie King, he was 'almost second in the knowledge pertaining to the atomic bomb', and that he knew 'practically all that has been done in Canada and the United States' in atomic weapons research. Incidentally the importance of Canada in the construction of the atomic bomb lay in the fact that there was a uranium mine beside the Great Bear Lake in the Mackenzie District of the North West Territories in the far north of the country, and it was the principal source within the control of the western allies of the bomb's essential raw material. In this context there was a nuclear energy plant at Clinton, British Columbia, and also at Chalk River, near Petawawa, Ontario, which latter Nunn May was known to have visited. He had also visited the metallurgical laboratory in Chicago University.

Furthermore, in a telegram from Zabotin to Moscow dated as recently as 9 August 1945, it was stated that according to 'Alek' a secret test of the atomic bomb had taken place in New Mexico, that the bomb dropped on Hiroshima was made of uranium 235, and that it was known that the output of uranium 235 amounted to 400 grams daily at Clinton. 'The scientific research work in this field is scheduled to be published, but without the technical details', Zabotin went on. 'The Americans have already published a book on this subject.'* Finally 'Alek handed over to us a platinum with 162 micrograms of uranium 233 in the form of oxide in a thin lamina'. Nunn May also handed over a sample of uranium 235 to his contact Lieutenant Angelov in Zabotin's office. Zabotin considered these samples to be so important that he despatched the Assistant Military Attaché, Lt-Colonel Motinov, with them to Moscow. Consequently on 22 August, Moscow instructed Zabotin to 'take measures to organise acquisition of documentary materials on the atomic bomb! The technical processes, drawings, calculations.' Nine days later Zabotin asked to be informed 'to what extent has Alek's materials on the question of uranium satisfied you and our scientists (his reports on production etc.). This is necessary for us

---

* H. D. Smyth, *Atomic Energy* (US Government Printing Office, 1945).

to know in order that we may be able to set forth a number of tasks on this question to other clients.'[21]

MacDonald told Cockroft that it was not proposed to arrest his colleague immediately, but in the meantime he wished Cockroft to keep a very cautious eye on him. He should be allowed to continue his work, so as not to arouse in him any suspicions that he was being watched, but care should be taken to ensure that no new significant knowledge came to his attention. Cockroft thereupon remarked that the scientist was due to leave for England almost immediately to take up his new appointment in London. This had been arranged some time before, probably at Nunn May's instigation, since on 28 July, a few days before the first atom bomb was dropped on Japan, Moscow instructed Zabotin to try to get from Nunn May information on the progress of work on uranium.

Discuss with him: does he think it expedient for our undertaking to stay on the spot? Will he be able to do that, or is it more useful for him and necessary to depart for London?[22]

On 10 September, Mackenzie King noted in his diary:

The most appalling statement which Robertson gave me this morning was that at Potsdam, when the 3 Great Powers were re-assembled there, Churchill brought up the question of the Balkan States and what was developing, and said they would have to thrash this out by process of argument and reasoning. Stalin had replied they would be settled by power. This caused Churchill to speak to Truman about the necessity of letting the Russians see where power really lay. The atomic bomb had been brought into action sooner on this account than would otherwise have happened. Russia itself came into the war in consequence of the atomic bomb sooner than otherwise would have happened . . .

This man, Gouzenko, had said that the day the atomic bomb was first used, there was tremendous excitement at the Embassy. They were accustomed there to talking about the next war. This had seemed to anticipate and possibly delay what might have been part of the plan. Combined with what Stalin had said at Potsdam, it will look as if the Russians had in mind no delay in asserting their further power. One of the most serious of all the documents found revealed that they had been asking for their men in the secret service here to give them a report on the strength of the American army and forces. The extent of demobilization; where they are and where located today, to give also the strength as regards to other of the Defence services. Robertson pointed out getting this information from Canada may have been to check on reports they were getting from other sources in the US.[23]

Should Nunn May be allowed to return to England, or should he be picked up before he was due to leave? 'The balance of argument seemed to be in favour of the latter argument', MacDonald recalled afterwards, 'because unlike Miss Willsher, Nunn May was a direct, conscious informer for the Russians; and examination of the legal position showed that, whereas under Canadian law it would be simple to arrest and detain him in Canada, under British law it would be impossible to do so in England for such an offence committed in another country. We therefore decided that he and all the rest of the Soviet agents should be picked up before the date of his flight across the Atlantic Ocean'.[24]

Apparently this decision was reached later, on 11 September, when MacDonald and Robertson saw Mackenzie King in the Parliament buildings before the sitting of the House of Commons, since the Prime Minister noted in his diary later that day the outcome of this meeting.

Robertson and Malcolm both represented that if he got away to Moscow he would be able to inform the authorities there of everything within his knowledge. He already has priorities leaving on a plane for England this week.

The question was what should be done with him. Robertson strongly advised the passing of a special Order in Council very secretly which would re-enact certain clauses of the Defence of Canada Regulations, so far as May personally was concerned, which would enable us to have him watched by the police and if necessary arrest him; also to see that he did not get away with papers, etc. To this I agreed and signed the recommendation to Council which was to get the signatures of four Ministers: Ilsley, Howe, Abbott* and myself,—only enough to be told the others to justify their signing. Nothing to be said to the rest of the Cabinet. The Order to be kept in the vault of the Council. I immediately signed the recommendation which was subsequently signed by the other Ministers . . .

Robertson told me that the head of the British Secret [Security] Service [Sir Percy Sillitoe] had sent two of his men to Ottawa. They had been given particulars and one at least was leaving by plane to give the information to [Sir Alexander] Cadogan, the Under-Secretary at the Foreign Office, the Foreign Minister [Ernest Bevin] to be advised, and he to advise Mr Byrnes, Secretary of State of the US. The FBI representatives arrived this morning and were given information by Robertson.[25]

During the next forty-eight hours or so, the translation of another Gouzenko document led the Robertson-MacDonald committee with the

---

* J. L. Ilsley, Minister of Finance, C. D. Howe, Minister of Munitions and Supply, and D. C. Abbott, Minister of National Defence.

Prime Minister's concurrence to reverse the earlier decision to arrest Nunn May prior to his departure, but instead to allow him to proceed to England as he had planned. The new document was a telegram from Moscow to Zabotin dated 18 August which revealed arrangements for Nunn May to establish contact with another and unknown agent referred to simply as 'the contact man'. They were to meet on three dates in October in front of the British Museum in London, and Nunn May was to carry a copy of *The Times* newspaper under his left arm, while the contact man would have a copy of the magazine *Picture Post* in his left hand. The latter would then ask 'What is the shortest way to the Strand?' and May would reply, 'Well, come along, I am going that way'. Before they began to talk business May would also say: 'Best regards from Mikel'.[26]

'We propose allowing May to leave on the plane, putting a secret service man with him', Mackenzie King consequently noted in his diary.

He will be followed when he reaches London and will be shadowed when this meeting takes place so that the other man may also be known. Whether the meeting will take place now that these papers have been stolen from the safe is considered a chance. The Russians will know they are gone but they do not know they are in the hands of the Government. They might suspect this and not carry on further.

'The whole business makes clear a vast espionage system', the Prime Minister added. 'Churchill was right when he said it would not do to let the Russians have the secret of the atom bomb. I thought Roosevelt was right when he said he felt an ally should know what we are doing in that regard. I can see that Churchill had the sounder judgment; had keener perceptions of what was at stake, what was going on.'[27]

Nunn May was due to take off for England from Dorval Airport, Montreal, in the early evening of 16 September. An amusing incident took place in connection with his departure. The station commander at Dorval was an English group-captain whom the British High Commissioner described as 'a charming fool'. He happened to be a personal friend of one of the detectives in the RCMP who was due to fly in the same aircraft. MacDonald thought that, as the passengers were preparing to embark, the group-captain might blurt out some such greeting to the detective as 'Hello, Charles! What on earth are you doing here out of uniform?' Since this might 'tip off' Nunn May and put him on his guard, MacDonald invited the group-captain to have tea with him in Ottawa. The officer accepted with profuse thanks for the honour which the High Commissioner had done him.

When the group-captain arrived at Earnscliffe, he was warmly received and entertained by the High Commissioner, who spent the next couple of hours, eating and drinking and discussing 'all sorts of trifling matters', such as football games, Wild West films and war scares. Eventually the telephone rang beside the High Commissioner's chair and MacDonald, on lifting the receiver, heard the message he had been expecting. The aircraft with Nunn May and the other passengers on board had just left Dorval. MacDonald thereupon got up and told the group-captain that it was a great pleasure to meet him but that he should not keep him away from his work at the airport any longer.

The aircraft landed safely in Britain next morning and Nunn May went off to take up his new appointment at King's College in the University of London.

Meanwhile the Russian Embassy in Ottawa had followed up their original request with a further note requesting Gouzenko's apprehension and surrender for deportation. To gain time Norman Robertson of the External Affairs Department asked for particulars of the money which it was alleged Gouzenko had stolen. 'You will, of course, understand that under the laws in force in Canada, it is impossible to comply in all respects with your request.' Robertson added: 'The Canadian police have no legal authority to arrest Mr Gouzenko and hand him over to your Embassy for deportation. If they adopted such a course they would be open to civil action and the effectiveness of the proceedings could be challenged by habeas corpus, involving a complete enquiry into the circumstances and the release of the accused if it were established that the arrest was designed to enable him to be handed over within this country to a foreign authority.'[28]

To this letter the Embassy never returned any answer. However, Pavlov did settle for the damage which had been caused to the door and frame of the Gouzenko apartment when he and his colleagues broke in on the night of 6 September, the owner of the premises being content with the sum of $5 which Pavlov paid him. At the same time, to put the Russians off the scent, the RCMP in Ottawa and the FBI in Washington pretended to accede to the Russian request to apprehend Gouzenko and hand him over to them by ostensibly instituting a nation-wide search for him in both countries. Also the fact that the Canadians had made no arrests was calculated to convey the impression that they were still unaware of Gouzenko's whereabouts. Furthermore, Stephenson sent two of the most experienced members of his staff to Ottawa to help the RCMP with their inquiries, while he put his telecrypton facilities at the disposal of the Canadian Government for the purpose of communicating with London, Washington, New York and elsewhere, since there was a danger that the Canadian secret cypher had been compromised and was known to the Russians.

On Sunday evening, 23 September, Mackenzie King kept an appointment at Earnscliffe with Malcolm MacDonald and Norman Robertson, together with Stephenson, who had come up again from New York, and several other Canadian and British intelligence officers, including Roger

Hollis of MI5, to discuss the Gouzenko case. According to Hollis, 'the Russians have got a lot of information on the atomic bomb'. Next day the Prime Minister dictated a short account of the meeting:

> The first question discussed was the alternative methods re security. One was to allow everything to be hushed up and not proceeded with further; another was to take action at once and let the British and US Governments know the situation with a view to taking what steps might be taken to prevent further developments. The third was adopting a course which would make the whole thing public, immediate arrests made and getting additional information at trials, etc. . . .
>
> My own view was that the second course was the appropriate one, and I found that was the view that appeared to be generally held. It was discussed in relation to the larger question of what was wisest from the diplomatic and political points of view. We all agreed that it would not do to let the matter pass as though it were something which should not be disclosed to the Russians, nor would it do to have publicity given to the whole business at this time. That the best course would be to have the British and United States Governments and ourselves work together on the highest level, and let the Russians know what we knew with a view to discovering from them whether they intended to really try to be friends and work for a peaceful world, or whether a course should be taken toward them which would lead to having all nations against them.
>
> I strongly favoured the direct approach to them, once everything had been worked out at the highest level.[29]

Thus general agreement was reached on the second course outlined above. Finally, someone suggested that the case should be given a cover name in all future conversations and reports concerning it. Norman Robertson pointed to the label on the bottle of Corby's Canadian rye whisky which stood on the desk nearby and which had been sustaining the group during their lengthy deliberations. Thus by general consent it was agreed that henceforward the case was to be known as 'the Corby case', and Gouzenko should likewise be known as 'Corby'.[30]

[6]

On 24 September, Mackenzie King spent two hours reading the complete statements which the Canadian secret service had so far obtained from Gouzenko, together with the translations of the documents he had supplied showing the extent to which official Canadian secret activities had been penetrated by Soviet espionage. The Prime Minister then dictated in his private diary:

It is all very terrible and frightening. It is strange how this business should have come right into my room in the East Block on the morning of the opening of the 20th Parliament. I can see that from now until the end of my days, it will be with this problem more than any other that, in all probability, I shall be most closely concerned . . .

As I dictate this note, I think of the Russian Embassy being only a few doors away [from Laurier House] and of there being there a centre of intrigue. During this period of war, while Canada has been helping Russia and doing all we can to foment Canadian-Russian friendship, there has been one branch of the Russian service that has been spying on all matters relating to location of American troops, atomic bombs, processes, etc. This first having to do with the army—reporting to army circles; another branch having to do with diplomatic and political questions, keeping headquarters of Russia informed of what might be going around by way of communications between the Americans, the British and ourselves, and yet another branch intended as a secret service, spying on themselves. It seems perfectly clear that chauffeurs, messengers, etc., are all part of a political organisation related to a system of espionage. The amazing thing is how many contacts have been successfully made with people in key positions in government and industrial circles.

I am sure the whole business extends much further than we begin to know. I am also sure that what has taken place in Canada is taking place even upon a vaster scale in the United States and Britain. I am almost certain also in other countries as well. All this helps to explain the Russian attitude at the Council of Foreign Ministers. Something very sinister there. Also at San Francisco [with the formation of the United Nations] in blocking what seemed to stand in Russia's way to increase her power and world control.[31]

Next day the Prime Minister had an engagement in his constituency. When he returned to Ottawa he saw Robertson, who was holding a telegram in his hand and appeared 'greatly concerned'. The telegram was from Cadogan, Robertson's opposite number in the Foreign Office in Downing Street, to the effect that the British authorities were prepared to arrest Nunn May at once and suggesting that arrests might be made simultaneously in Canada and also possibly in the United States, since 'it is apparent that the United States have discovered there has been similar penetration into the bomb business as has taken place here'.

Mackenzie King noted in his diary:

Robertson felt, as I felt, that to have arrests made at once would be a mistake. I said before I saw the telegram that I saw that the British had become exasperated at [the Soviet Foreign Minister] Molotov's behaviour at the Council of Foreign Ministers. The telegram stated that His Majesty's Government was prepared to take the step and all that might grow out of it and asked whether we would agree to a similar step and the United States taking a similar step.

Robertson and I conferred together and, after conference together, we held the same view as Robertson had set out in a message in reply, stressing that it would be unwise to take the step before we could get the whole case worked out by our police and had further evidence, but also that there should be a conference between myself, the President [of the US] or the Secretary of State, and Bevin as to how the whole matter should shape up . . .

We must move very slowly and cautiously. We were not ready in Canada to take proceedings and our leading advisers up to the present say it would be very difficult to get a conviction on the material we have considering its source, etc.[32]

A message was immediately sent to the White House and after some chopping and changing owing to their respective engagements, President Truman, whom the Canadian Prime Minister had not previously met, intimated that he would be pleased to see him on the following Sunday morning, 30 September. Before leaving Ottawa by air the previous afternoon, Mackenzie King saw the three Ministers who had signed the Order in Council, Ilsey, Howe and Abbott. Robertson and Wrong were also present and Mackenzie King told the Ministers for the first time the whole story of Gouzenko's defection. 'The three Ministers were naturally greatly surprised and impressed', King noted after their meeting. 'I let them know that my first information came the day of the opening of Parliament. That I had been carrying the secret ever since—known only to St Laurent. That it was really the factor which made it necessary for me to leave immediately. They all appreciated the situation.'

Robertson, who accompanied the Prime Minister to Washington, had made up a dossier on the Corby case which Mackenzie King read and re-read on the plane and also in the Canadian embassy, where they stayed the night with the Canadian ambassador, Mr Lester Pearson. At Robertson's suggestion, Mackenzie King took the dossier with him in an ordinary brown envelope to the White House next morning so as to refresh his memory if necessary, and he was actually photographed with it under his arm as he entered the building.

President Truman received him in the Oval Room; the Prime Minister arrived alone, as he thought it better to leave Robertson in the Embassy with Pearson, but the President had Dean Acheson, the Assistant Secretary of State, with him, since Byrnes was apparently away. After the usual exchange of courteous preliminaries, they got down to business. The

interview lasted for nearly two hours. The main preliminary points made by
Mackenzie King are set out below in his own words:

> Narrated the incidents regarding Corby. What had subsequently been
> obtained in the way of information. Told them of the extent of espionage in
> Canada. What we had learned about espionage in the United States.
> Mentioned particularly request as to information as to United States
> troops, etc., shipping to Russia; of information regarding the atomic
> bomb. The visit by a courier to the United States by one who turned out to
> be an Inspector of the Red Army and of his having sized up the espionage
> system in the United States. Had sent out his report from Ottawa. Spoke of
> the [Vice-] Consul at New York [Anatoli Yakovlev] who apparently had
> charge of the espionage business in the United States. Of the connection of
> that office with the organisation in Switzerland; of large sums of money
> having gone from that office to Switzerland.*

The President intervened at this point to say that he felt every care must
be taken to get full information before anything at all was disclosed,
repeating his view several times that nothing should be done without
agreement between them and Attlee in London and 'above all nothing
should be done which might result in premature action in any direction'.
He also said two or three times that he was particularly interested in
anything the Canadian Prime Minister could tell him of what had happened
in the United States or would give evidence of espionage there. Mackenzie
King then remarked that it would be best if he were to read from the report
he had with him, and to this the President was agreeable.

> I then read the preliminary statement concerning the espionage system
> in Russia. Read early portions about the system as it worked in the
> Embassy. Read about Primrose [Nunn May] and others in key positions.
> Went particularly to the passages concerning the Russian Consulate in
> New York. The statements re the atomic bomb; information gained from
> the United States. What was thought to have gone from Chicago. Also
> the statement that an assistant secretary of the Secretary of State's
> Department was supposed to be implicated, though I made perfectly

---

* After the break-up of the Soviet spy organisation in Switzerland towards the end of the war,
an important Swiss who worked for the Russians named Rachel Dubendorfer (code-name
'Cissie'), who was very short of funds, sent an *en clair* telegram in veiled language to a former
'cut-out' Hermina Rabinovitch employed by the International Labour Organisation in
Montreal, asking Hermina to go to the Soviet Embassy in Ottawa and ask for $10,000 to be
sent to her through the medium of a New York watch company whose Geneva agent would
pay the money to 'Cissie'. The money was transferred to Washington where Hermina
collected it, since it was considered too dangerous to cross the border with such a large sum.
See Rabanovitch's testimony in *The Report of the Royal Commission* (Ottawa, 1946) and
Alexander Foote, *Handbook for Spies* (London 1949), *passim*, on the connection between the
Canadian and Swiss espionage organisations.

clear this was only what Corby had said but I had no information to back it up. The President did not seem surprised. He turned to Acheson, then said that they had thought the report had reference to an assistant to an assistant secretary. I said of course I knew nothing but what was in the statement as recorded there. Probably he was right and there might even be no foundation.*

At the President's suggestion Mackenzie King called on the British Ambassador Lord Halifax the same afternoon. The visit was brief since there was a garden party taking place in the embassy grounds which the Ambassador left to receive the Canadian Prime Minister in the library. Mackenzie King did not enjoy their talk, since the Ambassador invited him to be seated on a sofa and himself took a seat to the right of the sofa, where the light shone in Mackenzie King's eyes so that the visitor could not see Halifax's face. This may well have been unintentional on the Ambassador's part though Mackenzie King thought otherwise, and felt rather offended. ('It seemed a poor type of practice for a man like Halifax to adopt. It is I know a way that some people of the Mussolini type and others take. They must watch the countenance of the men they are talking to and have their own in the dark.') The Prime Minister put his hand over his eyes to shade them in the short time they had to review the Corby situation. The Ambassador said he knew some of the particulars from Malcolm MacDonald, to which Mackenzie King replied that he felt he should give the Americans the same information as he was prepared to give Britain, with which Halifax agreed. The Ambassador then remarked that he was sure that Mr Attlee, who was going to come over from England to meet President Truman, should work out the matter between them. 'I at once interjected I thought it should be worked out with Canada as well', Mackenzie King noted in his diary, adding that 'the three of us were equally interested . . . and perhaps we [the Canadians] were in the most serious position of all as information was coming from Canada and if there was to be suffering from consequences, we should get most of it. Halifax later took care to refer to the three as being essential.'[33]

Later the same afternoon, Mackenzie King and Robertson left for New York where they embarked next morning, 1 October, on the *Queen Mary*. When the ship docked in Southampton at noon on 7 October, Roger Hollis of MI5 came on board and showed Mackenzie King a telegram from Halifax to the Foreign Office, stating that Dean Acheson had given him (Halifax) a

---

* The individual in question was Alger Hiss, who had been special assistant to Edward Stettinius at the Yalta Conference and later acted as first Secretary-General of the United Nations. He was convicted of perjury in 1950 and sentenced to five years' imprisonment of which he served 44 months. He had previously been accused by an admitted Communist agent named Whittaker Chambers of having Communist associations.

message from the President to the effect that the President was anxious that Nunn May, who was due to meet his Russian contact outside the British Museum the same evening, should not be arrested 'unless it was obviously necessary for security reasons and then only if he were discovered to be communicating some document of a Top Secret nature to the man he was to meet . . . That the President felt very strongly that there should be agreement on the matter. That every effort should be made to secure further information in the US and also in Britain before action was precipitated. Also most important to have complete understanding between the countries immediately concerned first.'[34]

On the Foreign Office wanting to know if the Canadian Prime Minister would give approval to an arrest being made that night, Mackenzie King stressed his agreement with the President's view and said, as Truman did, that he 'would not stand in the way of an arrest being made if the conditions were to be found to exist and observed'.

In the event no arrest was made, since Nunn May did not turn up at the agreed rendezvous either that night or on either of the other two nights specified in the same month.

During the four weeks or so that Canada's Prime Minister spent in England, he had many discussions and meetings with British Cabinet ministers and others, but the Gouzenko affair continued to prey on his mind. His first meeting was with Attlee, with whom he spent the night of his arrival at Chequers so that he could brief the British Prime Minister on his meeting with Truman. According to Mackenzie King, Attlee's immediate reaction was that he was in entire agreement with the American President's view, 'namely, that as much information should be secured both in the US and here before the case was opened up to the public'. Attlee also agreed that an approach should be made in the first instance to the Russians themselves, and that the espionage matter should be linked up with the atomic bomb secret. Attlee added that he felt the time had come when there must be a 'show-down' with the Russians.

> He said he really could not understand the Russians and what was behind their line of action. They were exceedingly difficult. He said Stalin was the only one who had a final say. Molotov could not go any distance in anything. Kept getting authority from Stalin. He said he did not think there was anything in the statement that Stalin was going to retire because of ill-health. He thought that the Russian successes had gone a little bit to their head; also that they had a strong inferiority complex. That both forces were operating to make things difficult. He added that they really had not any true conception of democracy. That both were talking about different things while they used the same words.[35]

The following afternoon, Lord Addison, the Dominions Secretary, called on Mackenzie King at his suite in the Dorchester, and they talked about the Gouzenko affair in the context of Russia's policy of what appeared to be 'power politics, pure and simple'. Apparently Addison had not appreciated that a Russian courier had taken back to Moscow a piece of uranium from Nunn May in Canada.

It may have been something that was acquired in Chicago. He [Addison] said he felt quite sure that Russia would very soon come to acquire the secret of the atomic bomb. The scientists, once they were working on a matter which had been successful elsewhere, were pretty certain to discover the processes which led to their final result. He believes we must count on Russia getting that secret.

He told me as a significant fact that in all the parts of Germany which are occupied by the Russians and which include many of the former great centres where research was carried on, the Russians had taken all the scientists and their equipment, etc., away and removed it to Russia. He was amazed at the extent of their organization for espionage purposes. Said he felt perfectly sure it was exercised here and in the US as we had discovered in Canada. He could not explain the whole Russian attitude on any basis other than one of real opposition.

I outlined to him the three courses which we thought could be pursued; one, indifference; the other, extreme publicity at once, and the third, confronting the Russians with the information we had and seeking to work out a basis of co-operation.

He was sure that the last of the three was the preferable course. He said we must remember they are Orientals. (Montgomery had told Salisbury that he regarded them as savages.)

Lord Addison thought we must be infinitely patient. He felt sure, however, that if we did not let the Russians see that we were in earnest, where a wrong had been done, they would think we were soft and themselves take advantage of the course of procedure and that nothing should be done which would endanger the situation until the course was agreed on. He regarded as the main factor in a situation of the kind what was in the mind of the other man; how he really thought and felt.

I had been mentioning that at San Francisco, Molotov was like a bit of bronze, or more accurately like a bit of marble, in his appearance and attitude. I said I thought at first it was due to his determination to see that Russia was put on an equality with every country, which I thought was right enough. I told him how completely he changed when a certain knotty question had been gotten out of the way. He said of the two men, he himself thinks better of Stalin, who sees things more quickly than Molotov, has a larger vision . . .

Lord Addison agrees, however, and we come back to that, that another war would mean a total destruction and this must be worked against at all costs. This is the view that Attlee holds. It is quite an appalling outlook.[36]

Addison impressed Mackenzie King favourably. 'I felt he was a very wise man', King noted afterwards in his diary. 'A good counsellor for the government. I also felt, however, that the British Government has really not as yet wholly tackled this problem or realised or begun to realise the implications of the whole espionage system.' This was confirmed by Norman Robertson in his talks with various officials of the Dominions and Foreign Offices the same day when, according to Mackenzie King, he discovered that 'they had not been thinking beyond the arrest of criminals as something which came as a matter of course, finding some official guilty of particular crimes, but they had never asked themselves how this all related itself to the atomic bomb. Robertson has suggested lines of thought which they are now exploring . . .' Two days later, when Mackenzie King dined with Ernest Bevin, he found that the British Foreign Secretary 'seemed to have very little knowledge or appreciation of the situation in a large way. He was inclined to think that an arrest or two might be made here and assumed that we would adopt a similar course.' After Mackenzie King had told Bevin of Truman's view that the three countries should act in concert, Bevin 'quite changed his attitude' and said he would see Attlee in the morning on the subject.[37]

On 18 October, Mackenzie King was the guest of the physician Lord Moran at a dinner of the Harveian Society. Several government ministers and ambassadors were also present including Fedor Gousev, whom Mackenzie King knew previously since he had been Zarubin's predecessor in Ottawa, but who ignored him on this occasion and deliberately refrained from speaking to him. Nor did Gousev call on him at the Dorchester as he might have been expected to do. 'That I thought was significant', Mackenzie King remarked at the time.

Three nights later the Canadian Prime Minister dined with the Attlees at 10 Downing Street. After dinner Attlee took his guest downstairs to the library and immediately re-opened the question of arresting Nunn May. He said:

That he had not turned up on Wednesday evening [for the second rendezvous] and their intelligence officials were feeling that they ought to disassociate him from the work that he is doing in connection with atomic energy and if there was much longer delay, the whole business would be getting cold and blame might attach for not having taken some immediate action. They propose as what they would like to do, to examine him privately under some military protectionist measure—I have forgotten the name of it—not with a view to publicity being given but simply to bring out information which would be helpful in discussing the matter later with the Russians. He thought it was as well to have the information first.

He then asked me if we could not begin an immediate inquiry. I told him that I agreed it was not well to delay much longer in getting information. I doubted, however, if we had the same authority at law for examining individuals on the score of suspicion. Attlee himself referred to the girl in the High Commissioner's office [Kathleen Willsher] and I mentioned the clerk in our own External Affairs [Emma Woikin] and said that, quite recently, some papers in our passport office were missing which we had been a little suspicious about. I told him I would communicate with the Minister of Justice and see if some way could not be arranged whereby we could immediately question the different persons involved in what we had discovered. Attlee stressed the point of not giving publicity to the matter at present but of having the information where it could be given to the Russians.[38]

Both men agreed that the Russians were probably already aware of the Canadian Prime Minister having some of the information, a deduction which had been reinforced by the Soviet ambassador's ignoring him at the Harveian Society dinner, at which Attlee had also been present. They also agreed to keep the American President informed of their plans and that they would try to meet him in Washington in the following month, on or about Armistice Day.

Mackenzie King wrote next day:

October 22, 1945. Spent a considerable time with Robertson going over what should be done at Ottawa regarding Russian espionage . . . I am strongly taking the position that we should not attempt any arrests at the outset but have employees of the Government questioned in the presence of the Minister of Justice. If they refused to allow searching, then they should be apprehended under warrants. I doubt the wisdom of attempting any general inquiry by a Royal Commission until we have got some evidence other than Corby's on which has been based the line of action to be taken when the conference is held in Washington between Attlee and the President.

The letter I sent to Attlee today made clear the desirability of my going to Washington with him and of the conference we were having together.[39]

'This evening', Mackenzie King noted in his diary for 23 October, 'I had a talk with Robertson who began by telling me that he had been talking with the Chief of the Secret [Security] Service here and they had come to the conclusion it was better not to take any action on Russian espionage until after the meeting in Washington; also that it was felt if we took action before, especially giving publicity, it might spoil the chance of getting a settlement on the atomic bomb and might arouse public opinion in a very serious way . . .'

> I tried to emphasise to Robertson that there would be great difficulty in getting proof and that unless we had entire proof, the whole thing would backfire in a very serious way, where I thought members of the Canadian government service should be questioned but care taken not to start any legal proceedings or inquiry by a Royal Commission.[40]

Meanwhile Gousev, the Soviet Ambassador in London, had been in touch with Moscow and had evidently been told not to ignore the Canadian Prime Minister but to invite him to the embassy in Kensington Palace Gardens. The result was an invitation to lunch on 31 October, which Mackenzie King immediately accepted. On his arrival at the embassy he received 'a very warm welcome' from the Ambassador, while 'Mrs Gousev also came running along the hall and extended an equally warm welcome'. The only other person present was the Commercial Counsellor, 'quite a pleasant substantial fellow'. It was a lavish meal with caviare and other delicacies accompanied by vodka and various wines which Mackenzie King, according to his own account, was 'careful not to do more than taste'.

In the course of conversation the Ambassador raised the subject of scientific research and referred to Attlee's recent announcement that he was shortly going to meet President Truman in Washington. Canada had a good deal to do with the making of the atomic bomb, Gousev went on to suggest; also Canada knew the secret. There had been a lot of research work done at McGill University, and British and American and Canadian scientists had met there for this purpose. Mackenzie King agreed that there had been research into the discovery of the release of atomic energy both at the research laboratories in Ottawa and at the Canadian universities. 'So far as Canada was concerned, however', he continued, 'it was not correct to say that we had the secret of the bomb because we had not had to do with its manufacture at all'. He added that he thought the scientists everywhere knew pretty much what there was to be known about the release of atomic energy but that 'the question of manufacturing for purposes of destruction—the process of manufacture—was something that we had no knowledge of'. At Petawawa they had been working on some of the substances that had to do with the release of atomic energy, but this was only incidental to general research.

The Commercial Counsellor broke in to ask whether Mackenzie King had seen the cartoon by Low in the previous day's *Evening Standard*. This depicted Truman carrying a little bomb under his arm, the bomb being marked 'secret'. Mackenzie King said he recalled having seen something of the kind the night before, but he was not too clear about it.

'You and I are old friends', he said to the Ambassador as they parted. 'We must do all we can to see that good-will is promoted between different countries—particularly our respective countries.' At the same time Mackenzie King felt sure that Gousev knew about Nunn May and that he must have known that the Canadian Prime Minister did too. Afterwards he noted in his diary:

> From what he said, I could see that the Russians may come back on any disclosure we make, presenting the view that the bomb was really conceived in Canada and worked out there by scientists of Britain and the US. That this was done at Montreal. This will be the excuse they will make for having found it necessary to have espionage.[41]

In the event, as will be seen, Mackenzie King's conclusion was to prove not very far from the mark.

[7]

The Canadian Prime Minister sailed from Southampton on 3 November and disembarked at New York on the 9th. He travelled overnight by train to Washington where he arrived about the same time as Attlee, who had flown from London. There is a gap in Mackenzie King's diaries between 10 November and the end of the year, but it is possible to piece together the gist from other sources of the outcome of the summit discussions. No official transcript was made at the time, and there was naturally no public mention of the Corby case, although no doubt it was discussed privately between the President and the two Prime Ministers and the others who sat in on the talks—they were, with the President, Secretary of State Byrnes and Admiral William Leahy, Chief of Staff; with Attlee, the British Ambassador Lord Halifax and Sir John Anderson, Chairman of the United Kingdom Atomic Energy Committee; and with Mackenzie King, Lester Pearson, the Canadian Ambassador in Washington.

On 15 November President Truman announced publicly that the three government heads had agreed on the need for international action, under the auspices of the United Nations, for the provision of controls over atomic energy to ensure its use for peaceful purposes only. 'We agree', he added, 'that there should be full and effective co-operation in the field of atomic energy between the United States, the United Kingdom and Canada'.

Unfortunately, as Attlee was later to comment ruefully, in American politics 'the Administration proposes but Congress disposes'. A strong 'lobby' was formed in the Senate opposed to the sharing of atomic information with any other country in spite of the wartime Anglo-American agreement on sharing which had been concluded by Churchill and Roosevelt at Quebec in 1943. The result was the introduction of a Bill by Senator Brien McMahon placing atomic energy in the United States under civilian control and prohibiting the disclosure of information to any foreign power. In spite of British protests the McMahon Bill became law, and it was more than a decade before the damage to Anglo-American relations and collaboration caused by this legislation was repaired. This meant that Britain was forced to undertake its own development of atomic energy through the experimental and research establishment which had already been set up by Sir John Cockcroft at Harwell on the Berkshire downs.

'I don't blame Truman', Attlee admitted later. 'He showed himself very aware of the need for co-operation in our Washington talks, and we did in fact fix up what looked like a pretty good agreement. The trouble was they couldn't get it through the Senate. The Senate wanted to have everything for America. Once Congress proceeded to pass the McMahon Bill we had to go ahead on our own. And although we were involved in a very much bigger expenditure than if we'd had the help and information due to us from America, we actually got ahead of them . . . in technical work generally at that time. A considerable achievement by our scientists.'[42]

Furthermore, although the Soviet Union subscribed to the British resolution unanimously passed at the first United Nations assembly establishing the UN Atomic Energy Commission, which outlawed the use of atomic weapons capable of mass destruction and providing effective safeguards through inspection, Soviet policy was afterwards effectively directed towards nullifying the work and objectives of this body. By this time, as will be seen, Russia had acquired the secret of the construction of the bomb.

While Mackenzie King was in London, Gouzenko wrote out a long statement in Russian for the RCMP, giving the reasons for his defection. 'The last elections which took place recently in Canada surprised me', Gouzenko observed, in a passage which particularly impressed the Prime Minister when he read it. 'In comparison with them the system of elections in Russia appear as a mockery of the conception of free elections. For example, the fact that in elections in the Soviet Union one candidate is put forward, so that the possibilities of choice are eliminated, speaks for itself.' The translation concluded with these telling words:

During my residence in Canada I have seen how the Canadian people and their Government, sincerely wishing to help the Soviet people, sent supplies to the Soviet Union, collected money for the welfare of the Russian people, sacrificing their sons in the delivery of these supplies across the ocean—and instead of gratitude for the help rendered, the

Soviet Government is developing espionage activity in Canada, preparing to deliver a stab in the back of Canada—all this without the knowledge of the Russian people.

Convinced that such double-faced politics of the Soviet Government towards the democratic countries do not conform with the interests of the Russian people and endanger the security of civilisation, I decided to break away from the Soviet regime and to announce my decision openly.

I am glad that I found the strength within myself to take this step and to warn Canada and the other democratic countries of the danger which hangs over them.[43]

Since Igor, Anna and young Andrei had been whisked off in a hurry to northern Canada with little more than the clothes they were wearing at the time, one of the first duties of the detectives who accompanied them was to measure them for warmer clothing, making records of their vital statistics and tracing on sheets of paper the exact size of their feet. These were duly despatched from Ottawa and, as the time for Anna's confinement was approaching, orders were also sent for maternity dresses. At the appropriate moment she was removed to a local hospital where she posed as the wife of a Polish immigrant farmer, while an RCMP officer disguised himself as the expectant father, visiting the hospital every day and talking at his supposed wife's bedside in carefully rehearsed broken English. At the request of the RCMP, a complete layette for the baby, who turned out to be a girl, Svetlana, weighing seven pounds and six ounces, was specially ordered and sent up from Stephenson's office in New York as a gesture of cordial welcome for the latest addition to Canada's population.[44]

It was originally intended that Nunn May's arrest in London and the arrest of Fred Rose and Sam Carr, the secretary of the Labour Progressive Party in Canada, should be carried out towards the end of November, but the FBI's need to investigate the activities of the Russian Vice-Consul Anatoli Yakovlev in New York, which Gouzenko's documents had revealed, led to a postponement until the time was ripe for the police in all three countries to swoop on the spies. Meanwhile the Soviet embassy in Ottawa, which by now strongly suspected that Gouzenko was in the hands of the Canadian authorities and that their spy network had consequently been 'blown', played down their covert operations. At the same time orders came from Moscow recalling Zabotin and the two assistant military attachés, Motinov and Rogov; also Pavel Angelov, who had been Nunn May's contact and who, it will be remembered, had been a member of the party which broke into Gouzenko's apartment in Somerset Street. The ambassador himself, Georgei Zarubin, also departed for home on what was stated to be a 'routine visit'.

One day in December Zabotin and the others boarded a Soviet merchant vessel, the *Alexandrov*, in New York and the ship sailed without going through the normal clearance procedures, since it appears to have enjoyed diplomatic immunity. None of the Russians ever returned to Ottawa, although some years later Zarubin was appointed Ambassador to Great Britain, an appointment which he took up in due course. As for Zabotin, although he had recently been awarded two high Russian decorations, the Order of the Red Star and the Order of the Red Banner, there are grounds for believing that he never reached the Soviet Union. 'Rumour whispered soon afterwards', Malcolm MacDonald subsequently told me, 'that he had jumped overboard when the vessel was at sea, preferring death among the waves to the fate which was likely to greet him on disembarking in his native land. I felt very sorry at the news, for I knew the Colonel well, and respected him not only as a charming man and a competent soldier but also as a devoted servant of his country.'[45] *

Incidentally the new Military Attaché, one Colonel Popov, did not make a particularly good impression when he arrived. Shortly afterwards, in January 1946, he was arrested in Toronto on a charge of drunkenness and, according to Mackenzie King, was 'found to be carrying a loaded revolver' and 'a receipt for money paid over to one of the agents whose name appears in the record'. By this time the Prime Minister was sure that the Soviet Government was 'pretty well aware that we have knowledge of some of the things which have been going on which could not stand the light of day. What may grow out of the inquiry we shall have in Canada, I cannot say, but there can be little doubt that a very heavy responsibility is now on our shoulders, and that it will grow into one of the major sensations of the day.'[46]

On 1 February 1946, Admiral Leahy, President Truman's Chief of Staff, visited Ottawa and lunched with Mackenzie King. 'In the course of conversation I spoke to him about the atomic bomb', the Prime Minister wrote afterwards.

> He was quite outspoken in saying that he did not think it should have been used as the United States had used it, against defenceless women and children which was the case in the two cities that were bombed. He also stated the destruction was due more to intense heat than explosion. He told me how examination had revealed curious evidences of this. Believed only the UK, the US and Canada should for the present know the effect of the use of the atomic bomb, at sea, against ships, etc. He felt the whole system of warfare might have to be changed.

* Writing to the Dominions Secretary Lord Addison on 22 August 1946, Sir Alexander Clutterbuck, who had succeeded Mr Malcolm MacDonald as British High Commissioner in Ottawa, stated that Colonel Zabotin was 'reported . . . to have paid for the disclosures with his life': PRO DO 35/1207. According to a report in the American Socialist weekly *New Leader*, Zabotin died of 'heart failure' four days after his arrival in Moscow.

We talked a little of the Corby case. He felt that we ought to go on with our inquiry if it involved our own civil servants. He also agreed that it might have far-reaching repercussions.[47]

Three days later some sketchy details of the case became public knowledge for the first time. During the afternoon of 4 February, Robertson telephoned the Prime Minister to say that in the previous evening the American broadcaster, Drew Pearson, had gone on the air, with an account of how Mackenzie King had gone to Washington in the first instance 'to tell President Truman about a situation in Canada which disclosed Russian intrigue. The report went on to speak of the Russians making plans of rivers, etc., round about Calgary.' How the information was 'leaked' to Drew Pearson the Canadian Prime Minister did not know, but he suspected that someone in the State Department was responsible. (In fact it was Stephenson.) 'As Robertson said', Mackenzie King noted, 'this business has become known to too many people—the President's office, the Secretary of State's office, the FBI, etc. However, this may be all for the best, as it gives us a special reason for starting immediately with our investigation.'[48]

Robertson added that during the morning he had met Malcolm MacDonald, some senior officers of the RCMP, and Mr E. K. Williams, the President of the Canadian Bar Association, all of whom had known of the details of the Corby case for some time. The Prime Minister 'suggested having the Commission appointed at once to take evidence in secret wherever Corby may be. Then make the arrests necessary of our own people and defer to that moment my having a word with the Russian Ambassador.'

Next day the Prime Minister reviewed the whole situation with Robertson who told him that 'suspicions are directed right up to the top of the United States Treasury, naming the person [Harry Dexter White];* also that it is directed against another person who was very close to Stettinius at San Francisco and who took a prominent part in matters there [Alger Hiss]'. With regard to the latter Mackenzie King said he was not personally surprised at Hiss's treachery, but he confessed he was surprised when he saw Hiss filling the position he did. His diary for the same day continued:

The lady Corby named [Elizabeth Bentley]† had for two years been

---

* Harry Dexter White was Assistant Secretary of the Treasury under Henry Morgenthau, who was largely responsible for the Bretton Woods monetary plan, the Morgenthau Plan for Germany, and the World Bank. According to the defector Elizabeth Bentley, White used his influence to place Communist Party members and fellow travellers in strategic positions in the US Government.

† Elizabeth Bentley, an American Communist underground worker, who defected to the Government, testified at length before the House Un-American Activities Committee in 1948, incriminating Harry Dexter White and other US Government officials.

employed as liaison between the Soviet headquarters in New York and officials in different government departments, from whom she was securing documents. These documents were taken to New York and copied there and then returned to departmental files, so that there was nothing to show they had been abstracted. The evidence went to show that the Russians knew everything about the invasion of Europe before it took place. Material had apparently come from the service departments. There was also evidence of the expenditure of much money.

After he had read the text of Drew Pearson's broadcast, Mackenzie King confided to his diary the feeling that it had been in some way inspired. 'I may be wrong', he wrote, 'but I have a feeling that there is a desire at Washington that this information should get out; that Canada should start the inquiry and that we should have the responsibility of beginning it and that the way should be paved for continuing it in the US. This may be all wrong but I have the intuition very strongly. It is the way in which a certain kind of politics is played by a certain type of man.' He was quite right. The man was Intrepid, although Mackenzie King did not know it at the time.

The Prime Minister next informed the Cabinet of the outlines of the story, and told the members of the secret order-in-council which he had signed and which he now activated by appointing two judges of the Suprene Court, Mr Justice Robert Taschereau and Mr Justice R. L. Kellock, as Commissioners to take evidence with the assistance of Mr E. K. Williams and other counsel; also that Corby would be brought to the Justice Department or the Commissioners would go to where he was located to get his evidence. 'It is most important his evidence should be gotten at once in case anything should happen to him', the Prime Minister emphasised. 'It is all important we should have his statements re documents, etc.' He later read the text of the public announcement he proposed to make, constituting the Royal Commission to investigate the fact that 'information of un-doubted authenticity has reached the Canadian Government which estab-lishes that there have been disclosures of secret and confidential informa-tion to unauthorised persons, including some members of the staff of a foreign mission in Ottawa'. Prosecutions would follow if considered necessary. He described what he had told the Cabinet in his diary:

> We were the most vulnerable of any country in our proximity to the USSR. That I had hoped, and had so said to the President and Bevin, that we might find a way of communicating the facts to the Russian government itself without disclosing them in court, giving the govern-ment the chance to clean up the situation itself. I pointed out, however, on the other hand, that there was the need to clean up our own service, and that now that Drew Pearson's statement was out, there would be questioning and we would not be able to conceal the situation effectively.

Howe [Minister of Supply] asked whether it was Drew Pearson's disclosure that was responsible for the timing. I replied it was not. That the timing was based on the return of Mr St Laurent after his talk with both Bevin and Byrnes in London [during the meetings of the United Nations General Assembly]. St Laurent then reported on these conversations and stated that both Bevin and Byrnes thought we ought to make an inquiry. It was of course our own business to decide, but it was their view that the matter should be gone on with now.

I explained that we had waited to give the US an opportunity to follow up the revelations that they had received. They had now told us it was better we should proceed without delay. They were of the view that the USSR might not take the matter too seriously. That they might simply feel that spying was a practice all countries adopted and that they had done nothing more than what other countries might be doing. *My own feeling is that this whole business goes much further than any one of us begins to realise.* (Author's italics)

Gouzenko was now brought down from his hide-out in the north and the RCMP began to take his evidence on 13 February. 'Arrests will have to follow at the end of the week', Mackenzie King noted the same day. 'I can see where a great cry will be raised, having had a Commission sit in secret, and men and women arrested and detained under an order-in-council passed really under War Measure powers. I will be held up to the world as the very opposite of a democrat. It is part of the inevitable.' Next day Robertson told the Prime Minister that 'the examination of Corby was proceeding morning, noon and night and will probably be concluded tonight, and tomorrow a number of civil servants will be taken into custody. A statement will have to be given out in the evening.'

R. wonders if it would not be better given out by the Minister of Justice. I told him no. That while I would personally prefer the Minister of Justice doing it, not to forget that the Catholic Church was a bitter enemy of the Soviets and this would add fuel to the flame. I had better take full responsibility. I could of course mention legal actions being taken at the instance of the Minister.

The Russian ambassador is not yet back, nor have I yet replied to communication regarding Popov in Toronto, which has come from the Embassy. A terrible document they have sent. Just the kind of thing that was attempted before in regard to some priests. Typical Soviet method of doing things.[49]

Thirteen people in all were arrested at seven o'clock in the morning of 15 February. Among them was Kathleen Willsher, who was picked up following a written request from Malcolm MacDonald. They were all taken to the police barracks at Rockliffe and detained there for questioning and subsequent trial where it would found that they had been disclosing material to the Russian embassy. By arrangement with London, Nunn May was questioned by Scotland Yard Special Branch officers, although he was not arrested, since he denied all knowledge of any espionage.

Mackenzie King had asked the Soviet Chargé d'Affaires, in the ambassador's absence, to come to his office in the afternoon, as he wished to speak to him before issuing the particulars of the constitution of the Royal Commission to the press. Accordingly Mr Belokhvostikov, accompanied by Vitali Pavlov, the Second Secretary and NKVD man, arrived shortly after four p.m. The Prime Minister, who had Robertson with him, began by asking the Chargé d'Affaires if he had any word as to when the ambassador was due to arrive. He replied that about a week or ten days ago they had received word from London that he was coming, but that there had been no news of him since. (In fact he never did come.) Mackenzie King went on to say that he wished to speak to them on a very important matter on which he was issuing a statement to the press later in the day and which he would like to read to them. This he proceeded to do, remarking at the same time that he had purposely refrained from making any statement as to the foreign mission referred to, but he thought they should know it was the USSR embassy. Mackenzie King also observed that Mr Belokhvostikov would notice that 'we were dealing only with members of our own civil service', adding that the statement would not go beyond reference to our own people except in the particular he had mentioned, which was to a foreign mission.

> When I began to read the statement [the Prime Minister noted afterwards] I noticed the young Chargé d'Affaires coloured up quite perceptibly. His countenance became very pink. There was no other evidence of particular emotion and his face gradually assumed its natural colour. The other man, Pavlov, however, sat throughout with his hands clenched tight and a sort of dour, determined, indifferent appearance. I noticed that he kept pressing his thumbs on his fingers as I was reading. He had a way of throwing back his head and looking more or less into the open.[50]

When he had finished reading, the Prime Minister handed the Chargé d'Affaires a copy of the statement, which the latter looked over. He then had a word with Pavlov, talking to him in Russian. Pavlov then said that 'this was a surprise to him, that it was not a matter of which he knew anything. As it of course concerned his government he would report the matter at once to them.' Mackenzie King then raised the incident of the arrest of the new Military Attaché Colonel Popov by the police. Robertson read the reply to the Russian communication which latter was a protest in offensive language at the breach of diplomatic immunity occasioned by

Popov's arrest in Toronto, and expressing an apology which the Prime Minister afterwards said he thought went rather too far, but in view of Gouzenko's statement and other evidence he thought on reflection that 'we could afford to go that far'. Again Pavlov spoke to the Chargé d'Affaires in Russian. Mackenzie King could not, of course, understand what was said. However, Mr Belokhvostikov immediately stated that he would see that his government was informed at once of what had appeared concerning the Popov matter in the Canadian newspapers.

The Prime Minister's account of the interview concluded:

> The young men were about to rise when I stopped them for a moment to say how sorry Robertson and I were to speak of these matters at all; that we were all close friends, and that nothing should destroy that relationship. I wanted to repeat again what I said about the care we had taken not to deal with other than members of our own public service. Disclosed nothing further of the offence which justified the action we had found it necessary to take against them. Robertson and I then shook hands with both of them.
>
> The Chargé d'Affaires I know quite well and have always joked with him about his marriage to Olga, who was an attractive secretary in the embassy under Gousev [Zarubin's predecessor as ambassador]. He had his happy smile in shaking hands. The other man was quite indifferent. When we closed the door, Robertson said to me 'Pavlov is the villain of the piece'. He did not think the Chargé d'Affaires knew much about the situation.

'There has never been anything in the world's history more complete', wrote Mackenzie King next day in his diary, 'than what we will reveal of the Russian method to control the continent as a result of Corby fleeing to the Department of Justice and the course then taken under direction of my office. As Prime Minister I have had to take the responsibility. The world now knows that I went to see the President and that I also went to see Bevin.'[51]

When Mackenzie King read Gouzenko's testimony which had been given before the Commissioners, it came as 'an astounding revelation' to him. 'It will be a terrible shock to the free nations of the world', he noted on 17 February. 'I think even more to Russia for it discloses their whole method of espionage in a more convincing manner than it has ever been exposed.' Later that day, far from being denounced for pursuing an undemocratic policy in appointing the Commission and ordering the arrests, the Prime Minister was interested in hearing over the radio the expression used that others should have the courage and initiative that Canada had shown.

Finally, he noted in his diary:

It can be honestly said that few more courageous acts have ever been performed by leaders of the government than my own in the Russian intrigue against the Christian world and the manner in which I have fearlessly taken up and begun to expose the whole of it. I see the full significance. I am certain that America now cannot hold back, but I myself know of what has taken place there. Britain cannot hold back what is known to the British Government with respect to Primrose [Nunn May], which links him up to what pertains to disclosures regarding the atomic bomb. What has been unearthed in Canada will lead each country to begin to examine its conditions in the light of this evidence. We are only at the beginning of the real disclosures . . . There will be certain major sensations.

Had Gouzenko defected a month or two sooner, Mackenzie King opined, it would have been too early. 'What we got in the last few weeks of cables to and from headquarters at Moscow', he concluded, 'brings in the US, Britain, as well as disclosing how far espionage has gone in Canada and how substantial were the beginnings of the fifth column organisation here. When the evidence is published, and that must be as soon as possible, it will fairly tear the roof off the American nation. It will rouse public opinion as nothing has done since the beginning of the war.'[52]

CHAPTER TWO

The Royal Commission

[1]

On 20 February 1946, while Nunn May was being questioned in London, Mr Solomon Lozovski, Deputy Commissar for Foreign Affairs in Moscow, sent for Mr Leon Mayrand, the Chargé d'Affaires at the Canadian Embassy there and read him the following statement which was the Soviet Government's reply to Mackenzie King's recent action in Ottawa.

> Soviet organisations have become aware that in the later periods of the war certain members of the staff of the Soviet Military Attaché in Canada received, from Canadian nationals with whom they were acquainted, certain information of a secret character which did not, however, present great interest for the Soviet organisations. It has transpired that this information referred to technical data of which the Soviet organisations had no need in view of more advanced technical attainment in the USSR: the information could be found in technical works on radio location, etc., and also in the well-known brochure of the American, H. D. Smyth, *Atomic Energy.*
>
> It would therefore be ridiculous to affirm that delivery of insignificant secret data of this kind could create any threat to the security of Canada.
>
> None the less, as soon as the Soviet Government became aware of the above mentioned acts of certain members of the staff of the Military Attaché in Canada, the Soviet Military Attaché, *in view of the inadmissibility of acts of members of his staff in question*, was recalled from Canada. On the other hand, it must be borne in mind that the Soviet Ambassador and other members of the staff of the Soviet Embassy in Canada had no connection with this. (Author's italics.)

The statement concluded by accusing the Canadian press and Government of deliberately making bad blood between the two countries.[1]

No doubt the Canadian Prime Minister's announcement of the appointment of a Royal Commission to investigate the unauthorised communication of secret and confidential information to a foreign power, which could only mean Soviet Russia, and the press and radio comments which followed, had this effect. But it was palpably untrue to state, as the Deputy Commissar did, that the information was either insignificant or available in official publications such as Smyth's *Atomic Energy*, which had been published by the US Government in the previous year. Furthermore, it will be noted that the statement only referred to Canadian nationals; nothing was said of any British national, and Nunn May's information went far beyond anything that had appeared in Smyth's work. Indeed, far from it being of no 'great interest' to the Russians, the telegrams which passed between Zabotin and the Director of Military Intelligence in Moscow, and which were subsequently published in the Royal Commission's Report, showed that the Russians were extremely anxious to get it.

This seems a convenient point in the narrative at which to mention briefly how the atomic bomb was developed. The process began in December 1938, when a German chemist working in Germany named Otto Hahn succeeded in splitting the nucleus of the uranium atom, thereby releasing an immense amount of energy. The details of his work were communicated to the West by a Jewish fellow worker, Lise Meitner, who had succeeded in fleeing from Nazi Germany. It is now known that she also passed this information to the Soviet Union which had facilitated her escape, it is believed by bribing German officials. Although the chain reaction had been discovered by Otto Hahn, he had misinterpreted what he had discovered, according to Dr Albert Einstein. 'It was Lise Meitner who provided the correct interpretation, and escaped from Germany to put the information in the hands of Niels Bohr,' Einstein wrote afterwards. And the Russians too, he might have added, although he was probably unaware of this. It was from the Danish physicist and Nobel prizewinner, Dr Bohr, that the celebrated mathematician was eventually to learn the details of the momentous atomic discovery.[2]

Although the bulk of the world's uranium supplies came from the Belgian Congo and a little from Canada, some were mined in Czechoslovakia which by this time had fallen under Hitler's control. At the same time the only commercial producer of 'heavy water' was the Norsk hydro-electric plant in Norway, in which the great German chemical combine I. G. Farben had a substantial interest.* Following sensational reports in the press of the new discovery, Winston Churchill, then a backbench MP, asked his scientific adviser, the Oxford professor F. A. Lindemann, later Lord Cherwell, to make an independent inquiry, which he did. Churchill passed the result to the British Air Minister, Sir Kingsley Wood. 'At first sight this might seem to portend the appearance of new explosives of devastating power,' Churchill wrote to the Minister on 3 August 1939. 'In

---

* Heavy water was not a component of the atom bomb but it was essential in experiments with substances required for use in the manufacture of the bomb.

view of this it is essential to realise that there is no danger that this discovery, however great its scientific interest, and perhaps ultimately, its practical importance, will lead to results capable of being put into operation for several years.' Churchill followed this up a week later with another letter to the Air Minister in which he referred to stories of Hitler's allegedly new secret weapon being spread by Herr Von Ribbentrop, the German ambassador in London.

> There are a lot of rumours going about this atomic explosive, and Ribbentrop has made remarks to people on the subject. I expect Lindemann's view is right, i.e. that there is no immediate danger, although undoubtedly the human race is crawling nearer to the point where it will be able to destroy itself completely.[3]

With the outbreak of the war, work on atomic energy at Cambridge and other English universities was pushed forward in a relatively small way compared with other scientific projects such as radar. It was helped by refugees, particularly two French physicists who managed to bring over a quantity of 'heavy water' from Norway. When Churchill became Prime Minister in May 1940, he was pressed to accelerate the atomic research programme and some funds were made available. However, by 1941, matters had reached a stage where independent research in the universities by men like Professor Cockcroft needed to be centrally co-ordinated. Thus a secret directorate was set up in London in October 1941 under Sir Wallace Akers of Imperial Chemical Industries and given the seemingly innocuous title of Tube Alloys, while additional equipment was ordered from industrial firms and substantial grants of money made towards research in the laboratories. Shortly after this, two leading American scientists, George Pegram and Harold Urey, both of Columbia University, visited England to exchange ideas, and the result was that Britain and the United States agreed to pool their resources and 'know-how' in the construction of the atomic bomb. This arrangement was duly ratified by Churchill and President Roosevelt, when they met at Hyde Park, the President's country house. 'I told the President in general terms of the great progress we had made,' Churchill recalled afterwards, 'and that our scientists were now definitely convinced that results might be reached before the end of the present war.'

> He said his people were getting along too but no one could tell whether anything practical would emerge till a full-scale experiment had been made. We both felt painfully the dangers of doing nothing. We knew what efforts the Germans were making to procure supplies of 'heavy water'—a sinister term, eerie, unnatural, which began to creep into our secret papers. What if the enemy should get the atomic bomb before we did! However sceptical one might feel about the assertions of scientists,

much disputed among themselves and expressed in jargon incomprehensible to laymen, we could not run the mortal risk of being outstripped in this awful sphere.[4]

On the day before Churchill arrived at Hyde Park—18 October 1942—four agents of the British Special Operations Executive (SOE), the so-called Baker Street Irregulars, were dropped by parachute on a mountain plateau separated by peaks and glaciers from the Norsk Hydro plant. A few days later the leader signalled back a message to the effect that the Germans were preparing to ship out the entire stock of heavy water, a 'quantity believed sufficient to satisfy the present demands from Berlin.' Meanwhile, two gliders containing thirty-four British commandos were towed by bombers across the North Sea from Scotland. Unfortunately the gliders crashed in bad weather, and all the occupants were killed by the Germans either on landing or later, some by the injection of air bubbles into their veins in a German field hospital, the remainder being shot.

On 16 February 1943, Knut Haukelid and five other Norwegians were parachuted into Norway, where they succeeded in joining up with the original four agents who had managed to survive the first attempt, although the latter were on the verge of starvation and suffering from frost-bite. After a long ski journey and a rock climb, they crossed a half-frozen torrent and attacked the Norsk plant, where they caught the German guards unawares and demolished the plant, thus destroying a year's production of 'heavy water'. Five of the agents reached Sweden safely, while one remained behind in Norway with his radio set. 'What rewards are to be given to these heroic men?' Churchill asked Lord Selborne, the political head of SOE, when he heard the news. Luckily all were able to continue with other sabotage activities and all survived the war.[5]

Meanwhile a secret message contained in a bunch of keys was conveyed to Niels Bohr in Copenhagen, inviting him to continue his scientific work under allied auspices. But the physicist declined, feeling he must stay and help the scientists who had sought refuge in Denmark. 'Any immediate use of the latest marvellous discoveries of atomic physics is impracticable,' he added. However, when the Germans began to round up Jews in Denmark, Bohr warned his English friends that the German scientists were increasing their demands for heavy water and uranium and were now submitting 'proposals for the use of chain reactions with slow neutrons for producing bombs.'* However, as Churchill had correctly anticipated, they later turned their attentions towards pilotless aircraft and rockets on which they tended to concentrate rather than on the atomic bomb.

Eventually, when it looked as if he would be arrested, Bohr was

---

* A neutron has been defined as 'an electrically neutral particle consisting of an electron and a proton in close association.'

persuaded to escape in a rowing boat to Sweden, whence with Stephenson's help he was flown to England in a Mosquito plane made of wood so as to avoid enemy identification by radar. He nearly died on the flight owing to the failure of the oxygen supply which led the pilot to skim the waves for much of the journey. Fortunately Bohr recovered and later went to America, to give what help he could or work on the bomb, while passionately concerned with the world problems which would arise after its use.[6]

Because of the immense facilities offered by the United States and Canada, the bulk of the experimental work on the bomb was transferred to North America, together with a scientific team which among others, besides Niels Bohr, included Nunn May and a German refugee named Klaus Fuchs.

At the same time as Nunn May crossed the Atlantic from England early in 1943, an Italian nuclear physicist named Bruno Pontecorvo, who had succeeded in making his way to the United States after the fall of France, was also invited to join the Anglo–Canadian research team in Montreal. He accepted and for the next six years was to work on the Chalk River heavy water project in Ontario. On the other hand, Fuchs, who became a naturalised British subject in 1942, joined the British team in New York at the end of 1943 and some months later was posted to the atomic laboratory in Los Alamos, near Santa Fé in New Mexico, where the bomb was finally assembled. According to one of the secret embassy documents purloined by Gouzenko, there was an 'auxiliary group of Montreal activists' in touch with Fred Rose, and these included two agents, 'Gini', a Jew, and 'Golia' who was stated to be working closely with Gini. These were two of the very few agents whom Gouzenko was unable and Rose refused to identify. French sources later established that 'Golia' was a cover name for Fuchs. In the circumstances, although it was never established, 'Gini' may well have been Pontecorvo.

It was in the desert at Alamogordo air base, about one hundred and twenty miles south-east of Albuquerque, New Mexico, that the first and only test was made on 16 July 1945. This was witnessed by the British team which included Fuchs.

The bomb had been placed on a tall steel tower while the scientists and military experts occupied observation posts ranging from 10,000 to 17,000 yards distant from the tower. They had been told to lie down with their feet towards the tower at a distance of ten miles and to protect their eyes from the blinding flash which was expected from the explosion. When it came, the explosion caused a flash that lit up the surrounding mountain peaks. Then came a tremendous, sustained noise, heard two hundred miles away and accompanied by a violent wind approaching the force of a tornado. Where the tower had stood there was a great boiling, surging cloud of many colours rising into the stratosphere to a height of more than 40,000 feet. When the cloud had dispersed, it was noted that the tower had completely disappeared, having been vaporised by the heat of the explosion which was estimated at several millions of degrees, and leaving in its place a huge crater. Indeed the explosion caused such curiosity in the neighbourhood that the commander of the air base was obliged to issue a press release to the effect that an explosion had occurred in a remotely located ammunition magazine.[7]

The Potsdam Conference was then meeting, and Henry Stimson, the US Secretary for War, immediately flew there to inform President Truman of the news of the success of the test. For the moment Truman said nothing about it to Stalin, but after he had consulted Churchill, who was at first reluctant to give any information to Stalin, it was agreed that Stalin should be told and that this should be done quite casually by the President after one of their meetings. The occasion arose a week later when Truman walked up to Stalin who was standing alone with his interpreter and told him that the Americans had a new bomb far more destructive than any other known bomb, and that they planned to use it very soon unless Japan surrendered. 'That's fine,' said Stalin, apparently unimpressed. 'I hope you make good use of it against the Japanese.'*

Truman and Byrnes were surprised by Stalin's evident lack of interest. Afterwards this was attributed to the Soviet leader's cunning, when it became known that the Russians had long been kept informed of the American experiments in nuclear fission by Klaus Fuchs. But Stalin's apparent lack of interest may not have been so contrived as was supposed, since there is some evidence that Fuchs did not believe the Alamogordo test would be successful. Byrnes, who concluded that Stalin had not grasped the importance of the discovery, thought that he would be certain to ask for more information about it. But he did not. Nor did he suggest that Soviet

---

* This was confirmed by Churchill's physician Lord Moran, who accompanied the British delegation to Potsdam, in a conversation he had with Mackenzie King in London in 1948. 'One place where I knew there had been a difference of view between them (Churchill and Truman), because each had spoken about it, was in regard to sharing the knowledge of the atomic bomb with Russia before Russia had come into the war against Japan. That Churchill had been very strong that Stalin should be told nothing. The President had thought it might possibly be a mistake in not telling Stalin, that he was an ally and later he might resent not being told. However, I had learned from each of them that at Potsdam, when Stalin was told, he seemed to treat the matter as one of course, was pleased to know the bomb existed, but did not seem to feel any resentment at not having known in advance, nor did he seem to be particularly interested. What I thought concerned him most was getting his own forces into the fight against Japan before the bomb was actually employed. There certainly had been no resentment on Stalin's part at that time of withholding the knowledge.

'I said I thought it was very fortunate that knowledge had been kept by America. That, as Schumann had said to me at luncheon the day before yesterday, "Our security today is the atomic bomb in the possession of the United States."' King Diary, 7 October 1948: Canadian National Archives.

officers or technicians should be allowed to examine the bomb or witness its use. 'Later,' wrote the American Secretary of State, 'I concluded that, because the Russians kept secret their military weapons, they thought it improper to ask us about ours.'[8]

Incidentally, Fuchs was one of the last of the British scientists to leave Los Alamos, which he did in June 1946 on his appointment as head of the Theoretical Physics Division at Harwell. Although in fact he had been spying for the Russians since 1941, Fuchs made no attempt to get into touch with them nor they with him while he was in residence at Los Alamos. Yet he was probably the most dangerous spy of all, since it was he who gave the Russians the secret of the bomb's manufacture.

On 21 February 1946, the day after the Soviet Deputy Commissar for Foreign Affairs had made his statement to the Canadian Chargé d'Affaires in Moscow, Mackenzie King noted with a sense of satisfaction that Robertson had come to him 'with the best piece of news we have had yet.'

> He told me that Primrose [Nunn May], who had denied any knowledge of contact with Communists when first picked up, had now, since the Royal Commission had been appointed, made a full confession,—even admitting that he had given some of the samples of uranium to Russian agents to take to Moscow in connection with the atomic bomb research, giving as his reason that he felt that they had a right to share in the secret. He is an Englishman sent out from England for the work here to assist in the direction of the work here. A University man of high standard.
>
> I said to Robertson I thought it would be best to arrange for his trial in England. Let them see that everything is not put off on Canadians. When he is arrested, and his trial comes, bring home Britain's responsibility and this is certain to lead very far in the US.[9]

During the five days that had elapsed since Nunn May was first questioned by the English police and his second interrogation, further information had reached Scotland Yard about him from Ottawa so that he was confronted directly with the fact that, contrary to his initial denial, when he asserted that he had no knowledge of Zabotin or Angelov, he was known to have been directly in touch with Russian agents in Canada. When questioned about the appointment outside the British Museum, he broke down. 'No,' he told the Special Branch, 'I did not keep that appointment as when I returned I decided to wash my hands of the whole business.' Nevertheless he refused to identify any of his Russian contacts, still maintaining that what he had done was right according to his beliefs at the time. He went on to make the following written confession:

> About a year ago, whilst in Canada, I was contacted by an individual whose identity I decline to divulge. He called on me at my private

apartment in Swail Avenue, Montreal. He apparently knew I was employed by the Montreal Laboratory and sought information from me concerning atomic research.

I gave and had given very careful consideration to correctness of making sure that development of atomic energy was not confined to USA. I took the very painful decision that it was necessary to convey general information on atomic energy and make sure it was taken seriously. For this reason I decided to entertain a proposition made to me by the individual who called on me.

After this preliminary meeting I met the individual on several subsequent occasions whilst in Canada. He made specific requests for information which were just nonsense to me—I mean by this that they were difficult for me to comprehend. But he did request samples of uranium from me and information generally on atomic energy.

At one meeting I gave the man microscopic amounts of U233 and U235 (one of each). The U235 was a slightly enriched sample and was in a small glass tube and consisted of about a milligram of oxide. The U233 was about a tenth of a milligram and was a very thin deposit on a platinum foil and was wrapped in a piece of paper.

I also gave the man a written report on atomic research as known to me. This information was mostly of a character which has since been published or is about to be published.

The man also asked me for information about the US electronically controlled AA shells. I knew very little about these and so could give only very little information.

He also asked me for introductions to people employed in the laboratory including a man named Veale, but I advised him against contacting him.

The man gave me some dollars (I forget how many) in a bottle of whisky and I accepted these against my will.

Before I left Canada it was arranged that on my return to London to keep an appointment with somebody I did not know. I was given precise details as to making contact but I forget them now. I did not keep the appointment because I had decided that this clandestine procedure was no longer appropriate in view of the official release of information and the possibility of satisfactory international control of atomic energy.

The whole affair was extremely painful to me and I only embarked on it because I felt this was a contribution I could make to the safety of mankind. I certainly did not do it for gain.[10]

On the morning of 2 March 1946, Mackenzie King received an advance copy of the first of the Royal Commission's three interim reports. 'It is short,' he noted, 'but quite enough to stimulate fresh interest and activity and also to justify in the minds of the public generally the steps taken in secrecy to discover the extent of the espionage. What I regret is the examination has only proceeded far enough to justify the arrest of four persons. That one of them Mrs Emma Woikin should be a woman in the Department of External Affairs. The worst feature about her is that she should ever have been employed seeing that she is of Russian descent. . . . I am glad that along with her is an employee of the British Government [Kathleen Willsher] which brings the British into the picture and also that the report draws attention to efforts being made to secure secrets with respect to US Army and Navy as well as our own.'[11]

Two days later the first interim report was released to the press and a copy was delivered to the Russian embassy.[12] 'It names several members of the Embassy staff [Zabotin, Motinov, Rogov, Sokolov (on the staff of the Commercial Counsellor) and Angelov] and brings the whole business to a direct issue with Russia. Up to the present the name of the Embassy has not been specified. By this time, too, four civil servants [Woikin, Lunan, Mazerall and Willsher] will have been charged with having violated the Act respecting Public Secrets and will have been arrested. Trials will open in Ottawa before long. Primrose the scientist will have been arrested in London and trials will open there.'

> It is a moment in the history of international relations, the importance and evidence of which cannot be over-emphasised. I am only too conscious of the great gravity of the whole situation and of the tremendous responsibility that has come on my shoulders without any wish or desire on my part but solely discharge of my public duties at a moment when I should have been happy to have been relieved of them altogether.[13]

[2]

Nunn May was arrested on 4 March 1946, by Detective-Inspector William Whitehead, who went to King's College in the Strand at 3.30 p.m. and met May as he was coming out of a lecture. Not wishing to make the arrest on the college premises, the officer said to him: 'I have in my possession a warrant for your arrest, which I will read to you in a moment.' 'Very well,' replied May. 'I was expecting something like this.' The detective then asked May to step outside into the Strand, which the latter did and got into the police car which was parked there. Whitehead read the warrant to May, who made no comment. Next day, after spending the previous night in custody, May was taken to Bow Street Magistrate's Court and charged with having communicated information contrary to the Official Secrets Act,

1911, between 1 January and 30 September 1945, to a person unknown, 'information which was calculated to be or might be useful to an enemy.' Again Nunn May made no comment. He was remanded in custody for a fortnight, and was brought up again at Bow Street on 20 March. When formally charged, he pleaded not guilty, and reserved his defence. After the magistrate had heard a brief account of the prisoner's career, his confession and the circumstances of his arrest, he committed him for trial at the Central Criminal Court. Bail was refused.[14]

When the news of Nunn May's arrest reached the atomic research station at Los Alamos, it not unnaturally made a considerable impression upon the British scientists there and their families. One of the wives, who was the first to hear it on the radio, came running to tell Klaus Fuchs and the others. Questions were asked as to who knew Nunn May and what he was like. 'I knew him fairly well,' one woman remarked. 'But I don't know how you would describe him. He was like—why, he was rather like Klaus here!'[15]

Fuchs smiled politely but made no comment other than to express his opinion that he did not think Nunn May could have told the Russians very much. Also his opinion of May as a scientist was not very high, in spite of May's brilliant academic career at Cambridge, where he got a 'double First' in Mathematics and Natural Sciences, and the fact that he was a senior member of the British team working with the Canadians in Montreal.

Certainly there were some similarities between the two men, but they were largely superficial. Both had been born in the same year, 1911, although Fuchs was eight months younger; both were Doctors of Philosophy; they were both serious-minded, shy and reserved; both had strong Communist sympathies, and both spied for the Russians. On the other hand, Fuchs undoubtedly possessed the tougher and stronger character, and he was the abler scientist of the two. Furthermore, he knew the secret of the atom bomb's manufacture, which Nunn May did not. The latter was an experimental physicist, and after he had joined the Tube Alloys project in the Cavendish Laboratory in Cambridge in April 1942, and later in Canada, his work was concerned with the wider aspects of atomic research rather than with the bomb itself. Nevertheless he knew something of the processes by which it was constructed, particularly the production of plutonium and the heavy water pile at Chalk River as well as what was going on in the Montreal laboratory. Although he had been investigated for security purposes and cleared for access to any atomic energy work in America, General Leslie Groves, the military commander of the American atomic research organisation, felt that he was getting to know too much about later developments and for that reason, 'although I had absolutely no reason to suspect him', as Groves later admitted, May was not allowed to pay a further month's visit for which he applied to the Chicago laboratory in the spring of 1945—he had already been there three times.

Nunn May was tried at the Old Bailey on 1 May 1946, before Mr Justice

Oliver and a jury. On this occasion he changed his original plea from not guilty to guilty, so that the proceedings were relatively short and were concluded the same day. The Attorney-General, Sir Hartley Shawcross, KC, MP, who led for the prosecution, described it as 'a somewhat squalid case' of a man who had set himself above the law and policy of his country, although it was true that there were people who thought that the atomic discoveries should be shared between all nations, as indeed it was hoped that the United Nations Organisation would eventually make possible. Nevertheless, Sir Hartley pointed out, Nunn May had signed the Official Secrets Act. He had known what he was doing. He had given the Russians information and accepted money for it. His confession was then read out with the exception of the reference to the samples of uranium, since this was still considered to be secret.

Mr Gerald Gardiner, KC (later the Lord Chancellor, Lord Gardiner) for the defence, made a powerful plea in mitigation. While admitting that the agent to whom the defendant had given the information was a Russian, he stressed that he had not given away the actual secret of the bomb; his information had merely saved foreign scientists engaged on atomic energy research a certain amount of time. 'Doctors take the view, rightly or wrongly, that if they have discovered something of benefit to mankind,' he went on, 'they are under an obligation to see that it is used for mankind and not kept for any particular group of people, and there are scientists who take substantially the same view.' In doing what he did, counsel argued, May had not worked in concert with any other British scientists—he had come to this decision entirely on his own responsibility and without reference to anyone else. Also, when the acts were committed, in February 1945, the British Army had not crossed the Rhine, while the Russians were driving towards Berlin.* They were customarily referred to then as allies, and no one at that date referred to them as enemies or potential enemies.

'My Lord,' the Attorney-General broke in, 'I think I ought to make it abundantly clear that there is no kind of suggestion that the Russians are enemies or potential enemies. The Court has already decided that this offence consists in the communication of information to unauthorised persons—it might be to your Lordship or to me or to anyone else. . . . What is hit by this section of the Act is the fact that once information passes out of the control of His Majesty's Government, although in the first instance it may be to persons whose attitude to this country is entirely friendly, there no longer remains control over it and it may get into the hands of enemies.'

Before defence counsel sat down, he mentioned that Nunn May had been

* Although Nunn May may have begun to supply the Russians with information in February 1945, he continued to do so certainly until August of that year, as Zabotin's telegrams to Moscow prove.

influenced by a statement made by Mr Churchill to the effect that Britain
had offered the Russians any technical or economic knowledge within this
country's power likely to be of assistance to them. Rightly or wrongly, the
defendant felt full of indignation that the promises of communication of
technical assistance which had been given to one ally should have been
made the monopoly of another. 'He had nothing to gain,' counsel concluded, 'except what we all have to gain by doing what we believe to be
right; and he had everything to lose.'

Asked by the judge if he had anything to say why sentence should not be
passed on him, the prisoner in the dock answered: 'No, my Lord.'

'Allan Nunn May,' said Mr Justice Oliver, addressing the prisoner, 'I
have listened with some slight surprise to some of the things which your
learned Counsel has said he is entitled to put before me: the picture of you
as a man of honour who had only done what you believed to be right.' The
judge went on:

> I do not take that view of you at all. How any man in your position could
> have had the crass conceit, let alone the wickedness, to arrogate to
> himself the decision of a matter of this sort, when you yourself had given
> your written undertaking not to do it and knew it was one of the
> country's most precious secrets, when you yourself had drawn and were
> drawing pay for years to keep your own bargain with your country—that
> you could have done this, is a dreadful thing.
>
> I think you acted not as an honourable but as a dishonourable man. I
> think you acted with degradation. Whether money was the object of what
> you did, in fact you did get money for what you did. It is a very bad case
> indeed.

'The sentence upon you,' Mr Justice Oliver concluded, 'is one of ten
years' penal servitude.'

Dr Allan Nunn May was then removed to serve this sentence in
Wakefield Prison in Yorkshire. He did not appeal against it.

A month or two later, the Association of Scientific Workers in Britain, an
organisation which included a number of Communists and the editorial
board of whose official journal the *Scientific Worker* Nunn May had joined
in 1936, on his return from a trip to the Soviet Union, issued a statement
demanding the reduction of the 'extremely harsh' sentence passed on May.
'It is noteworthy,' the statement went on, 'that the maximum sentence
under the proposed Atomic Energy Bill is penal servitude for a period of
five years. It is clear that no account was taken of Dr May's positive
contribution to the winning of the war by his scientific work, and that the
sentence is out of all proportion to the magnitude of the offence committed.'

A few days later, Mr W. J. Brown, an Independent MP, formerly

Labour, as well as a popular journalist and broadcaster who had visited Russia, asked Mr Chuter Ede, Home Secretary in the Labour Government, if he would review the sentence. Was the Home Secretary aware, the MP further queried, that it was perfectly obvious that May was no common traitor in the ordinary sense of the word? He had suffered a much heavier sentence than had been passed upon many people who had sold their country for money. The whole issue of atomic bomb secrecy, Mr Brown went on, constituted an extremely doubtful ethical area, and would the Home Secretary have another look at the case?

'It was open to this man to appeal against the sentence, although he would have run certain risks had he done so,' Chuter Ede stated in a reply which had been obviously drafted by a senior civil servant in the Home Office. 'It is still open to him to apply for an extension of time within which to lodge an appeal.' Chuter Ede went on to say that he did not accept Mr Brown's statement and its implications. He went on:

I can understand although I cannot condone the attitude of a man who said he was willing to make knowledge he had acquired generally available. But this man did sell knowledge he had acquired in the service of this country to a foreign Power for their private and particular use.

The Home Secretary's reply was greeted with loud cheers from most quarters of the House.

On the other hand, Sir Wallace Akers, who had been in charge of Tube Alloys when Nunn May was there, had wished to produce in court a statement about the prisoner's 'excellent work' on the wartime project, but was probably prevented by security considerations. At the same time Akers was reported to be 'flabbergasted' by the sentence and the general attitude of the judge. Also, a group of scientists, including Cockcroft, most of whom had been in Canada, put their names to a letter to the Home Secretary, appealing for clemency, after the letter had been redrafted, since Cockcroft felt that the original draft seemed to imply that Nunn May was a martyr to scientific freedom. While Cockcroft believed that Nunn May deserved a 'substantial' sentence, he felt that five years would have fitted the case better, although he agreed that May's offence was 'very serious and had done much to discredit scientists and to add to anti-Russian feeling.' But he did not join the deputation which delivered the letter to the Home Secretary in August 1947 after most of the Canadian spy trials had finished. Mr Chuter Ede listened 'with sympathy' and although he refused to review the case 'at present', he gave the deputation the impression that another approach in the future might have a more favourable result.

In the following year the Association of Scientific Workers had another try. This time they formed a deputation to the Home Secretary led by Professor Harold Laski. Again Chuter Ede said no.[16]

No further attempt was made to reduce or quash Nunn May's sentence.

Since he was a model prisoner, he gained full remission, and in 1952 after serving six years and eight months of his ten-year sentence he was released from Wakefield Prison. He then returned to Cambridge where his Viennese wife, Dr Hildegarde Broda, who subsequently became the town's deputy medical officer of Health, was living with their seven-year-old son in the family's flat in Chesterton Lane. It is significant that he expressed no remorse for the offence of which he had been convicted. On the contrary, he was reported to have declared that he had 'acted rightly.' In January 1962, shortly after the Gold Coast Colony received its independence and was renamed Ghana, Dr Nunn May was appointed Professor of Physics in the University of Ghana, and thither he departed with his wife and son.

[3]

The Russians had been making enquiries about nuclear energy in Canada for some time before Nunn May was 'contacted.' This was done through the Scotsman David Lunan, who was recruited by Major (later Colonel) Rogov in March 1945 and who was assigned to 'control' the B group of agents, Durnford Smith, Ned Mazerall and Israel Halperin. The latter was born in Quebec Province of Russian parents and was Professor of Mathematics at Queen's University, Kingston, Ontario. He had, incidentally, kept Fuchs supplied with newspapers and magazines when Fuchs was interned in Canada in the early months of the war.[17]

Discussing the work of the National Research Council in general, Lunan had written to Rogov in his first report dated 28 March 1945, 'Badeau [Durnford Smith] informs me that the most secret work at present is on nuclear physics (bombardment of radio-active substances to produce energy). This is more hush-hush than radar and is being carried on at the University of Montreal and at McMaster University at Hamilton. Badeau thinks that the government purchase of a radium producing plant is connected with this research. In general, he claims to know of no new developments in radar, except in minor improvements in its application.'

No doubt it was for this reason that Durnford Smith asked for permission to work on uranium. 'There is a possibility either by being invited or by applying himself,' Lunan told Rogov, 'but he warned that they are very careful in the selection of workers and that they are under strict observation.' Since Durnford Smith's information was largely technical, Rogov felt that he should be in direct contact with him, and accordingly a meeting was arranged through Lunan which took place in July in a parked car in the Ottawa Driveway. Rogov afterwards noted that Smith 'brought valuable material' and 'we agreed on further work.'

Durnford Smith was constantly asked if he could obtain a specimen of

Uranium 235. 'Ask Badeau whether he could obtain Uranium 235,' Lunan was told. 'Let him be cautious. If he can, let him write in detail about the radium-producing plant.' There is no evidence that Durnford Smith was successful in this proposed assignment.

About the same time Motinov drafted a telegram for Zabotin to send to Moscow from information supplied by Fred Rose:

> The Professor [Raymond Boyer] reported that the Director of the National Research Committee told him about the new plant under construction: Pilot Plant at Grand-Mère in the Province of Quebec. This plant will produce uranium. The engineering personnel is being obtained from McGill University and is already moving into the district of the new plant. As a result of experiments carried out with uranium, it has been found that uranium may be used for filling bombs, which is already in fact being done.
>
> The Americans have developed wide research work, having invested in this business 660 million dollars.

It is possible that this telegram was not sent, since the Russians found out shortly afterwards that the plant in Quebec Province produced RDX and not uranium, which was produced at Chalk River. The two plants and their purposes had been confused by Rose.[18]

On 5 July, Lunan reported that Halperin ('Bacon') had expressed curiosity about the Chalk River plant and the manufacture of uranium.

> He claims that there is a great deal of talk and speculation on the subject but that nothing is known outside of the small and carefully guarded group completely in the know. He emphasised that he himself is as remote from this type of information as I myself.

However, Halperin was unable or rather unwilling to attempt to obtain a specimen of Uranium 235, which Lunan had asked him to do.

While at first appearing co-operative, Halperin refused to give any other than oral information, or to provide photographs. In one of his reports to Rogov, Lunan wrote of Halperin:

> It has become very difficult to work with him, especially after my request for Uranium 235. He has said that, as far as he knows, it is absolutely impossible to get it. Thus for instance he declared that perhaps it is not available in sufficient quantity. Bacon explained to me the theory of nuclear energy which is probably *known* to you. He refuses to put down in writing anything and does not want to give a photograph or information on himself. I think that at present he has a fuller understanding of the essence of my requests and he has a particular dislike for them. With such a trend of thought as he has, it is impossible

to get anything from him except verbal descriptions, and I am not in a position to understand fully where it concerns technical details.

I asked him what is taken into consideration in the construction of the very large plant (Chalk River, near Petawawa, Ontario), in the general opinion, the principle of production of which is based on the physical properties of the nucleus; with regard to his expression of opinion that it is impossible to get Uranium 235. He replied that he does not know. He believed that the project is still in the experimental stage.

In the event, Smith's request to transfer his sphere of activities to uranium was turned down, doubtless because by this time Nunn May with his expertise on the subject had already been 'contacted' and had begun to work for the Russians in Canada.

A few days after May had handed over the uranium specimen of Uranium 233, as already mentioned, Colonel Zabotin paid a social visit to a friend living in the vicinity of Chalk River. This gave him an opportunity of seeing the plant from the river during a cruise in his friend's motor boat, and he reported to the Director of Military Intelligence what he had seen. Klaus Fuchs is known to have visited Montreal and other places in Canada at this period, and it is possible that he met the Soviet Military Attaché during this visit.

On 14 August the Director cabled Zabotin:

If possible give a more detailed description of the exterior of the plant.

The Commission's second Interim Report, which incriminated Fred Rose MP and Sam Carr, the Canadian Communist Party secretary, was released on 14 March, the day the second session of Parliament opened.[19] The Prime Minister thought that Rose might try to stay within the parliamentary precincts so as to avoid arrest, but although he went to Parliament on that day, Rose did not seek to take advantage of any privilege and he was arrested as he left the Parliament Buildings the same night. Sam Carr, however, could not be found anywhere; in fact, he had already fled the country.

The Commission's third and final Interim Report, which incriminated Halperin and Eric Adams, among others, was tabled in the House of Commons on 29 March.[20]

'I must confess,' noted Mackenzie King when he read through the last report, 'I felt amazed at the attitude of some of these university men in having no regard for the sanctity of the oath, apart, altogether, from their readiness to give secret information to another country at the time they were sworn into the public service.'

On the following day the Prime Minister informed the House that the order-in-council justifying the arrests under the wartime regulations, had been revoked, an action which Mackenzie King admitted was 'an immense relief' to him. 'I feel the Commissioners have thought more of themselves and doing a fine bit and of the Report they are making than of the position in which they have placed the Government and our party,' he noted in his diary the same day. 'It will always be held against us and the Liberal party that we sanctioned anything that meant so much in the way of deprivation of liberty for a number of people. However, as I saw it at the start, it has raised an issue in the minds of the people even more important than that of espionage and will probably result in several persons being freed altogether when they come before the Court, or given trifling sentences. It will be an interesting study in the power of public opinion and the preservation of freedom.' The Prime Minister was right. For example, although Adams and Halperin were clearly incriminated on Gouzenko's evidence, they both pleaded not guilty when they came to trial and were acquitted. In fact seven others, out of a total of twenty-one defendants, were likewise found not guilty.

Mackenzie King continued to worry about the detention of so many individuals before they were brought to trial. On 7 April he wrote:

> I continue to feel more and more put out at the course adopted by the espionage Commission in detaining the persons whom they had before them. It has done irreparable harm to the party and my own name will not escape responsibility. Only the documentary knowledge I had in advance and its bearing on the safety of the State could have excused the course taken. Even there I think the ends of justice would have been better served by risking more in the way of possible loss of conviction.[21]

Four trials took place before the Commissioners completed their Report at the end of June. The first two were those of Emma Woikin (12 April) and Kathleen Willsher (3 May) who both elected to be tried summarily. In the event both pleaded guilty and were sentenced to two and a half and three years respectively. Two interesting admissions were made by these women to the Commissioners before their trials. Woikin testified that she made use of a hiding place (*dubok*) in the lavatory of a dentist who was looking after her teeth; the documentary information she left there would subsequently be picked up by Zabotin's chauffeur Captain Gorshkov. This practice was borne out by Gouzenko in his testimony. As for Kay Willsher, she believed (as Fuchs was to do later) that she could be hanged or shot for commiting a breach of the Official Secrets Act. 'Do they not execute people?' she asked. 'I have not heard of that myself in this country,' one of the Commissioners observed.[22]

On the other hand, E. W. Mazerall ('Bagley') and Fred Rose MP ('Fred' or 'Debouz') each pleaded not guilty. Mazerall, who was charged with passing top secret information on the latest radar developments to Lunan for the Russians, was clearly guilty on his own admissions before the Royal Commission and also on Lunan's evidence. He was tried before a jury in the Supreme Court of Ontario, found guilty and sentenced to four years' penal servitude. He appealed, but his appeal was dismissed by the Ontario Court of Appeal (16 October).

Of all the persons mentioned in the Russian documents which Gouzenko procured, as well as by the witnesses who testified before the Commission, none (with the exception of the Soviet officials) were more repeatedly and prominently mentioned, either under their real names or under their cover-names than Fred Rose and his fellow spy and conspirator Sam Carr, the Secretary of the Canadian Communist Party. This explains why they received the heaviest sentences, six years each, on conviction, although Carr, who had succeeded in getting away, was not picked up until January 1949 in New York, and brought to justice in the following April.

Rose, whose real name was Rosenberg, was born in the Polish town of Lublin of Russian Jewish parents in 1907. He came to Canada in 1920 with his father Jacob Rosenberg and, being still a minor, was included in the latter's naturalisation certificate when the latter took out Canadian citizenship in 1926. Fred Rosenberg soon dropped the second and third syllables of his surname and henceforth was known as Fred Rose.[23] He became a member of the Canadian Communist Party in 1927, spent a year in jail for sedition in 1931–2 and was interned for 'disloyal activities' as a Communist in 1942. He was released in the following year on giving an undertaking to refrain from participating in any illegal organisation including the Communist Party, but he lost no time in violating this undertaking. His key rôle behind the scenes was in organising the group of agents in the National Research Council, and to that extent he was responsible for the disclosure of atomic research secrets although, as we have seen, he mixed up the plants at Chalk River and Grand Mère. Rose's activities extended outside Canada's frontiers, since one telegram from Zabotin refers to his association with an American geneticist named Arthur Steinberg, who was working on a research project for the US Navy in Washington. Another telegram referred to his association with a Canadian agent named Samuel Sol Burman, who went to London and arranged to communicate with Rose. Burman may possibly have been the agent who was designated to meet Nunn May, but who failed to keep any of the appointments which the Russians had arranged. Rose's cover was broken by two documents, one of which acknowledged information about a secret session of the Canadian Parliament in 1944, dealing with the redeployment of Canadian forces following Germany's collapse, and the second dated 12 July 1945, stating that 'Debouz' had been re-elected for the second time as a member of the Federal Parliament. In the event, Fred Rose was convicted in the Quebec Courts on 20 June 1946, and sentenced to six years. He appealed against both conviction and sentence and his appeal was dismissed. Consequently he automatically ceased to be a member of the Federal Parliament and his seat was vacated.

The principal 'contact' used by Rose for communicating with Professor Boyer and other agents was a Jewish girl whose name was Freda Linton or Fritzie Linden, originally Lipchitz, who had been born of Polish parents in Montreal in 1916. She also appears to have been Rose's mistress. For a time she worked for the late John Grierson, the Scottish Chairman of the Canadian Film Board in Ottawa, and a request in one of Moscow's telegrams to Zabotin that she be placed in a more useful position in the National Research Council 'through Grierson', was so ambiguously worded as to cast suspicions on Grierson's loyalty, and he was cross-examined at some length before the Royal Commission on his Russian associations. However, there never was the slightest foundation for these suspicions against Grierson, who did a first-rate job both as Chairman of the Film Board and as General Manager of the allied wartime Information Board, as the present writer well recalls.[24]

As for Freda Linton, she was promoted to a post in the Distribution Branch of the Film Board in Montreal, but she did not succeed in getting into the Research Council although she seems to have been used as a 'contact' between Rose and Boyer, with whom it is also suggested that she slept. It proved impossible to subpoena her to testify before the Royal Commission, since she disappeared from her lodgings in Montreal at the end of April 1946, taking all her belongings with her. 'The inference is obvious,' in the words of the Commission's final Report. 'The flight of Linton is, in our opinion, as significant as that of Sam Carr. The reasons are doubtless the same in both cases.' Although Carr was eventually arrested and brought to justice, as we have seen, no information has come to light as to Freda Linton's subsequent history. Among the smaller fry she would appear to have been one who 'got away'.

Although the full report of the Royal Commission, which amounted to some seven hundred and thirty-three pages, was published under the date 26 June, it was not tabled in the House of Commons and so made generally public until 15 July, as a courtesy to the Soviet Embassy.[25] 'As the Report names additional persons of the Embassy involved,' Mackenzie King noted at the time, 'Robertson and I felt it desirable to tell them in advance who these people were and to say that the Government thought they might wish to have these people return themselves of their own accord instead of having the Government make a formal request.' The Prime Minister went on in reference to the visit he had requested from the Russian Chargé d'Affaires:

I had a memo before me of the numbers involved in the Embassy—— some seventeen in all with some six new names. Belokhvostikov came as

Chargé d'Affaires. He had with him a lady member of the Embassy whom I met with Mrs Zarubin and who acted as interpreter. The Chargé d'Affaires coloured up quite a bit as the additional names were mentioned. They were relieved when I said I hoped they would let Mrs Zarubin know that the Commission had directly stated that the Ambassador was not involved.

I gave him a list of the names as given in the Report and a memo of the particulars I had stated orally. He said he could see that the matter was one the Government at Moscow would have to deal with and he would advise them at once. He said the attitude of the Moscow Government had been set out in a communication received in February and then later he spoke of a communication in April. I said nothing about those excepting to identify the one of February which made use of the expression that the same things that were inadmissible had been done by the Embassy officials here.[26]

[4]

Of all the witnesses who were questioned by the Royal Commission during its sittings, which extended over approximately four months, Igor Gouzenko was by far the most important, since not only could he testify on the secret documents which he had removed surreptitiously from the Soviet Embassy when he sought asylum with the Canadian authorities, but he was able from personal knowledge, notwithstanding his relatively subordinate position as a cypher clerk, to give the Commissioners a clear idea of the inner workings of the secret side of the Russian mission. 'He has undoubtedly been a most informative witness,' the Commissioners reported, 'and has revealed to us the existence of a conspiratorial organisation operating in Canada and other countries. He has not only told us the names and cover-names of the organisers, the names of many of the Canadians who were caught '*in the net*' (to employ the phrase used by the documents) and who acted here as agents, but he has also exposed much of the set-up of the organisation as well as its aims and methods here and abroad.'

The utmost secrecy was the standard practice impressed upon all members of the confidential branches of the embassy. 'Burn after reading' was a common instruction on written assignments from the Intelligence Director in Moscow to Colonel Zabotin and by Zabotin to his associates and agents. Meetings with agents usually took place at night on street corners and in motor vehicles, while cover-names and intermediaries or 'cut-outs' were frequently used for security purposes. The cover-names were used by the Russian leaders of the espionage system not only for themselves, and their Russian assistants and agents, but also for places, organisations and things. Thus Canada was usually referred to as *Lesovia*; the Soviet Embassy as *Metro*; the NKVD or secret police as *The Neighbour*, passports as *shoes*; the Communist Party of Canada and other countries except the USSR as *The Corporation* and its members as *corporants* or *corporators*, any hiding place as a *dubok*; a legal 'front' for illegal activities as a *roof*; and the military espionage organisation itself as *Gisel*. Zabotin's cover-name was 'Grant', and each of his agents or sub-agents had his or her own separate cover-name.

Here is a typical instruction from 'Jan' (Rogov) for 'Back' (Gordon Lunan), who operated the B group, to pass on to his sub-agents:

I beg you to instruct each man separately about conspiracy in our work . . .

All the materials and documents to be passed by *Bagley* (Mazerall), *Bacon* (Halperin) and *Badeau* (Durnford Smith) have to be signed by their cover names as stated above . . .

Any meeting with *Bacon, Badeau, Bagley* must not take place indoors, but on the street and, moreover, separately with each one and once a month . . .

The materials from them must be received the same day on which you must meet me in the evening. The materials must not be kept with you even for a single night . . .

Their wives must not know that you work with and meet their husbands.

Warn them to be careful.[27]

There had been some form of Communist organisation in Canada as early as 1924, when the most active individuals were Fred Rose (born Rosenberg) and Sam Carr (a native of the Ukraine born Kogen or Cohen). Carr was fluent in Russian and he took a course at the Lenin Institute in Moscow in such practical subjects as political 'agitation', fomenting strikes, sabotage and espionage.

Prior to Russia's entry into the war, there had been no official Soviet mission in Ottawa. The first Minister and head of the Legation—the mission had not yet been raised to the status of an embassy—was Fedor Gousev, whose acquaintance we have already made when he was ambassador in London. 'When I think of the welcome I gave to Gousev, his wife and children at the time of their arrival, how we secured this embassy for them [in Charlotte Street] etc., and all the time they were planning out means of having Canada subsequently seized by the Russians,' Mackenzie King was to write later, 'it all seems quite beyond belief. I will have quite a story to tell there if still spared.'[28] Unfortunately, so far as is known from his papers, he was never able to do this.

Before Gousev arrived the preliminary work was carried out by Major

Sokolov, whose cover-name was 'Davie' and who arrived ostensibly as a Soviet inspector to work in the Canadian factories on the Canadian Mutual Air Programme with the USSR. So far as the evidence discloses, the first head of the military espionage system in Canada was Sergei Koudriavtzev (code-name 'Leon'), who was nominally First Secretary of the Legation, and it was from him that Sokolov took his instructions and it was to him that he reported. On Zabotin's arrival in June 1943, Koudriavtzev handed over his organisation, such as it was—it consisted of Rose, Carr and a few others including Professor Boyer—to the new Military Attaché.

According to Gouzenko, there were four parallel undercover organisations operating from the embassy—the NKVD, which reported to the NKVD headquarters in the Lubianka in Moscow; the Political Section under the Second Secretary Goussarov, which was in direct contact with the Central Committee of the Communist Party in Moscow;* the Commercial Section under the Commercial Counsellor Ivan Krotov, which communicated with the Commissariat for Foreign Trade, and the Military Section under Colonel Zabotin, which reported to the Director of Military Intelligence at the Soviet Army Moscow Headquarters at 19 Znamensky Street. It was not until after Zabotin's arrival that the 'net' was considerably expanded and Zabotin was supplied with the necessary funds to do this in Canadian dollars, for which he specifically asked, as being unlikely to attract attention, as 'we are carrying out repairs, buying a car and there are people coming, etc.' There was also some evidence of the operations of a naval intelligence system, since a Captain Patzerney came up from New York and co-operated with Zabotin in obtaining information about the shipyards and shipping in Halifax and Vancouver.

This method of maintaining several distinct espionage networks had obvious advantages from the security point of view for those operating them, since nobody, even among the directing Soviet personnel, would know the names of the agents in more than one of the networks, a factor which was calculated not to facilitate investigation by the Canadian authorities. As Gouzenko told the Commissioners:

What has transpired is only a modest or small part of all that is really here. You may have discovered fifteen men but it still leaves in Canada

---

* Although Goussarov only held the rank of Second Secretary, his authority was on the level of the ambassador according to Gouzenko. He had formerly been assistant to Malenkov when the latter was Head of the Foreign Section of the Central Committee of the Communist Party in Moscow. Gouzenko testified that he had reason to believe that in addition to this Goussarov had the task of transmitting political directives from his superiors in Moscow to the leaders of the Canadian Communist movement. These directives would include not only general political lines to be taken up in Communist propaganda, but also instructions on techniques of operation e.g. getting control of such organisations as the Canadian Association of Scientific Workers.

this dangerous situation, because there are other societies and other people working under every Embassy, under every Consul in each place where there is a Consulate. It is just like a number of small circles. There are parallel systems of spies or potential agents . . .

The last telegram asked about the mobilisation of resources in Canada. They wanted to know everything possible about everything concerned in Canada. They wanted to know the natural resources that Canada could mobilise in case of war, her coal, oil, rare metals and so on.[29]

The existence of these parallel systems sometimes led to misunderstandings, particularly when two of them tried to develop the same agent. Pavlov for instance tried to develop the Canadian Communist Party Secretary for the NKVD and was peremptorily ordered by Moscow: 'Don't touch Sam Carr.' There was a good deal of friction from time to time between Pavlov and Zabotin. Nor was Pavlov noted for his diplomatic finesse. On one occasion he sent two of his agents named Matrenichev and Zhukov, who worked in the Commercial Attaché's office, to the Canadian Patent Office to obtain information about radar equipment, which was on the secret list. Since the Russians spoke such poor English, the Canadians in the Patent Office thought they were German agents and called the police. They were arrested but released when their credentials had been verified. Major Sokolov, who had been transferred to the Commercial Section, immediately told Zabotin about the episode. As Gouzenko put it in his evidence, 'Zabotin became very angry and he wrote a big telegram to Moscow. He said that the "Neighbour" should not work with such hooligan methods. He described what had happened and he said that these were the Neighbour's people, Pavlov's people.'

This was confirmed by Gouzenko when he was questioned by Counsel for the Commissioners:

Counsel: So the NKVD system, started as early as 1942, has been operating continuously here and is operating at the present time apart from Zabotin?

Gouzenko: Yes.

Counsel: And you think the NKVD system is much larger than Zabotin's?

Gouzenko: Yes.

Counsel: And both are actually working?

Gouzenko: Yes.

In their Report the Commissioners stressed that they were impressed by Gouzenko's sincerity and with the manner in which he gave his evidence which they had 'no hesitation in accepting.' They concluded with this tribute:

In our opinion, Gouzenko, by what he has done, has rendered great public service to the people of this country, and thereby has placed Canada in his debt. (Author's italics)[30]

This opinion was endorsed by Mackenzie King, who met Gouzenko for the first time on 16 July, the day after the complete Report and the evidence with a considerable number of omissions was released and published to the world. Mackenzie King asked the police to bring Gouzenko to the Prime Minister's office, where he talked to him in the presence of the RCMP and Norman Robertson. 'I told him that I was very pleased at the way in which he had conducted himself throughout the period of great anxiety,' the Prime Minister noted afterwards in his diary. 'I thought he had done a great service and wanted him to know that I appreciated his manliness, his courage and standing for the right, etc.' The Prime Minister continued:

I asked him if he had read the book *I Chose Freedom* [by Victor Kravchenko]* He said he had. I asked him if he thought of writing himself. He said that he was writing something, bit by bit. I said to him I thought he ought to have in mind not to do it too quickly but to begin with his own life; his ancestors and early bringing up. His ideas; his training; what caused him to change his views, etc. He told me afterwards he was very pleased to know I had thought well of his writing his life.

I asked him a number of pointed questions, among the number as to whether the atomic bomb had made any difference to the espionage business, so far as Canada was concerned, or a difference between America and Russia. He said he did not think so. That the espionage had been going on for years. It began immediately after the Russian revolution. Plans were then made for training men . . . So far as the bomb was concerned, it was just one more weapon that had to be considered. They believed that Communism would have to conquer the world. That they would not let any information in to Russia and would not give the Russians much information about the outside world. They did not want democracy to develop there. . . .

He thought writers in America made a mistake in not distinguishing between the Soviet Government and the Russian people. It was a trained minority that really governed. It was a tyranny.

I asked him if he thought the Ambassador was really without knowledge of what was going on. He said that Russia's policy was to choose as Ambassadors men who were either very innocent or were

---

* Kravchenko, who worked in the Soviet Purchasing Commission in Washington, defected in April 1944. His book, which quickly became a bestseller, was first published in New York in 1946.

nonentities, depending on the place to which they were going. They were chosen so as to keep them out of being in the 'know' of things. He felt, however, that the present Ambassador [Zarubin] had had a wider knowledge than the Commission had assumed; for example when two Generals came over from Russia, went through Canada, the US and Mexico and returned to Canada, the Ambassador had promised to help them in any way he could.

He said sometimes the real Ambassador was the chauffeur. As Ambassador he would have to report to the chauffeur at the end of the day's proceedings if the chauffeur happened to be a General or whoever was in charge.

In conclusion the Prime Minister noted that Gouzenko, whom he described as youthful in appearance ('Clean cut. Steady eyes. Keen intellect.') made 'a fine impression' on Robertson and himself. Gouzenko 'spoke well of the support his wife had given him. I spoke nicely about her and the children. Told him the Government would keep an eye on them all and to keep his faith strong. He said he would certainly do that.' Mackenzie King added:

I noticed when I shook hands with him as he was going away that he had apparently been under a strain in talking with me. His hand was warm, perspiring a little. He showed no sign of it as we conversed. I let him see that I believed in him as I do and felt him to be a real person with a mission. I would have liked to have had an afternoon with him instead of an hour . . . He certainly reveals a condition of things that is alarming.[31]

Although it is out of strict chronology, this seems the most appropriate stage in the narrative at which to round off the tale of Igor Gouzenko. He continued to live with his wife and two children under the protection of the RCMP in a secret location and under an assumed name. Occasionally he would consent to be interviewed on Canadian television, but understandably he always insisted on appearing with a black hood over his head and his full face photograph has never been seen outside the Soviet Union. He took Mackenzie King's advice as to how he should write the story of his life until the date of his defection and that he should take his time over it. The result was *This Was My Choice*, which came out in 1948 on both sides of the Atlantic and later formed the subject of the film *The Iron Curtain*. He still lives incognito with his family under police protection, and in the words of the editor who wrote the introduction to his book, only a few high government and police officials know what dot on the Canadian map represents his home. Unfortunately his health is not good and he suffers from diabetes. Nevertheless he has been able to produce some further literary work including a novel, *The Titan*, based on Stalin's life. Nor can he

ever forget what a narrow escape he had with his life and how close he was
to falling into the hands of the NKVD. ('In the mysterious way small
happenings so often lead to big happenings, influencing the lives of
individuals and nations,' he wrote in the concluding words of his autobio-
graphy, 'it was Pavlov's jemmying open of my apartment door that
convinced the authorities Igor Gouzenko really had a story to tell.'[32]

Some years later, after the Soviet spies Guy Burgess and Donald Maclean
had fled to Russia, and Harold ('Kim') Philby had been cleared of the
charge of being the 'third man' who 'tipped them off', Gouzenko was again
questioned by the same authorities, this time on the subject of Soviet
espionage in Britain. On 6 May 1952, he wrote a memorandum for RCMP
Intelligence in which he revealed an astonishing piece of information,
namely that the Russians had a spy working in the British counter-
espionage service (M15) in London. 'The case of the member of MI5 was,
in my opinion, much stronger than that of Rose or Hiss, and there was
much more to go on,' he wrote. 'In the first place I was not told by
somebody but saw the telegram myself concerning this person. And then,
as a second confirmation, I was told by Lieutenant Liubimov. With these
two pieces of evidence there is not the slightest doubt in my mind that there
was a Soviet agent inside MI5 during the period 1942–3 and possibly later
on.' Liubimov, it should be explained, was a comrade of Gouzenko's in the
Moscow Intelligence Directorate and they took the same course in codes
and cyphers in Moscow during the war, when they became friendly.

'This member of MI5 was not contacted personally, but through a *dubok*
[secret hiding place or letter drop],' Gouzenko went on. 'This showed that
Moscow took special precautions in dealing with him . . . In this particular
case the *dubok* was at a certain graveyard in a split between certain stones of
a certain tomb. I remember that the telegram struck me as unusual and we
had a short talk about it. It is most probable that Liubimov deciphered it
himself since he was usually working on telegrams from London. . . .
Liubimov said 'This man has something Russian in his background.'
According to Gouzenko, the words 'something Russian' were capable of a
number of interpretations such as that he had Russian relatives or had
visited the Soviet Union and had some knowledge of the country and its
people. Gouzenko added, 'Of course, the locality of the *dubok* could and in
practice was frequently changed.' Gouzenko's account continued:

> In 1944, Zabotin received a long telegram from Moscow of a warning
> character. In it Moscow informed him that representatives of the British
> 'Greens' (counter-intelligence) were due to arrive in Ottawa with the
> purpose of working with the local 'Greens' (RCMP counter-intelligence)
> to strengthen the operations against Soviet agents. Now it could be that
> Moscow just invented these representatives . . . in order to make Zabotin

more careful. On the other hand, it might have been genuine, in which case it would mean that Moscow had an inside track on MI5 . . . The mistake, in my opinion, in dealing with this matter was that the task of finding the British MI5 agent was given to MI5 itself, so that the results could be expected to be nil.[33]

Gouzenko was unable to remember the spy's cover-name but he did not attach much importance to this, since, as he pointed out, cover-names like *duboks* were changed from time to time. However, in all the circumstances it is practically certain that the spy in question was Anthony Blunt, who occupied a senior post in MI5 between 1940 and 1945, was successively Professor of the History of Art in London University, Director of the Courtauld Institute, Surveyor of the King's and later the Queen's Pictures, and a Knight of the Royal Victorian Order, before confessing to being a Russian spy in 1967 and being granted immunity from prosecution in return for the information with which he supplied the security authorities. He was eventually revealed in his true colours in November 1979 and stripped of his knighthood by the Queen. Thus the one-time Sir Anthony Blunt was conclusively shown to be the so-called 'fourth man' in the case of the missing diplomats Burgess and Maclean, about whom Gouzenko was questioned for possible leads by the RCMP in 1952.

[5]

From the time that the Commissioners published their first interim report at the beginning of March 1946, the Gouzenko affair caused the greatest possible sensation in Canada. When the story broke, it was in the newspaper headlines every day for a month and the press was led into all sorts of speculations and guesses about the intrigues that had been going on. Later the press struck a more responsible note, taking the line that while the menace must be dealt with effectively and promptly, at the same time the civil rights of the individual must be safeguarded, which could hardly be the case when numbers of people mentioned in the various reports were detained by the police and held in Rockcliffe barracks, some for several months, before they were eventually brought to trial. As Sir Alexander Clutterbuck, who had succeeded Malcolm MacDonald as British High Commissioner in Ottawa, wrote to the Dominions Secretary Lord Addison:

In Canada, as a whole, the news first came as an intense surprise and shock. There was amazement that Canada should have become overnight the scene of so dramatic a spy story. At first there was some pride at this example of Canada feeling free to take so strong and independent a line in an important matter of foreign policy (though it was generally and rightly assumed that this action was not being taken without consultation with the Governments of the United Kingdom and the United States). This feeling was mingled to some extent with an uneasiness that, if this was the price of being a great Power, then many Canadians would prefer her to remain as she was.

The impact on the Canadian public of the shock at the news of the Russian espionage network was particularly severe in the light of Canada's previous relations with Soviet Russia. Canada had taken no particular part in the campaign against the Bolsheviks after the 1914–18 war and had not participated in the 'Intervention' which followed, and in the following years, especially during the decade preceding the end of the Second World War, there was in Canada a growing feeling of sympathy and understanding for Russia. In Clutterbuck's words, 'much had been made of the common interests of Russia and Canada, both being regarded as young, vast and undeveloped territories, with similar problems in the Arctic north.'

This feeling of sympathy received a strong fillip with Russia's entry into the war against Germany. As in other Allied countries, the Canadian authorities were at pains to emphasise, indeed, to over-emphasise, the role of 'heroic' Russia, and there was widespread admiration for her part in the war. This was evidenced by the growth of numerous Canada–Soviet friendship societies, which held many successful and widely attended rallies. The establishment of a Soviet Legation in Ottawa in 1942 and its elevation to an Embassy in 1944 were regarded as fitting: the embassy, by scattering invitations to its mammoth parties far and wide, and in other ways, seemed anxious to establish the friendliest relations with Canadians generally.

The most obvious effect of the Commission's inquiry was to cause a sharp reaction against Communism in Canada. Mackenzie King, who sought to avoid causing unnecessary embarrassment to the Soviet Union, regretted that the Report was such 'a huge volume', and he was afraid that it would be made use of by Russia 'as an effort on the part of Canada to destroy Communism and may hinder rather than further the object we have in mind.' On the other hand, the Prime Minister went out of his way to discredit the argument that the action on the part of those detained was due to the secrecy with respect to the atomic bomb. 'I had a letter only yesterday from the secretary of one of the councils of Soviet–Canadian friendship,' he said in the House of Commons on 18 March 1946, 'stating that all this had grown out of the fact that Russia was being denied information which the United States, Great Britain and Canada had with respect to the atomic bomb.' He went on:

May I impress this fact upon the House that the disclosures of which I have been speaking tonight go back to 1943 and 1944. The organisation for the purpose of espionage of which I have been speaking has been in existence for three or four years in this country, and the greater part of the information which it obtained was secured before anyone knew anything about the atomic bomb.

It may be observed that of the twenty-six persons mentioned in the Report as being involved in dealing with Soviet Embassy personnel, ten had a foreign background (mostly Russian or Polish) and six had an English or Scottish background; most of the remaining ten were of Canadian parentage. There was no reason to doubt that the main attraction was purely ideological and that the technique employed by the Russians was to attract persons with Communist sympathies to study groups or 'cells' and in due course, after 'suitable development' to arrange for them to be approached by Canadian Communists with a view to their communicating information. Money played little part in these arrangements and relatively small sums changed hands, mostly for expenses and the like. It is remarkable, too, that there was no case, according to the evidence, of such a request to co-operate with the Russians being refused, and certainly no case in which such an approach was reported to the responsible Canadian authorities.

The duality of the Report of the Royal Commission was analysed in general terms in a hitherto unpublished despatch dated 22 August 1946, from Sir Alexander Clutterbuck, the British High Commissioner, to the Dominions Secretary Lord Addison, from which the following is an extract:

As to the Report itself, this has so far been generally praised as a masterly uncovering of the spy organisation. The Report is indeed a brilliant study. It is thorough, clear and forceful. It is a courageous and outspoken piece of writing and minces no words in speaking of the activities of the Soviet authorities. Altogether it is a most readable document and misses no point in the drama of the story. On the other hand, one cannot avoid the impression that the attempt to give dramatic effect has led at times to unjustifiable extravagant language; the search for brilliance has not always led to an impartial judicial conclusion. Indeed, on close examination it appears remarkable that the document should have been issued over the signature of two judges of the Supreme Court. . . .

There is, of course, a difficulty which the Commissioners were up against. None of the information concerning the espionage activities would have reached them but for the action of Gouzenko. This is inevitable, but it is a pity, because in spite of the fact that the Commissioners were able in the end, by close questioning of various witnesses, to build up a closely connected story, the point still remains that the whole story hangs on the single thread of Gouzenko's evidence and on the documents which he produced. There can be no doubt that the documents are genuine; there is little doubt that Gouzenko himself was sincere and probably told the truth so far as he knew it. But he was merely a subordinate official who was probably very far from knowing anything like all the story and yet the Commissioners tended to see the whole matter through Gouzenko's eyes (though it is fair to add that when corroboration from other sources was secured, Gouzenko was invariably supported on questions of fact and that he was, in fact, a good witness, and distinguished sharply between what he knew at first hand and his own inferences). This criticism might, perhaps, not have been so valid had not the Commissioners themselves fallen into the trap of writing their Report in such a manner as to give the appearance that they regarded Gouzenko's evidence (e.g. about such important matters as the existence of the Comintern) as statements of fact.

It must be recognised, too, that the Commissioners were placed in a dilemma by having a dual task thrust upon them. According to their terms of appointment, their primary duty was to report on who, in the public service, was involved: but they also had the wider function of investigating the whole espionage system. But this inevitably means that their Report takes on two self-contradictory qualities—it is not only a commission appointed to report to Parliament on a general question, but also it inevitably constituted itself a judicial tribunal, in effect, to try certain persons of suspected illegal activities, without any actual charge being laid against them. It is fair to the Commissioners to say that this difficulty was inherent in the problem and was an insuperable one. But it has led them to make comments in a public document which cannot fail to be prejudicial to the individual if and when proper judicial proceedings are taken. In certain cases, for example, the Commissioners frankly state that the person questioned was furtive and evasive and that they did not accept his answers.[34]

Indeed the duality between the Royal Commission inquiry and the trials in the courts which followed the publication of the full Report was strikingly illustrated when the *Montreal Gazette* serialised the Report under the title 'The Red Shadow over Canada,' while publishing the proceedings of the trials, often on the same page.

Eighteen persons in all were brought to trial on the basis of the information contained in the Report. Of these eight were found guilty and served prison sentences, one was fined, and the rest were acquitted either in the court of first instance or on appeal. On the other hand, several defendants, who were flatly reported by the Commission to have played an important part in the Soviet spy organisation, were acquitted. One of these was Eric Adams, an employee of the Industrial Development Bank, who was allegedly referred to in Gouzenko's documents by the code name 'Ernst', and was also incriminated by Kathleen Willsher in her confession made prior to her pleading guilty. However, Adams's counsel argued that the description of 'Ernst' could not by any stretch of the imagination apply to his client. So far as Miss Willisher had allegedly given confidential information to Adams, the defence insisted that this evidence had been 'twisted and torn from her' while she was at the RCMP barracks at Rockcliffe. Adams admitted that he knew Kay Willsher and that on one occasion he had given her money, but stated that this was to pay her expenses of attending a convention of a group in Montreal in which they were both interested. He also admitted that he had met Fred Rose but said, somewhat implausibly, that he had merely been interested in obtaining his views on political happenings in Canada. At the same time, when Adams's rooms were searched by the police, they were found to be full of Communist literature.

Similarly strong evidence was adduced before the Commissioners against a Squadron-Leader in the RCAF named Matt Nightingale for having given Rogov information on monitoring methods and plans of aerodromes, but the jury refused to convict after the judge in his summing up had warned them that it would be dangerous to do so on the uncorroborated evidence of an accomplice (Gouzenko). Professor Halperin ('Bacon') was acquitted on similar grounds in the face of strong documentary evidence put before the Commissioners. Incidentally, although it was not disclosed by the Commissioners in their public Report, a notebook kept by Halperin was found to contain the name and Edinburgh address of Klaus Fuchs.

'But whatever damage may be done to the Government or to the reputation of the Royal Commission by the acquittals in the courts of persons deemed guilty in the Report,' the British High Commissioner wrote to the Dominions Secretary in London on 25 November 1946, 'they have at least been some comfort to those who have feared for the future of civil liberties, for although those found innocent in the courts of law will not easily free themselves from the stigma of the Royal Commission's findings, the acquittals have shown that justice in the Canadian courts continues to be meted out without fear or favour.'[35]

Perhaps the last word on the Royal Commission may be left with the man who originally instituted it. 'Certainly it is a little short of providential that we made the discovery we did, and were so successful in handling the whole matter through the Supreme Court, etc.,' wrote Mackenzie King in his diary, looking back in May 1948. 'While I always felt worried and sorry for the delay the investigation took, and also thoroughly disapproved of some of the methods adopted by the police, I do think events justify what was done.'[36]

[6]

Emil Klaus Julius Fuchs, the naturalised English traitor who gave the secret of the atom bomb to the Russians and presumably enabled them to manufacture it sooner than they otherwise might have done, was born in a West German village called Russelsheim, near Darmstadt, on 29 December 1911. His family was not Jewish but Protestant, and his father Dr Emil Fuchs was a Lutheran pastor, who joined the Society of Friends when Klaus was thirteen, so that the boy was brought up in a poor but strictly pious Quaker home. He studied mathematics and physics at the University of Leipzig and later at that of Kiel after his father had been appointed Professor of Religious Science at the Teachers' Training College in that town. Like his father he joined the Social Democrats but gradually moved more and more to the left, eventually deserting his family's Christian beliefs and becoming an atheist. Finally he joined the Communist Party, a fact which became known to the student Brownshirts at Kiel University because they beat him up and threw him into the river. This experience only served to make him a dedicated Communist, since he had now suffered for the Party cause. He also hated the Nazis because they put his father in prison for his socialist views, although he was released shortly afterwards as the result of a strong protest from the Quaker community. Klaus's home life was clouded by further misfortunes. His mother committed suicide, while his sister Elizabeth threw herself on to the track of the Berlin underground railway and was killed.[37]

Very early on the morning of 28 February 1933, Klaus Fuchs got up and caught a train for Berlin. It was a great stroke of luck for him that he did so. He had been chosen to attend a Communist students' conference in the capital and what he did not know was that the Nazis were searching for him in Kiel. But, when he bought a newspaper he realised that he was a marked man and in danger of being arrested and thrown into a concentration camp as a Communist. On the previous night the Reichstag had been burned down and the fire was immediately blamed on the Communists, although it was the Nazis themselves who were responsible for it and used it as a pretext against their political opponents.

'I remember clearly, when I opened the newspaper in the train, I immediately realised its significance,' Klaus later recalled, 'and I knew that the underground struggle had started. I took the badge of the hammer and sickle from my jacket lapel which I had worn until that time.' He knew the hunt would be on for all known Communist Party members, and as soon as he reached Berlin he arranged to go into hiding. His elder brother Gerhard, who was also a Communist sympathiser, managed to avoid arrest and for a time he and his father ran a hire-car business for getting anti-Nazi refugees out of the country. Eventually Gerhard escaped to Switzerland where he was treated for a tubercular infection. As for Klaus, the Gestapo never caught up with him, although he attended the Communist students' conference where he was warmly praised for his work at Kiel. He was advised by the party to try and make his way out of the country so that he could complete his studies abroad, and then return one day in the future and help in rebuilding a new Germany when the Hitler régime had collapsed. As a first step he was asked to attend a United Front rally, which was being organised by the French Communist writer Henri Barbusse in Paris in August.

In July, after five months in hiding, helped by a girl who became his mistress, Klaus secretly crossed the frontier into France and succeeded in making his way to Paris, where he participated in the United Front rally. But he was destitute. He had no money and no friends in the French capital outside the French Communist Party. But he knew that a certain German girl, with whom he was friendly and who in fact was engaged to one of his cousins, was living with an English Quaker family in England. Fortunately he had her address in Somerset and he wrote to her from Paris, telling her of his circumstances. When the Quaker family heard of this, they sent him a generous invitation to come and join them in England so that he could complete his studies there. And so he arrived, pale, thin and virtually starving, and with nothing besides the clothes he was wearing and a bundle of dirty linen in a canvas bag.

Klaus Fuchs, who arrived in England in September 1933, told the immigration officer who interviewed him at his port of entry that he had come to England to study physics at Bristol University and he gave as a reference the name of the Quaker family in Somerset, saying that they were friends of his father. Accordingly he was registered in the official records of the Aliens Branch of the Home Office as a refugee, and since there was a constant stream of refugees coming from Germany at this time he was given permission to land and to stay for the time being. At the same time he was told that after a certain period of time, if he wished to remain in England, he would have to apply to the Home Office to have his residence permit extended.

A few weeks after his arrival in Somerset, he was taken down to the University at Bristol, where he met Professor Nevill Mott of the physics department, who spoke German. When the Professor heard Fuchs's story, how he had almost completed his studies for a degree at Kiel before being forced to go into hiding, Mott was able to arrange for Fuchs to enrol at the university free of charge, and he also helped him to get a grant from the Academic Assistance Council and the Society for the Protection of Science and Learning. In October Fuchs became Mott's first research student. About the same time the Quaker family moved to Bristol, and Fuchs continued to live with them for most of the next two years before, with the help of a further financial grant, he was able to take rooms of his own in the Redland district of the city. Meanwhile he proved a model student, methodical, persistent and showing outstanding ability in his chosen field of study. In 1937 he was awarded his Ph.D. degree in mathematical physics and, at the same time was given a research scholarship to continue his studies under Professor Max Born in Edinburgh.

Although he associated with other students of left-wing views, and his Quaker friends made several visits to the USSR under the auspices of Intourist, he never joined the British Communist Party nor did he admit his allegiance to the Communist creed, although he had by this time become a convinced Marxist. At this period the Nazi authorities kept lists of known Communists who had escaped abroad, and in November 1934, the German Consul in Bristol informed the Chief Constable of the city that Klaus Fuchs was a Communist. The Chief Constable duly forwarded the Consul's report to London with the comment that Fuchs was not known to have taken part in any Communist activities in Bristol, nor had he come to the unfavourable notice of the police. As an alien whose residence permit needed to be extended from time to time, Fuchs was investigated on three separate occasions by the Bristol constabulary, each time with the same negative result. His record, both personal and academic, was equally satisfactory in Edinburgh, where he began to contribute accounts of his original research to scientific journals. He also wrote a thesis on 'Some Problems of Condensation Quantum Dynamics and Stability of Nuclei', and within two years gained a Doctorate of Science in theoretical physics. On obtaining this degree in 1939, he was awarded a Carnegie Research Scholarship and continued to work in Edinburgh. He was now twenty-seven, he spoke fluent English with a German accent, and he had made a number of English and Scottish friends. On 17 July 1939, he applied for English naturalisation, being supported by the Quakers and his university teachers and associates. However, the war broke out before his application could be processed by the Home Office and from now on applications for naturalisation from enemy aliens were suspended. In November, 1939, he was summoned to appear before the Aliens Tribunal in Edinburgh, although he had been classified by the Home Office as a refugee from the Nazis. There was no evidence before the Tribunal that he was a Communist, only a letter from Professor Born that he had been a member of the Social Democratic Party in German between 1930 and 1932. In view of his excellent record in Britain, the Tribunal exempted him from any special restrictions apart from having to report regularly to the police, and he was allowed to return to his work at the University. Unfortunately for him he was caught by the General Order of May 1940 which followed the German breakthrough to the Low Countries, and he was interned with other enemy aliens and suspected enemy sympathisers.

At first he was sent to the Isle of Man and then shipped off to Canada with a mass of other internees. Luckily for him he travelled on the *Ettrick* which reached Quebec safely, and not the *Arandora Star*, which was torpedoed by a U-boat with considerable loss of life. Also lost in this vessel were the papers of the internees on board the *Ettrick*, so that when they arrived at Sherbrooke camp near Quebec nobody seemed to know exactly who they were. Indeed someone assumed that they were Nazi parachutists who had been dropped in disguise on Rotterdam during the frightful raid which destroyed much of that city, and in the event they were treated as avowed Nazis and prisoners-of-war. It is worth noting that while he was in the camp Fuchs used to receive newspapers and magazines from Professor Israel Halperin. He had never met Halperin and, so far as is known, he never did meet him. It is possible that Fuchs's name as an internee may have been given to Halperin by Fuchs's sister Kristel, who was living with her husband in Massachusetts and who knew the Professor. It is also not without significance that when Halperin was arrested as the result of Gouzenko's disclosures, an address book was found in his possession which among other names contained that of Fuchs and his Edinburgh address.

Fuchs remained in internment in Canada for the remainder of 1940, thus escaping the Nazi air 'blitz' on England. However, his friends were working on his behalf, particularly Professor Born in Edinburgh who greatly missed the loss of his brilliant research assistant. This led to a further check by the Home Office authorities on Fuchs's credentials, and as a result he was released from internment in January 1941 and returned to Britain to resume his research work at Edinburgh University.

In the spring of 1941, Dr (later Sir) Rudolf Peierls, German-born Professor of Mathematical Physics at Birmingham University, wrote to Fuchs in Edinburgh, asking him if he would be interested in undertaking some work of 'a special nature' in Birmingham. The salary was modest, £275 a year, and the job temporary, although he was told that it might continue for some considerable time. Peierls had only a slight personal acquaintance with Fuchs, but he had read some of his scientific papers which had impressed him favourably and his professorial colleagues Mott and Born had spoken highly of his abilities. After an interview in Brimingham, Fuchs was offered the job and accepted it. He was not told what it was beyond the fact that it was secret and connected with the war. First he had to be 'vetted' for security, since he still ranked as an enemy alien, but there was nothing recorded 'against' him except the report from the German Consul in Bristol and this was regarded as a tainted source. Otherwise his record was impeccable. However, it was recommended in the circumstances that he should not be given access to more classified material than was strictly necessary. Accordingly he signed the Official Secrets Act and began work in May 1941 on what it was immediately clear to him was connected with atomic energy. Since he was on his own and his financial means were very limited, the Peierls family let him have a room in their home, and he remained with them for the next eighteen months, after which he moved into lodgings. His work, like that of Professor Peierls, who was incidentally extremely satisfied with his help, was concerned with the gaseous diffusion process of separating the uranium isotopes, which was still in the experimental stage and was only one of a number of processes that were being explored in Britain and the United States.

With the setting up of Tube Alloys to co-ordinate the work of the atomic scientists at the different universities, the reports which Fuchs prepared and submitted on any question or problem put to him by Peierls were regarded as models of their kind. In 1942 Fuchs again applied for British naturalisation, and on this occasion he had the backing of the Tube Alloys directorate which was then supervised by Sir John Anderson, Lord President of the Council and a valued member of Churchill's wartime Cabinet. During the war enemy aliens were only naturalised in exceptional circumstances, but Fuchs's case was regarded as exceptional since he was engaged on work of national importance. He had to undergo another security 'vetting' and the German Consul's report was again brought up. However, he was duly cleared, since he had to become a British citizen in order to be given access to secret material and prohibited places for the purpose of his duties. His naturalisation was approved and he formally became a British citizen on 7 August 1942, when he swore the oath of allegiance to the British Sovereign. Yet at this time he was already in contact with the Russians and had begun to pass on secret information to them.

In fact Fuchs had made his initial contact with the Russians soon after his arrival in Birmingham in the previous year, and the initiative had come from him, no doubt stimulated by the fact that the Soviet Union was now at war with Germany. He was acquainted with several Communists, who like himself were refugees from Nazi Germany, and it was one of these who put him in touch with the Soviet Military Attaché's secretary in London. The secretary's name was Simon Davidovich Kremer, but throughout their association Fuchs never discovered it. He simply knew him by his cover-name of 'Alexander'.

What prompted Fuchs to turn traitor in 1941? In the account which he subsequently gave, he explained it quite simply. He began by stating that he doubted whether the fact that, when he took the job at Birmingham he was unaware of its precise nature, would have made any difference to his subsequent action. He went on:

When I learned about the purpose of the work I decided to inform Russia and I established contact *through another member of the Communist Party*.

Since that time I have had continuous contact with persons who were completely unknown to me, except that I knew they would hand over whatever information I gave them to the Soviet authorities. At that time I had complete confidence in Russian policy and I believed that the Western Allies deliberately allowed Russia and Germany to fight each other to the death. I therefore had no hesitation in giving all the information I had, even though occasionally I tried to concentrate mainly on giving information about the results of my own work. (Author's italics)[38]

Fuchs never revealed the identity of the other Communist. But reference to 'another member' of the Party is interesting, since it establishes that he regarded himself as a Party member, although he had no dealings with the small British Communist organisation.

During the twelve months between the end of 1941 and the end of the following year, it is known that Fuchs had at least four meetings with Kremer. Since it was not possible for Fuchs to get away from Birmingham on a week day, the meetings took place in London at week-ends in the evenings. The first was at a house near the Russian Embassy in Kensington Palace Gardens with a Russian who spoke English and called himself 'Alexander', and seemed to be familiar with his surroundings. Nevertheless Fuchs seems to have had doubts as to whether 'Alexander' was what he purported to be—he might have belonged to MI5 (British Counter-Intelligence) or was perhaps a 'double agent.' Anyhow, Fuchs did something which is strictly forbidden to an espionage agent. He called at the Russian Embassy and actually enquired whether 'Alexander' was genuine. However, he was reassured on the point, and he met Kremer again, but all the later meetings were in the street, in a quiet residential road, and on one occasion at a crowded bus stop. In October 1941, Fuchs began to supply 'Alexander' with carbon copies of his reports to Tube Alloys and also with manuscripts in his own handwriting on aspects of his work in which the Russians were particularly interested.

At the end of 1941, 'Alexander' departed on other duties and Fuchs was told that his new contact would be a woman. No doubt to suit his convenience his meetings with her were changed to Banbury, about forty miles from Birmingham, where the two would meet at two- or three-monthly intervals. Fuchs would take an afternoon train from Birmingham to Banbury at week-ends and would walk along a certain country road outside Banbury, where he would meet his woman contact. She did not live in Banbury, but in nearby Oxford, and after each meeting she would leave by train.* On one occasion they met at a café opposite Snow Hill in

---

* She was Ruth Kuczynski, code-name 'Sonya', a German Jewish refugee, whose English husband Len Brewer was in the RAF. *See* article 'The Housewife Who Spied For Russia' by Antony Terry and Philip Knightley, in the *Sunday Times*, 27 January 1980.

Birmingham. After about nine months Fuchs told her that their meetings must cease, since he had been chosen to go to the United States with Professor Peierls and others in a British team to continue work on the gaseous diffusion process in New York.

The content and importance of the information which Fuchs gave the Russians between June 1941, when he began work in Birmingham, and November 1943, when he left with Peierls and the rest of the team for the United States, is a matter of conjecture. Unquestionably he was able to tell them that the uranium atom bomb was a possibility and he certainly gave them the results of his own calculations on the theory of the gaseous diffusion process for separating the isotopes of uranium, and the fact that U235 produced in that way might be used in an atomic bomb. Dr Karl Cohen of Columbia took the view, which he expressed in a letter to the Joint Committee on Atomic Energy in Washington, that because of the visits of Peierls and others to the US early in 1942, when the relative merits of the Birmingham and Columbia versions of the diffusion process were discussed at length, as well as the established though inefficient channels of Anglo-American interchange of technical information, it was clear that even before his arrival in New York, Fuchs 'could have transmitted a very good outline of the American gaseous diffusion project.'

Before he embarked from Liverpool on the troopship *Andes*, Fuchs's woman contact gave him precise directions as to how he should communicate with the Russians. On a certain Saturday in January 1944, he was to make his way to a street corner on New York's lower East Side carrying a tennis ball in his left hand. There he would see a man carrying a book with a green binding and wearing gloves and carrying an additional pair of gloves in his hand. The man would at some point introduce himself as 'Raymond'. They would take a cab to a restaurant on lower Third Avenue, where Fuchs would hand over or otherwise disclose what information he had, and they would make arrangements for future meetings.

[7]

Fuchs landed with Peierls and the other members of the British team in New York early in December 1943. They immediately went to Washington to sign the usual security undertakings with the United States Government. Since Fuchs had already been cleared by the British authorities as an accredited member of the British mission, there was no further investigation of his credentials. Nor did anything of the kind take place during the next two and a half years that Fuchs was working in the United States. 'Our acceptance of Fuchs into the project was a mistake,' afterwards wrote General Groves, who was in charge of the American side. 'But I am at a loss when I try to determine just how much we would have avoided that mistake without insulting our principal war ally, Great Britain, by insisting on controlling their security measures.' Hence Groves had to be satisfied with the British statement that each member of the British team 'had been investigated as thoroughly as an employee of ours engaged on the same type of work.'[39]

On leaving Washington Fuchs put up first at the Taft Hotel in New York, after which he moved to the Barbizon-Plaza and finally to an apartment of his own at 128 West 77th Street. He also visited his sister Kristel at Cambridge, Massachusetts, where she and her husband, whose name was Robert Heineman, and their children were living.* So far as his official work went, Fuchs was kept extremely busy from the date of his first meeting with the Americans, on 7 December, when both teams of scientists exchanged views on the gaseous diffusion process and jointly planned their future operations. Further meetings followed both at Columbia University where the research was carried on and the Kellex Corporation where a large-scale gaseous diffusion plant was being designed, and Fuchs was specifically asked to make numerical calculations for its design. He also had an office in the British Centre in Wall Street and was a frequent visitor to both laboratories. The American project, to which the British thus contributed, was known as the Manhattan Engineering District, or more simply as the Manhattan Project.

Fuchs left the Barbizon-Plaza Hotel on the Saturday afternoon as previously arranged and took the subway to the lower East Side, holding a tennis ball in his left hand. He immediately recognised his contact with the book in green binding and together they took a cab to a restaurant on lower Third Avenue. Over lunch the other man told Fuchs his name was 'Raymond' and it was by that cover-name that Fuchs always knew him. His real name was Harry Gold, born Heinrich Golodnitsky of Jewish parents in Switzerland in 1910, subsequently becoming a naturalised American citizen after the family had come to the United States in 1914. Gold was a biochemist who worked for the Philadelphia Sugar Company in their laboratory. According to the FBI, Gold had been drawn into the Communist orbit by a Russian agent alternatively known as Troy Niles and Tom Black. When Gold was temporarily laid off work during the depression, Black helped him to get another job and also gave him money to get a college degree in chemistry. Gold began by supplying the Russians with industrial information such as that on solvents used in varnishes and lacquer. His chief Soviet supervisor, whom he only knew as 'John', was Anatoli Yakovlev, Vice-Consul in the Soviet Consulate in New York,

---

* Robert Heineman, who had married Kristel Fuchs in 1938 when he was twenty-one, owned a launderette in Cambridge. He also had some private means from his father, so that he and his wife lived fairly comfortably.

which, as has already been noted, was a centre of Soviet espionage. When Fuchs told Gold that he was working on the Manhattan Project with the object of harnessing the energy produced by nuclear fission for use in military weapons, Fuchs was probably unaware that he was being drawn into an espionage network of considerable proportions.[40]

Fuchs and Gold arranged to meet again, and it is known that they had at least five meetings in New York before Fuchs left for Los Alamos towards the end of 1944. After their first meeting Fuchs would let Gold know in advance what he proposed to give him at their next meeting; normally it would be a number of papers which he had typed or handwritten himself. He would also answer questions orally put to him, no doubt on Yakovlev's instructions, which Gold would go home and write up and later give to 'John' at a pre-arranged meeting place. At their second meeting, which took place in the middle of June at Woodside, Queen's, Fuchs promised that at their next meeting he would bring information of the actual plans for the construction of the uranium bomb. This Fuchs did at the end of the same month when they met near the Borough Hall in Brooklyn. In the middle of July they had a further meeting at the corner of 96th Street and Central Park West, and on this occasion they spent an hour and a half walking together in the park. Mostly at this time Fuchs passed over his own original manuscripts which his office assumed had been destroyed after official copies had been made. They included details of the production plant at Oak Ridge, originally called the Clinton Engineering Works, near the town of Knoxville, Tennessee, and its equipment included an electronic computer for nuclear physics calculations. It is difficult to guage the precise value to the Russians of the disclosures of Fuchs, May, Pontecorvo and other traitors, each reporting on his own work within the project, since some of the relevant documentation still remains classified. The considered opinion of the American Joint Congressional Committee on Atomic Energy, shortly after the Russians had exploded their first uranium bomb in the late summer of 1949, was that it had advanced the Soviet atomic energy programme by at least eighteen months. Certainly the disclosures of Fuchs and the others, assuming they were used and evaluated correctly, must have saved Soviet scientists a great deal of work.

When they parted in Central Park, Fuchs and Gold arranged to meet again at the Brooklyn Museum of Art, or alternatively, in the event of either of them being unable to keep this appointment, at Central Park West again.

Gold was greatly worried when Fuchs failed to keep either of these appointments. It is always a matter of concern to any espionage organisation when something of this kind occurs, since the assumption is that the agent may have confessed his activities to his own people with possibly disastrous results for the spy masters. At all events Gold went to Fuchs's apartment in West 77th Street, the address of which 'John' had given him, only to be told by the doorman that Fuchs had gone away, he did not know where. Gold then tried Fuchs's sister Kristel in Cambridge, saying that he must see Fuchs urgently, but all Mrs Heineman could say was that he had gone off 'somewhere in the south-west.' However, she said he had promised to spend Christmas with her and her husband if he could. All Gold could do in the circumstances was to leave his telephone number with her and ask her to get her brother to call him if and when he arrived. He then reported the position to Yakovlev and prepared to wait.

The explanation of Fuchs's conduct was simple. He had been posted to Los Alamos, near Santa Fé in northern New Mexico, which had been selected for the final stages of the work of assembling and arranging to test the atomic bomb. The director was Dr Robert J. Oppenheimer of the University of California at Berkeley. Peierls was one of the first British scientists to arrive at 'the Hill', where the top secret work was being carried out. Meanwhile he had left Fuchs in charge of the New York office with instructions to follow on later, which he did.

Since Los Alamos was primarily a military establishment with a Commanding Officer, the American authorities wished to put the scientists into uniform, with appropriate ranks, thus bringing them under army discipline. The scientists objected to this and won their point, although the military remained at the station, where they were responsible for the maintenance of living conditions, and safeguarding government property, while the scientists answered for the technical and security aspects of the work programme. Fuchs soon felt thoroughly at home in this atmosphere. The dry desert air agreed with him, he took more exercise than formerly, and enjoyed mountain climbing and skiing. Since he liked motoring, Mrs Peierls persuaded him to go down to Santa Fé and buy a second-hand vehicle. He settled for an old Buick, in which he liked to drive round the countryside. It was probably the happiest period of his life.[41]

'Fuchs was popular at Los Alamos,' wrote a Hungarian colleague named Edward Teller, 'because he was kind, helpful, and much interested in the works of others. But his exceptional intelligence was combined with exceptional reticence. Mrs Peierls, at Los Alamos parties, called him 'Penny-in-the-slot' Fuchs, because in order to get a sentence out of him she had to drop a sentence into him. He never talked unless there was a reason for talking. Later, after he was arrested, I understood why.'

He did not go north to spend Christmas with his sister and brother-in-law in Cambridge, outside Boston, but he made the journey early in 1945, much to Harry Gold's relief when he received a telephone call from him at his New York number. Gold lost no time in coming to Cambridge, where he saw Fuchs in the Heinemans' apartment. Fuchs now agreed to put down in writing everything he had gleaned at Los Alamos and a second meeting was arranged in a Boston street for a few days later. On this occasion Fuchs was able to disclose information which was of the greatest value to the Russians. In the notes which he made and gave Gold, he revealed the details of the plutonium bomb (as distinct from the uranium bomb); this included its design, method of construction and the fact that the plutonium (which in the event was to be used in the bomb which was dropped on Nagasaki) was produced in atomic piles at Hanford in Washington State. These piles were water cooled, necessary for the transference of heat, while the pile at Oak Ridge was air cooled. The device used in detonating plutonium was an implosion lens, which exploded inwards, and Fuchs also described this device, which interested the Russians greatly, so that Gold was asked to get any further details he could from Fuchs. However, Fuchs had given all the information he could. But in the event Gold was able to obtain actual drawings of the implosion lens from a young American soldier named David Greenglass, who was also working at Los Alamos. His story emerges later.

Before Fuchs and Gold parted in Boston, they agreed to meet in the summer in New Mexico, since Fuchs said that his work made it unlikely that he could come north again. The rendezvous was arranged for 4 p.m. on 2 June 1945—the first Saturday in June—at the Castillo Bridge in Santa Fé.

Fuchs returned from his ten-day visit to the Heinemans in Cambridge at the end of February. Some of his friends noticed that he was looking harassed and depressed. But all he would say, when questioned, was that he was worried about his sister.

The next visit took place exactly as arranged. Gold travelled down from New York by train to Albuquerque, and thence by bus to Santa Fé, which he reached with over an hour to spare. He whiled away the time by visiting the local museum where he bought a map of Santa Fé, so that he would not have to ask anyone for directions as to the whereabouts of Castillo Bridge. He was later to regret that he kept the map, although he destroyed all other evidence of his visit to New Mexico. Gold was the first at the bridge. A few minutes later Fuchs appeared, chugging along in his old Buick.

They spent half an hour together, during which Fuchs told Gold that there had been great progress at Los Alamos and that the first test of the atom bomb would take place the following month. Nevertheless, Fuchs intimated that he did not consider that the bomb would be ready for use against the Japanese before the end of the war. Just before they parted, Fuchs handed over a package of relevant papers. This was standard espionage practice, since if the two men had been previously accosted by a security man, Gold would have nothing incriminating on his person while Fuchs had a right to be carrying secret documents. They arranged to meet again in Santa Fé three and a half months later, near a church on the way out of town.

After they parted, Fuchs returned to Los Alamos, while Gold caught a bus back to Albuquerque. Since it was late when he reached Albuquerque, Gold took a room for the night at the Hotel Hilton. Next morning, he called at 209 North High Street, where David Greenglass and his wife were living, and allegedly identified himself by saying 'Julius sent me.' Later in the day, Greenglass handed Gold the drawings of the implosion lens which he had stolen from Los Alamos. Gold left after giving Greenglass $500—Fuchs had waved aside Gold's offer of $1500, saying he did not need money. Three days later Gold, who was back in New York, met Yakovlev at a pre-arranged rendezvous in Brooklyn, where he handed over everything he had got from Fuchs and Greenglass.

Gold's next and last meeting with Fuchs, on 19 September 1945, took place without a hitch. By this time the atom bomb test had taken place at Alamogordo, the two bombs had been dropped on Hiroshima and Nagasaki, and the Japanese had surrendered unconditionally. Fuchs had written down all he knew, and the information was vital. He gave the size of the bomb, what it contained, how it was constructed, and how it was detonated. He also gave a vivid description of the test explosion and he conceded that he had grossly underestimated the industrial potential of the United States, besides admitting that he was mistaken in supposing that the bomb would not be ready in time for use against the Japanese. He also volunteered the information that he expected to be posted back to England fairly soon. This worried him as his father, who was still alive in Germany, would also probably come to England to see him. Old Dr Fuchs was apt to be over-talkative, and Klaus was afraid that the old man might talk about his son's pre-war Communist connections in Germany. Klaus had correctly deduced from the action of the German Consul in Bristol that there was a Gestapo dossier about him in Kiel, a town which he was sorry that the British and not the Russians had captured, and that was now in the British zone of occupation. It would be awkward, he surmised, if that dossier should chance to fall into the hands of British Intelligence. Nevertheless he agreed to go on working for the Russians and he arranged with Gold that, on the first Saturday of each month after his return to England, he would go to the street entrance of Mornington Crescent Underground Station at 8 p.m.* He would be carrying five books in one hand tied together by string, and two books in the other. His contact at the rendezvous would also be carrying a book by Bennett Cerf, *Stop Me If You Have Heard This*.

During the eight months which elapsed between Fuchs's last meeting with Gold and his final departure for England in the following June, the Russians made no attempt to get into touch with Fuchs nor he with them.

---

* Mistakenly described as 'Paddington Crescent'.

The Gouzenko affair had broken in Canada with repercussions in the United States and Britain, and pending the outcome of the Canadian inquiry Moscow may well have kept its espionage operations in a low key. In fact there was a general lull, no doubt accentuated by the agents themselves who were less disposed to action following their wartime exertions. Also there were fewer vital secrets to impart, although no doubt routine spying continued, and the Russians had allies in men like Maclean and Philby who were actually working for them in the British Embassy in Washington.

Towards the end of November 1945, Fuchs visited Montreal and Chicago on official business, and it was on this trip that he was interviewed for the appointment at Harwell which led to his being made head of the division of theoretical physics. In December he accompanied Professor Peierls and his wife on a motor trip to Mexico. As usual he was unimpressed by the tourist sights, but the Peierls noticed that he also seemed more abstracted than usual. Alan Moorehead has suggested in his book *The Traitors* (1952) that, since Mexico was one of the regular staging posts for Communist agents, Fuchs may have contemplated going on to the Soviet Union. However he returned to the United States with Peierls and his wife.[42]

On 16 June 1946, Klaus Fuchs left Los Alamos for the last time. He went first to Washington to report the accomplishment of his mission and then continued north to Boston for a final visit to his sister and her husband. On 28 June, after a week with them in Cambridge, he flew from Montreal to England to take up his appointment at the newly established atomic energy establishment at Harwell.

CHAPTER THREE

Klaus Fuchs and Bruno Pontecorvo

[1]

The British atomic research establishment at Harwell was hurriedly built on the site of a wartime airfield from which airborne forces took off on D-day in 1944 for the invasion of Normandy. 'We were given Harwell on a windy day of February 1946 on a flying visit from Canada,' wrote Sir John Cockcroft, the first scientist in charge. 'A start had to be made quickly and the only solution was to provide prefabs and to erect them on our own site where services and sewers were available and where the minimum of consents had to be obtained.' The laboratories and office blocks were located between two clusters of prefabricated buildings not unlike enlarged rabbit hutches, which accommodated the staff, the whole being enclosed by a high security fence, with warning notices such as 'Danger' and 'Radio-active Waste'. When Fuchs arrived in July 1946 he contributed to the original planning, recruiting the staff for the divisions of theoretical physics which he headed, ordering their work and largely setting out their programme. His salary was £1500 a year and at first he lived in the bachelors' quarters of the staff club, but later moved to a boarding house in Abingdon nearby, and finally, as befitted a departmental head, to one of the prefabricated houses on the site which were normally reserved for married couples. He bought a second-hand grey saloon MG car which he could easily afford to run on his present pay, and he began to make friends among senior members of the staff, notably Professor and Mrs W. H. B. Skinner from whom he bought his car, and Wing-Commander Henry Arnold, the station security officer, and his wife. He could afford to spend his leaves abroad, going to Switzerland with Professor Peierls and his wife and to the French Riviera with the Skinners. On the Swiss holiday, which was near Zermatt, he met his elder brother Gerhardt, who was a tubercular patient as well as a Communist, and who came over from Davos for a couple of days; they spent a lot of time together. But Gardhardt was in the final stages of the disease and his life was gradually ebbing away.[1]

Professor Margaret Gowing, the official historian of the British atomic energy authority, has given a fair assessment of Fuchs during his time at Harwell:

Fuchs was not an inspired or original scientist but, rather, a highly competent and omnivorous worker, with a remarkably good memory. He was the one ubiquitous scientist at Harwell, on almost every committee—whether about the design of the Windscale piles or the diffusion plant, or nuclear power, or declassification policy. He was the only Harwell scientist deeply involved in the weapon itself. Cockcroft had a special respect for him and thought his value to Harwell 'extreme'. Fuchs seemed to others, as well as to himself, indispensable to the establishment. Some colleagues found him intolerably arrogant, and one or two were on record as instinctively disliking him without knowing why, from the time they first knew him in the wartime project.[2]

Klaus Fuchs certainly seems to have had no small measure of self-conceit. 'Yes', he once remarked, 'I suppose it could be said that I *am* Harwell.' Thus it was quite natural that he should have been a member of the United Kingdom delegation which conferred with representatives of the United States and Canada during three days in November 1947, on the subject of declassification. The object of the conference was to examine the atomic knowledge which had been shared by the three countries in the war and to decide what material should be released for publication and what should not because of its connection with atomic weapons. No knowledge which any of the countries had acquired since the war was discussed. But Fuchs was a member of the sub-committee which specifically considered the Los Alamos period, and it has been recalled that on the whole he took a conservative line on the release of information. Later, however, according to Alan Moorehead, he worked out an elaborate scheme of declassification possibly with the idea of establishing that the information he had given the Russians was no longer secret.[3]

It is of some interest that the declassification conference in Washington, in November 1947, was attended among others by a representative of the British embassy whose name was Donald Maclean, and who four years later was to make a dramatic flight behind the Iron Curtain with his fellow diplomat Guy Burgess. Maclean had been working for the Russians for some years. He arrived in Washington at the beginning of 1947 with the rank of First Secretary and the following note about him appeared in the FBI files after his defection, dated 19 June 1951.

From January 1947 to August 1948 Maclean officially represented the British Embassy on matters dealing with political aspects of atomic energy. He reportedly had no access to classified scientific information, but he did have full knowledge of the discussions which took place during that period concerning co-operation between the United States, Canada and England. He had access to communications on such matters which passed between Washington, DC, and London, England. During the same period he had knowledge of the transactions of the Combined Development Agency and for arrangements for securing raw materials and estimates of future production which were made at that time.

Although the McMahon Act, which set up the US Atomic Energy Commission, in effect denied fresh nuclear information to Great Britain, it did not apply to declassification or raw materials. For this reason the British Embassy was interested, and Maclean was given a pass to visit the premises of the AEC on his own whenever he liked. This annoyed some of the senior officers in the American armed forces, who on their visits always had to be accompanied by an escort. Even J. Edgar Hoover required an escort, which riled him considerably. When the matter eventually came to be investigated, it was discovered that between 6 August 1947 and 11 June 1948, Donald Maclean had visited the AEC no less than twelve times, occasionally at night. According to a report of the acting head of the AEC dated 1 July 1951, after Maclean's flight with Burgess, Maclean had access to the estimates made of ore supply for the period 1948–52 and the uranium requirements in particular. 'Some of the information was classified as Top Secret and would have been of interest to the Soviet Union.' However, the report added, fissionable materials production schedules for the period in question had in fact 'expanded considerably' above the current estimates while Maclean was a member of the relevant committee, so that in the event the Soviet Union did not gain so much as might have been anticipated. So far as declassification was concerned the acquaintance of Maclean and Fuchs seems to have been confined to this subject, and it is unlikely that either knew that the other was working for the Russians.[4]

Fuchs would also attend regular meetings in the Ministry of Supply in London, where secret matters were often on the agenda. Here again Fuchs appeared strongly in favour of safeguarding security. 'You will remember,' he wrote to a colleague at this time, 'that last week I gave you a document on the understanding that it would be restricted to members of the Technical Committee and Sir John Anderson's Committee. In the meantime I have seen this document in other hands; no harm has been done in this particular instance and I do not intend to follow it up. However it does raise the question whether at present there is any machinery to ensure that such restrictions are observed.'

Fuchs did not keep any of the rendezvous which had been arranged for him outside Mornington Crescent Underground Station. Nor did the Russians for their part make any attempt to approach him or renew the contact in any way. The repercussions of the Royal Commission in Ottawa were still being felt throughout the western world, and no doubt the Russians had passed the word to the majority of their agents abroad to remain inactive. However, early in 1947, Fuchs felt the draw to Moscow again and in the result went in search of the Communist who had originally put him in touch with Simon Kremer at the Soviet Embassy in London. He failed in his search, but he did find another Communist, a woman, who was willing to put him in touch with the right quarters. This she did and contact was resumed, although Fuchs was again rebuked for his action by his new contact and he was warned, as he had been on the previous occasion, to keep absolutely clear of the British Communist Party, which was a constant object of interest to the security service.

Fuchs was instructed to go into the saloon bar of a public house in north London, carrying a copy of the weekly *Tribune* and take a seat on a certain bench. His contact would carry a red book. The meeting took place as arranged and, perhaps out of a feeling of guilt for having kept away from the Russians for so long, Fuchs accepted £100 in bank notes. Hitherto he had only taken small sums by way of covering his expenses, mainly from Harry Gold in the United States. But this was something different. Afterwards Fuchs admitted that he took the money as a symbol, as a formal act to bind himself to the cause. 'After this there could be no going back: he had taken money and he was committed for ever,' Alan Moorehead has written of his behaviour at this stage. 'That is his explanation, and since he is the only witness to his own thoughts it must be noted, if not accepted. He took no more money from the Russians after this.[5]

Elaborate arrangements were made by the two men in case Fuchs was unable to keep an appointment, but most of the meetings seem to have gone off all right—about eight spread over two years, usually in one of two pubs, the Spotted Horse in High Street, Putney, or the Nag's Head at Wood Green. On the whole Fuchs was no longer in a position to give the Russians anything like the material he had been able to hand over in America, since he was now cut off from the secrets of American research through the operation of the McMahon Act. Nevertheless he was able to give them various details of the British nuclear reactors at Windscale in Cumberland, and also the figures of American production up to the time he left Los Alamos. At this time the Russians were very interested in the hydrogen or so-called H-bomb, but Fuchs could say little on this subject beyond what had been discussed when he was at Los Alamos. The Russians now wished Fuchs to go to Paris and make contact there with certain agents who possessed some technical knowledge of this weapon. However, he refused, pleading that he could not get away. The fact was that he was beginning to have doubts about the Russians in spite of having previously committed himself by accepting their money, and he came to feel that he was cheating his friends at Harwell. He decided not to break altogether with the Russians but to give them less and less information, while he wrestled with his personal problem of the Russians versus Harwell. This is how he explained his position:

In the course of this work I began naturally to form bonds of personal friendship and I had to conceal them from my inner thoughts. I used my Marxist philosophy to establish in my mind two separate compartments: one compartment in which I allowed myself to make friendships, to have personal relations, to help people and to be in all personal ways the kind of man I wanted to be, and the kind of man which, in a personal way, I had been before with my friends in or near the Communist Party. I could be free and easy and happy with other people without fear of disclosing myself because I knew that the other compartment would step in if I approached the danger point. I could forget the other compartment and still rely upon it. It appeared to me at the time that I had become a 'free man' because I had succeeded in the other compartment in establishing myself completely independent of the surrounding forces of society. Looking back on it now the best way of expressing it seems to be to call it a controlled schizophrenia.[6]

Eventually, as Fuchs went on with this analysis, he came to the point where he knew he disapproved of many actions of the Russian Government and of the Communist Party, but he still believed that they would build a new world, that one day he would take part in it, and that on that day he would also have to stand up and say to them that there were things that they were doing wrongly. 'During this time I was not sure that I could give all the information I had,' he admitted. 'However it became more and more evident that the time when Russia would expand her influence over Europe was far away and that therefore I had to decide myself whether I could go on for many years to continue to hand over information without being sure in my own mind whether I was doing right. I decided that I could not do so. I did not go to one rendezvous because I was ill at the time. I decided not to go to the following one.' His illness was due to a spot which he developed on one of his lungs during a holiday in the spring of 1949 with the Skinners on the Mediterranean, and that was why he missed one appointment. Meanwhile, Mrs Skinner nursed him back to health in her house at Harwell.

During the following summer, the FBI in Washington were working on the theory that the Russians had been getting information about the atomic bomb from Los Alamos, and that it came from a British and not an American scientist. Among the British scientists at Los Alamos were Professor Peierls and Dr Fuchs.* At this time there was a brilliant young member of the British Secret Intelligence Service in the Washington embassy named Peter Dwyer, who had previously worked in William Stephenson's New York organisation. In the words of the super-spy H. A.

---

* On 17 October 1949, in response to a request from the Director of the FBI, the finger print cards of Fuchs and Peierls, which had been taken at Los Alamos in 1944, were despatched to Washington: FBI New York file 65–15136–5.

R. ('Kim') Philby, who was in Washington at the same time as Dwyer, and incidentally also with Burgess and Maclean, Dwyer, 'by a brilliant piece of analysis of the known movements of the two men, conclusively eliminated Peierls. Thereafter the finger pointed unwaveringly at Fuchs.'

Philby's words are taken from the book which his Soviet masters allowed him to publish after his defection and flight to Moscow.[7] The 'brilliant piece of analysis' is a euphemism for an intercept between the Soviet Embassy in Washington and Military Intelligence Headquarters in Moscow, which was forwarded by Dwyer to London after it had been decrypted by the Americans in Washington. Obviously Philby could not reveal the fact that members of the British service for which he once worked were reading Soviet coded signals which were being intercepted by the US Central Intelligence Agency (CIA). When this particular one was seen by Dick White, deputy director of the Security Service (MI5) in London, he could not understand it; but he suspected that it had something to do with atomic energy. According, on 5 September, he showed it to Mr (later Sir) Michael Perrin, who had been Assistant Director of Tube Alloys and who had stayed on after the war as deputy controller of the technical policy side of atomic energy when the department was transferred to the Ministry of Supply. Asked if he could throw any light on the message's meaning, Perrin replied: 'It looks very much as if Fuchs has been working for the Russians.' As a result the Prime Minister was informed, and the security officer at Harwell was alerted to keep an eye on Fuchs.

Meanwhile a momentous incident took place which was of the greatest interest both to the United States and Great Britain. On 10 September Perrin and an officer from the British Secret Intelligence Service (MI6) were asked to attend a top secret 'teletype' or telex conference in the US Embassy in London between the embassy and the CIA and military intelligence in Washington. The first message from Washington came through about 11 a.m. It was to the effect that on the previous day an aircraft of the US Air Force operating the Long Range Detection System had tracked a suspicious looking 'cloud' from the North-West Pacific and had succeeded in obtaining an air sample which was found to be highly radio-active. The 'cloud' was moving in the direction of the British Isles where it was expected to remain for a few days in the latitude of 70 degrees north. Could the British do anything to confirm the American finding? Perrin immediately replied that this was quite feasible, and the Americans were informed that a British aircraft operating the normal 'met' flights from Aldergrove in Northern Ireland could be fitted with a special filter and sent off on a reconnaisance flight at a height of 20,000 feet. Further questions to Washington elicited detailed information about times and strength of the activity, and it was clear that the Americans regarded the evidence as pointing conclusively to the recent detonation of an atomic bomb by the

Russians on their mainland, apparently some time during the last week of August.

In the result a Halifax fitted with the necessary filter took off the same evening, followed by several Mosquitoes next morning flying at heights between 20,000 and 30,000 feet and following a north-eastern course parallel with the Norwegian coast in case the 'cloud' should have passed earlier than expected by the Americans. These arrangements had been reported to Sir Stewart Menzies, the head of MI6, and the Chief of the Air Staff, and were approved by them. What the Americans had correctly anticipated was amply confirmed by the British flights.

The Prime Minister was spending the following week-end at Chequers and Menzies took Michael Perrin there on the Sunday (18 September) to brief him on the latest developments in the atomic field. Attlee assumed that a public announcement would be made by President Truman, probably within the next week, after the President had informed the members of the Congressional Joint Committee on Atomic Energy, of which Senator McMahon was chairman. So far as Fuchs was concerned, it was agreed that it would be necessary to move with great caution since if he were to be alerted in any way, Fuchs might take wing to Moscow, and there was no means of preventing him from doing this since there was nothing against him which could be brought out in court. After carefully considering the matter, Attlee authorised a circumspect interrogation. Curiously enough it was Fuchs himself who was shortly to provide a convenient pretext for his questioning.[8]

The President's announcement was made on the morning of 23 September 1949. 'We have evidence that within recent weeks an atomic explosion occurred in the USSR,' he declared. 'This recent development emphasises once again, if indeed such emphasis were needed, the necessity for that truly effective enforceable international control of atomic energy which this government and the large majority of the members of the United Nations support.'

About the middle of October, Fuchs approached Wing-Commander Henry Arnold, the security officer at Harwell, saying that he would like to have some advice from him on a personal problem. He had received word from Germany, he said, that his father, who had recently visited his son at Harwell and whom Arnold remembered well, had accepted an appointment as Professor of Theology at the University of Leipzig in the Russian zone. Suppose his father should get into difficulty with the Russians? Perhaps he ought to resign from Harwell, since the Russians might try to put pressure on him through his father. Arnold replied that the question of his resignation was one for the administrative authorities, and as security officer he was not competent to advise Fuchs. They met again, a few days later, on 20 October, when Fuchs repeated that he was in some doubt what to do if the Russians were to arrest his father. Asked what he might do, Fuchs said he did not know; he might do different things in different circumstances. There were two possibilities, though he did not mention them to Arnold. He might confess and get the whole business over with, since he had lost contact with the Russians and had not been approached by any agent since the beginning of 1949. Now that they had the bomb, maybe the Russians had lost interest in him. Alternatively, he might try deliberately to manoeuvre himself into a position which would oblige the security authorities to declare him a bad risk on account of his father's position, and so enable him (the younger Fuchs) to leave Harwell before he was discovered.

Klaus Fuchs felt that he could not stop his father from going to Leipzig. 'However, it made me face at least some of the facts about myself,' he admitted afterwards, looking back. 'I felt that my father's going to the Eastern zone, that his letters, would touch me somewhere and that I was not sure whether I would not go back [to Germany myself]. I suppose I did not have the courage to fight it out for myself and therefore I invoked an outside influence by informing security that my father was going to the Eastern zone. A few months passed and I became more and more convinced that I had to leave Harwell.'[9]

Arnold reported that Fuchs was undergoing a deep crisis of conscience, and if he were approached tactfully with an appeal to that conscience, there was some hope that he could be brought to confess his treachery. For this reason, one of the most experienced interrogators was chosen to question Fuchs on behalf of the Security Service (MI5). This was Mr William James Skardon, who had handled the case of William Joyce ('Lord Haw-Haw') and other traitors. He combined patience with tenacity in a remarkable degree, and he was to need both in abundant measure if he was to bring out the truth in the case of Klaus Fuchs.

On 21 December 1949, Skardon came down to Harwell and they met in Arnold's office. After introducing them, Arnold withdrew and left them alone together. Skardon began by referring to the information which Fuchs had given about his father. Was there something more that Fuchs cared to say?

For over an hour Fuchs discussed his family background and career with the utmost candour. He spoke of his sister Kristel, his brother Gerhardt, and he revealed that at the Social Democrat Party elections in Kiel in 1932 he had supported the Communist candidate in the absence of a Socialist. For that, Fuchs said, he was expelled from the SD party and 'drifted into the Communist camp'. He spoke about his work for Tube Alloys and of his visit to America in 1943. All this he spoke of calmly and frankly. Suddenly Skardon broke in with a loaded question.

'Were you not in touch with a Soviet official or a Soviet representative while you were in New York? And did you not pass on information to that person about your work?'

'I don't think so,' said Fuchs, with a look of surprise.

'I am in possession of precise information which shows that you have been guilty of espionage on behalf of the Soviet Union,' Skardon went on. 'For example, during the time when you were in New York you passed to them information concerning your work.'

'I don't think so,' Fuchs repeated, shaking his head.

Skardon suggested that, in view of the seriousness of the matter, this was rather an ambiguous reply.

'I don't understand,' Fuchs replied. 'Perhaps you will tell me what the evidence is. I have not done any such thing.' He went on to deny any knowledge of the matter, adding that in his opinion it had been wise to exclude the Soviet Union from information about the atomic bomb. Fuchs was then questioned about Professor Halperin, but he insisted that they had never met, though Halperin had sent him papers and magazines when he was interned in Canada. Had he ever returned to Canada? Yes, he recalled that he had made one visit to Montreal during the period when he was working in New York.

After lunch the meeting was resumed, when Fuchs repeated his denials but added that, in view of the suspicions about him, he felt he ought to resign from Harwell.

Two more meetings took place between the two men before Fuchs at last began to crack. Meanwhile, on 10 January 1950, Sir John Cockcroft sent for Fuchs and told him that in view of his father's departure for Leipzig it would be better for all concerned if Fuchs resigned from Harwell and took a university post, although he (Cockcroft) would be glad to retain him as a consultant.

Fuchs persisted in denying the espionage charge when he met Skardon for the second time at Harwell on 30 December and again on the morning of 13 January 1950, when Skardon came down again, this time at Fuchs's request. Fuchs looked pale and agitated. 'You asked to see me and here I am,' said Skardon. 'Yes,' answered Fuchs. 'It's rather up to me now.'

After a further inconclusive morning when Fuchs asserted that Skardon would never persuade him to talk, they broke off for lunch, which Fuchs suggested they should have together at Abingdon. Skardon was agreeable but somewhat concerned by the breakneck speed with which Fuchs drove, and the correspondingly slow return drive.

As soon as they got back to Arnold's office, Fuchs shut the door and told Skardon he had decided to confess. His conscience was clear, but he was worried about his friends on the station and what they might think.

'When did it start?' asked Skardon.

'About the middle of 1942,' Fuchs replied, 'and it continued until about a year ago.'

The fact that Fuchs's spying had gone on for seven years was Skardon's first shock, since he thought it had only involved a few facts and figures given over a relatively short period.

Skardon's second shock came when he asked Fuchs what exactly he had given the Russians. In this context, said Fuchs, he considered that the worst thing he had done was to tell the Russians how to make the atomic bomb.[10]

[2]

It was only towards the end of his long confession which Fuchs dictated and which Skardon took down by hand, that the Deputy Chief Scientific Officer at Harwell, as Fuchs now was, expressed contrition for his treachery. 'I know that I cannot go back on that,' he declared, 'and I know that all I can do now is to try and repair the damage I have done. The first thing is to make sure that Harwell will suffer as little as possible and that I have to save for my friends as much as possible of that part that was good in my relations with them. This thought is at present uppermost in my mind, and I find it difficult to concentrate on any other points.'

He went on:

> However, I realise that I will have to state the extent of the information I have given and that I shall have to help as far as my conscience allows in stopping other people who are still doing what I have done. *There is nobody I know by name who is concerned with collecting information for the Russian authorities.* There are people whom I know by sight whom I trusted with my life and who trusted me with theirs, and I do not know that I shall be able to do anything that might in the end give them away. They are not inside the project, but they are intermediaries between myself and the Russian Government. (Author's italics)

'At first,' he concluded, 'I thought that all I would do would be to inform the Russian authorities that work on the atomic bomb was going on. I concentrated mainly on the product of my own work, but in particular at Los Alamos I did what I consider to be the worst I have done, namely to give information about the principle of the design of the plutonium bomb.' Later on at Harwell he began to be concerned about the information he was giving, he added, and he began to sift it, 'but it is difficult to say exactly when and how I did it because it was a process which went up and down with my inner struggles.' The last time he had handed over any information, he said, was in February or March 1949:

> Before I joined the project most of the English people with whom I made personal contacts were left wing, and affected in some degree or

other by the same kind of political philosophy. Since coming to Harwell I have met English people of all kinds, and I have come to see in many of them a deep-rooted firmness which enables them to lead a decent way of life. I do not know where this springs from and I don't think they do, but it is there.

Fuchs came up to London by train on Friday, 27 January, without any police supervision. Skardon met him at Paddington Station and drove him to the War Office where Fuchs read through his confession and signed it after the security officer had administered the usual caution. He had one reservation which may strike the reader as somewhat odd in the circumstances. He would not tell Skardon the technical details of the construction of the atomic bomb or of the other scientific and technical information which he had given the Russians on the ground that Skardon had not been cleared for access to such information. But he agreed to confide them to a qualified person, and for this person he chose Michael Perrin, whom he had known since 1941 when Perrin was assistant to Sir Wallace Akers at Tube Alloys. An appointment was made for the following Monday, 30 January, in London, as Fuchs said he would like to rest over the week-end to collect his thoughts. He then returned alone to Harwell by train, since Skardon was evidently satisfied that he would not attempt to flee the country and get away to Russia.

The same night Arnold saw a light burning late in Fuchs's office and looking over the glass transom could see that Fuchs was poring over some papers. Was he planning an escape, taking the papers with him? Or was he thinking of suicide? Meanwhile Fuchs went on sorting his papers and putting them in neat piles on his desk. He left for a while but returned later and finally turned off the light about 12.30 a.m., locked his office and drove home. Arnold thereupon entered the room with a duplicate key only to find that his long vigil had been in vain, since the papers only concerned routine matters and were of no importance. The papers were still there spread out on the desk when Fuchs was arrested.

On Monday, 30 January, Fuchs went up by an early train which reached Paddington at 10.45. Skardon met him as before and together they drove to the War Office where they met Perrin in Room 055, customarily used by MI5. Skardon, who had now been cleared for access to atomic secrets, told Perrin that Fuchs had 'decided to reveal everything'. Perrin replied that he had plenty of writing paper and they set to work with Skardon sitting in on the interrogation which was mainly conducted by Perrin, although Skardon did occasionally ask a question. It was a long-drawn-out process, as Fuchs's confession had to be set down chronologically with all the relevant technical data, first, his monthly reports when he was working with the Tube Alloys in Birmingham in 1942; then, in New York, the details of the gaseous diffusion process; then, at Santa Fé, the principles of the plutonium bomb;

and finally, at Harwell, the information about the progress of the British post-war project, which was to culminate in the explosion of the first British atomic bomb in 1952.[11]

Fuchs repeated several times that he was sure the Russians had been getting material from other scientists. For example, quite early on, when he was in Birmingham, the Russians had asked him for details of the electro-magnetic isotope separation process, about which British scientists knew very little at that time. 'It's an alternative method of separating isotopes from the diffusion method,' Perrin explained for Skardon's benefit. 'The Americans had, at Oakridge, two very big plants—one for each method.'

After Fuchs got to New York and learned of the electro-magnetic separation process, he realised that the Russians had other sources of information. He was even more surprised, he went on, when at Los Alamos he was asked for information about what was called 'the tritium bomb' by his contact 'Raymond' (Harry Gold) in Santa Fé. This request clearly referred to the hydrogen bomb, to which some thought was being given by a small select group of the staff at Los Alamos, and Fuchs was consequently able to supply the Russians with some information of theoretical significance.

It should be explained here that tritium, or trebly heavy hydrogen, does not occur in a natural form but has to be made in uranium piles. It is extremely expensive to make, since eighty kilogrammes of plutonium must be employed to produce one kilogramme of tritium. It is radio-active so that half of it disappears every dozen years, and the heat of this radio-active decay has to be removed by cooling plants during storage. On the other hand, deuterium, or doubly heavy hydrogen, which can be separated from hydrogen in various ways such as by electrolysis and chemical exchange processes, is a relatively cheap substance and is commonly used for power producing piles. It was the water in which ordinary hydrogen was replaced by deuterium that became known as 'heavy water'. The hydrogen or fusion bomb in its original form consisted of a fission bomb surrounded by a ton or so of some mixture of light elements such as deuterium and tritium in a highly compressed or liquidised form. When the fission bomb detonates, the temperature of the light elements is raised sufficiently, to some tens of millions of degrees, to start the fusion process and so releases an immense amount of energy—many hundred times that of the fission bomb itself.*

After a couple of hours the interrogation was broken off for lunch, and the three men went to a pub behind the War Office, close to Scotland Yard. Finding all the tables occupied, they perched themselves on stools at

---

* The first American fusion bomb was exploded at Eniwetok in the Marshall Islands (Western Pacific) in November 1952, and nine months later, in August 1953, the Soviet Union exploded a fusion device.

the snack bar, which must have been one of the most bizarre lunch parties ever to take place in London. Afterwards they went back to Room 055 in the War Office to continue their work.

Questioned further about what he had given the Russians, Fuchs stated that they had never pressed him much about atomic piles or nuclear reactors.

'One thing which always surprised me, or rather surprises me now, is that they asked so little about piles,' said Fuchs. 'They never pressed me on the subject and I didn't give them much information on it.'

However, in the light of the recent announcement of the explosion of the first Soviet atomic bomb, he concluded that this must have involved plutonium produced in a nuclear reactor and not U235 from an isotope separation plant. He assumed that Nunn May had given the Russians information on this point from his work in Canada. He also admitted that the Russians asked him specific questions about 'mixing devices' in relation to the use of uranium rods.

The uranium piles, such as those at Hanford in the state of Washington, were so designed that the uranium was employed in the form of rods encased in metal containers. They were inserted into the piles by automatic machinery operated by remote control since no one could safely enter the chamber where a pile was located. They were subsequently removed by similar means and transported to the plants where the plutonium was separated. These likewise had to operate by remote control because of the radio-activity of the fission products in the uranium rods. Heavy concrete walls were built as shields to protect workers from the radiations released by the uranium piles and separation plants.

Questioned as to whether he had given any information with regard to raw materials, about ores, either rates of production or techniques, Fuchs shook his head. Then he added, by way of qualification, that he could not be certain whether the Russians had asked him any questions about ores, but if so he had said that he did not know. Fuchs went on to agree, when pressed, that, although he had passed on copies of some of the British Tube Alloys classified reports to the Russians, it seemed that they were content over a period of time to get really good first-hand information from him covering that part of the atomic field in which he specialised.

'The most important bit, really, was in the field of the Los Alamos period of your work?' he was asked.

'Yes,' Fuchs agreed.

'The rest, if they had that, wouldn't be of enormous significance and help?'

'Some,' said Fuchs rather weakly.

'It would be some, yes,' his interrogator agreed. 'But it couldn't compare with the work picture at Los Alamos?'

'No,' Fuchs had to admit.[12]

It was not until 4 p.m. that the interrogation was concluded, after which Perrin had to write his account, which he did in longhand marking it 'Top Secret' and keeping no copy. Meanwhile Fuchs returned to Harwell to await events. He still seemed to be under the impression that there was no question of his being arrested, since he had been giving all the help he could to improve the British knowledge of the Russian programme, and as soon as the matter had been cleared up with Skardon and Perrin he would be free to resume his work at Harwell, since he had decided not to take a university post—this now seemed to him unnecessary.

[3]

A General Election was about to take place in England at this time and Parliament had been dissolved. The Attorney General, Sir Hartley Shawcross was away campaigning in his constituency in the north of England, and it was necessary to obtain his authorisation in order to prosecute Fuchs under the Official Secrets Act. This caused a slight delay, as Fuchs's signed confession had to be sent to Shawcross, but by 2 February the necessary formalities had been completed and the police were ready to proceed with the charge. Since as yet nothing had leaked out at Harwell about the investigation, it was decided not to arrest Fuchs but to get him to come up to London allegedly for a further interview and to make the arrest in Perrin's office in Shell-Mex House. Somewhat reluctantly, as he was loath to treat a former colleague in this way, Perrin got through to Fuchs on the telephone on the morning of 2 February. 'Can you come up again this afternoon?' he asked. Fuchs agreed and suggested catching a train which was due to arrive in Paddington at 2.30 p.m.

The arrest was to be made by Commander Leonard Burt of Scotland Yard, who agreed to be in Perrin's room with the warrant. However, there was some delay owing to a last-minute difficulty in the wording of the charge which had to be agreed with the Americans, so that Fuchs arrived first and was kept waiting until Burt and another police officer arrived at 3.20. Perrin, who had insisted that he should not be present when the charge was read and the arrest made, quickly made the introduction and slipped off to another room.

Fuchs passed no comment when he was told that he was under arrest. But he asked if he could see Perrin again. This request was granted and Perrin came back to his room to find Fuchs slumped in a chair, looking ashen-grey. He gazed at Perrin appealingly and stammered out the words: 'You realise what this will mean at Harwell?' Perrin made no comment. The officers from the Yard then took Fuchs away to Bow Street Police Station. There he was formally charged with four separate breaches of the Official

Secrets Act and told that he would be brought up before the Chief Magistrate at Bow Street Court, Sir Laurence Dunne, on the following morning. Meanwhile he would be held in police custody.[13]

The appearance before the magistrate was brief and formal, the only witness being Commander Burt who gave evidence of arrest. After Fuchs had said he did not wish to put any questions to the witness, the magistrate asked him if he could help him on the question of legal representation. 'I don't know anybody,' answered Fuchs pathetically. Asked if he were a mean of means, Mr Christmas Humphreys, who appeared for the prosecution, replied that there was no reason to think that he could not pay for legal representation. 'He has a substantial salary,' Humphreys added. The magistrate then ordered that the prisoner's spectacles and other articles which had been taken from him at the time of his arrest should be returned to him. Fuchs did not ask for bail so that he was remanded in custody to Brixton Prison for a week.

The news of Fuchs's arrest made a considerable impression in the United States as well as Great Britain, particularly among those who remembered him in the Manhattan Project. One of them was a New York physicist named John M. Corson, who had worked with Fuchs in the early days and now cabled him on learning what had happened.

NATURALLY DO NOT BELIEVE THE ACCUSATIONS STOP
IF I CAN BE OF ANY SERVICE CALL ON ME STOP
CORSON

To which Fuchs replied:

THANK YOU STOP THERE IS NOTHING YOU CAN DO STOP
THE EVIDENCE WILL CHANGE YOUR MIND
FUCHS

It is significant of the feeling at this time, particularly after some of the hearings of the House Un-American Affairs Committee in Washington, that Corson had his United States passport withdrawn, although there was not the slightest evidence of any political involvement on Corson's part.

The prisoner's second appearance in the magistrate's court on 10 February was almost as brief as the first. Arnold, Skardon and Perrin all went into the witness box and testified briefly as to their connection with the case. Perrin in particular gave evidence as an expert witness to the effect that Fuchs had admitted passing on information to the Russians and that in his opinion as a scientist it was of a kind valuable to a potential enemy. Fuchs's confession was not read out in court, although it was shown to the magistrate and referred to by Humphreys in asking that he should be committed for trial.

'The mind of Fuchs may possibly be unique and create a new precedent in the world of psychology', said Humphreys. 'It is clear from his statement that we have half of his mind beyond the reach of reason and the impact of facts. The other half lived in a world of normal relationships and friendships with his colleagues and human loyalty. The dual personality had been consciously and deliberately produced. He broke his mind in two, describing it as controlled schizophrenia. He had produced in himself a classic example of the immortal duality in English literature, Jekyll and Hyde.'

Asked by the magistrate whether he had anything to say, the prisoner shook his head. He was then committed for trial at the Old Bailey three weeks hence and ordered to be kept in custody until then.

While Fuchs was in Brixton awaiting trial, Edgar Hoover, 'who had contributed nothing to his capture,' to quote Kim Philby, 'was determined to extract the maximum political capital from the affair for himself. To that end, he needed to show that he had material of his own, and such material could only be obtained through the interrogation of the prisoner by one of his own men.' The agent Hoover had in mind for this assignment was the head of the Bureau's anti-Communist section called Whitson, and according to Philby, Hoover announced his intention of sending Whitson to London to question Fuchs in his cell. Geoffrey Patterson, the MI5 representative in Washington, and Philby both received instructions to tell Hoover that such a course was quite out of the question. Fuchs was in custody awaiting trial, and it was impossible to arrange for his interrogation by anyone, let alone the agent of a foreign power. 'I found Hoover in a state of high excitement, and in no mood to be impressed by the majesty of British law,' Philby later recalled from his Moscow exile. 'He refused to budge. Whitson was sent to London, with peremptory instructions to see Fuchs, or else. The answer was "or else".'*

According to Philby, when he heard that Whitson was back, he called at his office, 'a fairly grand, carpeted affair.' Someone else was in his chair. Whitson himself Philby found a few doors further down the corridor, writing on the corner of a desk in a small room tenanted by four junior agents. 'The poor devil was bloody and very bowed. He looked at me as if it had been my fault. Such was life under Hoover.'[14]

On the advice of his leading defence counsel, Mr Derek Curtis-Bennett, KC, Fuchs decided to plead guilty. Indeed, in the face of his signed confession, he had no alternative. Curtis-Bennett, who saw him in the cells immediately before the hearing began at the Old Bailey, told him that he would put forward as strong a plea in mitigation of sentence that he could, but he had to be prepared for the maximum penalty. 'Yes, I understand,' said Fuchs.

'You know what the maximum penalty is?' counsel asked him. 'Yes, I

---

* 'Our relations with the British have been excellent and we furnished them a lot of information on Fuchs which brought about his arrest,' Hoover told Admiral Lewis Strauss, Chairman of the US Atomic Energy Commission, on 2 February 1950, the same day as Whitson arrived in London. 'They do not know the angles we know so I felt we should have a technical expert in our own right to interrogate Fuchs and keep us advised daily of any information he gives.'

know,' Fuchs answered. 'It's death.' Apparently he had believed all the time he was in Brixton that he would be sentenced to be hanged.

'No,' Curtis-Bennett reassured him. 'It is fourteen years.' However, Fuchs showed no sign of surprise at this news and took his place in the dock quite calmly, although his last-minute conference with his counsel had resulted in the Court being kept waiting for several minutes. The trial judge was the Lord Chief Justice Lord Goddard, while the Attorney General Sir Hartley Shawcross led for the Crown with the Senior Treasury Counsel, Mr Christmas Humphreys, and another Treasury Counsel Mr R. E. Seaton.

Fuchs was charged with having communicated information which might be useful to an enemy on four separate occasions contrary to the Official Secrets Act: namely (1) in Birmingham in 1943; (2) in New York between December 1943 and August 1944; (3) in Boston, Massachusetts, in February 1945; and (4) in Berkshire, England, in 1947. Fuchs pleaded guilty to all four counts. It is remarkable that the indictment did not contain any count referring to the information he had handed over while he was working at Los Alamos. This may have been due to the difficulty in wording the charge which has already been mentioned, due to the evidence supporting such a count being still top secret; or it may have been omitted at the request of the Americans, since their investigations into Fuchs's contacts in New Mexico had not been completed, and in any event there was more than enough to justify the award of the maximum penalty on the basis of the other admissions in Fuchs's confession.

The Court was crowded with interested spectators, among whom was seen to be the Duchess of Kent, wearing a veil.

'The prisoner is a Communist, and that is at once the explanation and indeed the tragedy of this case,' said the Attorney General opening the case for the prosecution. 'Quite apart from the great harm the prisoner has done the country that he adopted and which adopted him, it is a tragedy that one of such high intellectual attainments as the prisoner possesses, should have allowed his mental processes to have become so warped by his devotion to Communism that, as he himself expresses it, he became a kind of controlled schizophrenic, the dominant half of his mind leading him to do things which the other part of his mind recognised quite clearly were wrong. Indeed, my Lord, his statement (and so far as we have been able to check it, we believe his statement to be true) is a very object lesson in the meaning of Communism . . .'

In this country the number of Communists is fortunately very few, and it may be that a great number of those people who support the Communist movement believe, as the prisoner at one time apparently believed, that that movement is seeking to build a new world. What they don't realise is that it is to be a world dominated by a single power and that the supporters of the Communist Party, the true adherents of Communism, indoctrinated with the Communist belief, must become traitors to their own country in the interests—or what they are told to be the interests—of the international Communist movement.

'My Lord,' Sir Hartley Shawcross went on, 'it was because of those facts that this brilliant scientist as he is, now undoubtedly disillusioned and ashamed, came to place his country and himself in this terrible position.'

In going on, as he did, to give an account of Fuchs's career, with which the reader is already familiar, Sir Hartley quoted at length from the prisoner's confession. At the same time he stressed that his confession had not been obtained by any 'sinister pressure' nor 'after any long period of secret incarceration incommunicado.' Skardon confirmed this in the witness box and added that since his arrest Fuchs had done all he could to help the authorities.

'Is it right that before you took a statement from him,' Curtis-Bennett asked the witness, 'there was no evidence upon which he could be prosecuted?'

'That is right,' Skardon agreed.

In his plea in mitigation of sentence which Curtis-Bennett now addressed to the court, Fuchs's counsl submitted that, since the first three counts in the indictment were concerned with the period when Russia was fighting as an ally of Britain, it would be difficult to see how giving information to Russian agents could be interpreted as prejudicial to the safety or the interests of the State, and he pointed out, with some justification, that the English authorities had acquiesced in Fuchs's conduct with their eyes open since he had never pretended to be anything but a Communist.

'I don't know whether you are suggesting that was known to the authorities,' the Lord Chief Justice remarked.

'I don't know,' said counsel, 'but he made no secrecy of the fact.'

'I don't suppose he proclaimed himself as a Communist,' the judge went on, 'when he was naturalised or when taken into Harwell or when he went to the USA.'

'If I am wrong, Mr Attorney General will correct me,' observed Curtis-Bennett. 'It was on his records in this country at the Home Office that he was a member of the German Communist Party.'

Sir Hartley Shawcross explained at this point: 'It was realised when he was examined by the Enemy Aliens Tribunal at the beginning of the war that he was a refugee from Nazi persecution because in Germany he had been a Communist. All the investigations at that time and since have not shown that he had any association with British members of the Communist Party.'

'Anybody who has read anything of Marxist theory,' Curtis-Bennett continued his plea, 'must know that any man who is a Communist, whether in Germany or Timbuctoo, will react in exactly the same way when he comes into the possession of information. He will amost automatically, unhappily, put his allegiance to the Communist ideology first . . .'

Lord Goddard interrupted at this point, holding up the prisoner's confession. 'I have read this statement with very great care more than once,' he said. 'I cannot understand this metaphysical philosophy or whatever you like to call it. I am not concerned with it. I am concerned that this man gave away secrets of vital importance to this country. He stands before me as a sane man not relying on the disease of schizophrenia or anything else.'

'If your Lordship does not think that the state of mind a man acts under is relative to sentence—'

Counsel did not finish his sentence since the judge cut him short. 'A man in that state of mind,' said the judge in his customary down-to-earth style, 'is one of the most dangerous that this country could have within its shores'.

'I can only try to explain what your Lordship has said you fail to understand,' Curtiss-Bennett bravely persisted. 'Though I fail in the end, I can do no more, but do it I must.' And so counsel did his best to explain how the sieve of Fuchs's mind got wider until he gave the Russians all he knew, and then finally on his return to England the sieve closed up. He first gave the information because Russia was an ally and after the war it was only logical for him to continue to do so. Now, finally, he had recanted.

'There you have this man being logical, in my submission,' Fuchs's counsel concluded, 'having decided to tell everything, tells everything, makes it about as bad for himself as he can, and provides the whole of the case against him in this court. There is not one piece of evidence produced in this case which is not the result of the written and oral statements he made to Mr Skardon in December, and January of this year.'

Asked if he had anything to say before sentence was passed, the prisoner stood up in the dock and made the following statement, the first and only one he had uttered since his arrest:

> My Lord, I have committed certain crimes for which I am charged and I expect sentence. I have also committed some other crimes in the eyes of the law—crimes against my friends—and when I asked my counsel to put certain facts before you I did so not because I wanted to lighten my sentence. I did it in order to atone for those other crimes.
>
> I have had a fair trial and I wish to thank you and my counsel and my solicitors. I also wish to thank the Governor and his staff of Brixton prison for the considerate treatment they have given me.

The Lord Chief Justice looked very sternly at the prisoner as he proceeded to pass sentence. 'In 1933, fleeing from political persecution in Germany,' Lord Goddard addressed him in these carefully chosen words, 'you took advantage of the right of asylum, or the privilege of asylum, which has always been the boast of this country to people persecuted in their own country for their political opinions. You betrayed the hospitality and protection given to you by the greatest treachery.' He went on:

In 1942, in return for your offer to put at the service of this country the great gifts Providence has bestowed upon you in scientific matters, you were granted British nationality. From that moment, regardless of your oath, you started to betray secrets of vital importance for the purpose of furthering a political creed held in abhorrence by the vast majority in this country, your object being to strengthen that creed which was then known to be inimical to all freedom-loving countries.

There were four matters which seemed to him, said the judge, to be the gravest aspects of the prisoner's crime. First, by his conduct he had imperilled the right of asylum which this country had hitherto extended. Secondly, he had betrayed not only the projects and inventions of his own brain for which this country was paying him and enabling him to live in comfort in return for his promise of secrecy. He had also betrayed the secrets of other workers in this field of science, not only here but in the United States. Thirdly, he had imperilled good Anglo-American relations; and fourthly, he had done 'irreparable and incalculable harm' both to the United Kingdom and the United States, and he did it, as his statement showed, for the purpose of furthering his political creed, 'for I am willing to assume you have not done it for gain.'

Your statement which has been read shows to me the depth of self-deception into which people like you can fall. Your crime to me is only thinly differentiated from high treason. In this country we observe rightly the rule of law, and as technically it is not high treason, so you are not tried for that offence.*

'I have now to assess the penalty which it is right I should impose,' the Lord Chief Justice concluded. 'It is not so much for punishment that I impose it, for punishment can mean nothing to a man of your mentality. My duty is to safeguard this country and how can I be sure that a man, whose mentality is shown in that statement you have made, may not, at any other minute allow some curious working of your mind to lead you further to betray secrets of the greatest possible value and importance to this land? The maximum sentence which Parliament has ordained for this crime is fourteen years' imprisonment, and that is the sentence I pass upon you.'

Klaus Fuchs left the dock of No 1 Court at the Old Bailey without

* High treason, which is a capital offence, involves directly aiding an enemy. The information which Fuchs conveyed was given to an ally with whom Britain continued to have diplomatic relations after the end of the war.

uttering another word, escorted by two prison officers. The trial had lasted exactly one hour and twenty minutes.[15]

[4]

Two days after the Fuchs trial, Mr Attlee, whose Labour party had been returned to power, though with a greatly reduced majority, and who was still Prime Minister, saw Sir Percy Sillitoe, the head of MI5. They agreed that the documents in the case should be sent to President Truman and Mr Hoover in Washington. This was done and the FBI placed them before the Joint Congressional Atomic Energy Committee, thus further weakening American confidence in British security. The documents included Fuchs's first confession to Skardon and the second, technical confession, to Perrin. The Committee Chairman, Senator McMahon said he had been 'shocked' when he heard that Fuchs had been arrested, and now, 'having read his confession, including those parts which had not been made public for reasons of security, he was still shocked.'

The security service was also the target for attack in the British press to such an extent that Mr Attlee was obliged to come to the defence of MI5 in the House of Commons. 'It is a most deplorable and unfortunate incident,' he declared on 6 March, the day on which the new Parliament was assembled. 'Here you have a refugee from Nazi tyranny hospitably entertained who was secretly working against the safety of this country. I say secretly because there is a great deal of loose talk in the Press suggesting inefficiency on the part of the security service. I entirely deny that.' He went on:

> Not long after this man came into this country—that was in 1933—it was stated that he was a Communist. The source of that information was the Gestapo. At that time the Gestapo accused everybody of being Communists. When it was looked into there was no support for it whatever. And from that time onwards there was no support. A proper watch was kept at intervals . . . proper inquiries were made, and there was nothing to be brought against him. His intimate friends never had any suspicion. The universities for which he worked had the highest opinion of his work and of his character.
>
> In the autumn of last year information came from the United States suggesting there had been some leakage while the British Mission, of which Fuchs was a member, was in the United States. This information did not point to any individual. The security service got to work with great energy and were, as the House knows, successful.

'I do not think there is anything that can cast the slightest slur on the security service,' the Prime Minister concluded; 'indeed, I think they acted promptly and effectively as soon as there was any line they could follow up.' Mr Attlee added that he did not think any blame attached to his government or to that of Mr Winston Churchill who was Prime Minister when Fuchs was first employed in atomic research, or to any officials, for what occurred. 'I think we had here quite an extraordinary and exceptional case. I mention that because of the attacks which have been made.'[16]

Unfortunately Mr Attlee had not been too well briefed on this occasion, and it was a pity that he could not have been more explicit in revealing more of the facts of the case. His statement did little to allay the sense of public uneasiness about the Fuchs affair and the general feeling that the security service had been caught out badly on this occasion. Nor did anyone attach the slightest credence to the statement put out by the Soviet official news agency Tass on the day after Attlee's statement in the House of Commons, denying that Fuchs had passed information to the Soviet Union, as was alleged by the Attorney General during the trial, and stating that the Soviet Government had no knowledge of Fuchs and that no agent of theirs had any connection with him. Between 1941 and 1948 Fuchs had been investigated six times by the security service, and nothing was recorded against him apart from the German consular report that he was a Communist and a rumour in refugee circles in Britain in 1941 that he had been a well-known Communist, though it was not known whether he was a party member. At the time of his naturalisation the view was held that his importance to the war effort outweighed any slight security risk, but when he went to America two years later to work on the Manhattan project, General Groves was not warned, as he should have been, of the sense in which Fuchs's original security clearance was qualified.

Both the Prime Minister and the Home Secretary were very tight-lipped in answering the few questions which were put to them about the Fuchs case. The Home Secretary, for instance, refused to divulge the names of the persons who had sponsored Fuchs's application for naturalisation, saying that police inquiries were always relied upon and that no certificate was ever granted solely on the recommendations of sponsors no matter how distinguished they were. Asked whether the Government had received any warning about Fuchs from the Canadian Government at the time the Royal Commission was sitting in Ottawa, the Prime Minister replied that it had not.

In thanking the British Security Service for the Fuchs trial documents, Mr Hoover made a more tactful request than his previous one for two FBI agents to be permitted to interview Fuchs now that the trial was over. Two senior officers were despatched from the Bureau, Hugh Clegg, Assistant Director of the Bureau, and Robert Lamphere, a special agent, and in so far as they were able to see Fuchs in Wormwood Scrubs prison, they were more

The Soviet Embassy in Ottawa

The Soviet Ambassador Georgi Zarubin
and his wife receiving guests at a
reception in the Embassy, with a portrait
of Stalin in the background

(*Left*) Colonel Nicolai Zabotin, Soviet Military Attaché (code name Grant) in charge of espionage in Canada.   (*Right*) Vitali Pavlov, nominally Second Secretary in the Embassy but really representative of the Soviet Secret Police (NKVD)

Copy of telegram from Zabotin to Director of Military Intelligence in Moscow dated 12 July 1945. It reads in part:

1. Debouz (code name for Fred Rose) obtained data from conversations with officers on the Western Front . . .

2. Debouz was re-elected for the second time as a member of the Federal Parliament. Sam (code name for Sam Carr, national organizer of the Canadian Communist Party) and Tim Buck were not elected, although they were candidates. Thus from the corporators (code name for Communist Party members) there is one member of the Federal Parliament. The first session of Parliament meets on 26 August.

GRANT

This telegram was abstracted with other documents in the Embassy's secret files by the cipher clerk Igor Gouzenko when he defected in September 1945.

(*Left to right*) Malcolm MacDonald, British High Commissioner in Ottawa; Herbert Morrison, British Home Secretary and Minister of Home Security; and Mackenzie King, Prime Minister of Canada. In Ottawa during the war

Louis St Laurent, Minister of Justice in Mackenzie King's Government

The Rt Hon William Lyon Mackenzie King, PC., O.M.,
Prime Minister of Canada and Secretary of State for External Affairs

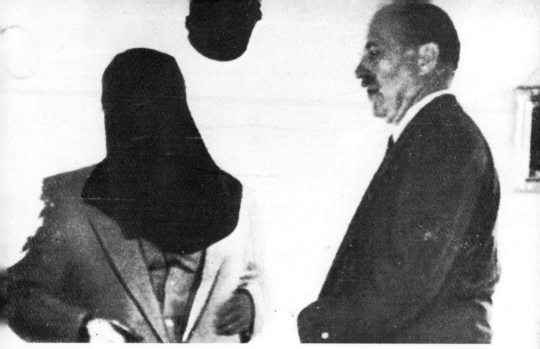

Igor Gouzenko, wearing a hood, being interviewed on Canadian radio by the American broadcaster Drew Pearson

Sir William Stephenson, MC, DFC, British Chief of Security Intelligence in the Western Hemisphere (British Security Coordination), who had his headquarters in New York and a field station for training agents in Canada. His timely intervention probably saved Gouzenko's life, since otherwise the defector would have been handed back to the Russians

Atomic bomb production plant at Oak Ridge, Tennessee

Sketch of first nuclear chain reactor, built on a squash court at Chicago University in 1942

Atomic plant at Chalk River, Ontario

Niels Bohr, Danish physicist and Nobel prize winner, with Sir John Anderson (holding hat), later Viscount Waverley

Allan Nunn May

Emil Klaus Fuchs

*Three who spied for the
Soviet Union*

Bruno Pontecorvo

*Four of the principal
Canadian spies*

Sam Carr, code name Sam or Frank,
national organizer of the Canadian
Communist Party. Convicted and sentenced
to 6 years

Fred Rose, code name Fred or Debouz,
Communist Member of the Federal
Parliament. In the dock at Ottawa where
he was convicted and sentenced to 6 years

David Gordon Lunan, code name Back,
organised a local spy ring. Editor of *Canadian
Affairs*. Convicted and sentenced to 6 years

Durnford Smith, code name Badeau, worked
in the National Research Council, Ottawa.
Convicted and sentenced to 5 years

Emma Woikin, code name Nora, cypher clerk in Department of External Affairs. Convicted and sentenced to 3 years

Edward Mazerall, code name Bagley, worked in National Research Council, Ottawa. Convicted and sentenced to 4 years

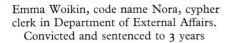

Four others who spied for Russia in Canada

Kathleen Willsher, code name Elli, worked in confidential registry of British High Commission in Ottawa. Convicted and sentenced to $2\frac{1}{2}$ years

Professor Raymond Boyer, code name The Professor, of McGill University, Montreal. Specialised in explosives. Convicted and sentenced to 2 years

Entrance to the British Atomic Research Establishment at Harwell, Berkshire

The Director and Heads of Divisions at Harwell, 1947. Sir John Cockroft, the director, is sitting on the right. Opposite with his hand on the chair is Professor H.W.B. Skinner (General Physics) and standing directly behind him is Klaus Fuchs (Theoretical Physics)

William Skardon, holding pipe, the MI5 interrogator who broke Fuchs, and Wing-Commander Henry Arnold, the Security Officer at Harwell

The Minister Sir John Balfour's office in the British Embassy, Washington.
Sitting on the edge of the desk on the right is Donald Maclean, First Secretary and liaison officer with the American Atomic Energy Commission, while he was spying for the Russians. Neither Balfour nor the ambassador, Lord Inverchapel, suspected Maclean of being a Soviet agent at this time (1947). Maclean defected to the Soviet Union with another member of the foreign service, Guy Burgess, four years later.

Sir Rudolf Peierls, Professor of Mathematical Physics at Birmingham University, who first engaged Klaus Fuchs on the atomic energy project

Sir Michael Perrin, Assistant Director Tube Alloys (Atomic Energy) and Deputy Controller Atomic Energy Technical Policy, Ministry of Supply. Interrogated Fuchs on technical details

Bruno and Marianne Pontecorvo in their flat in Moscow about 1955

Bruno Pontecorvo being greeted by reporters and friends at Rome airport in September 1978 when he had been allowed out of Russia to attend a scientific conference, for the first time in 28 years. His wife stayed behind in the Soviet Union. 'I have never worked on the bomb,' he told reporters, who plied him with questions

Judge Irving Kaufman, who tried the Rosenbergs and sentenced them to death

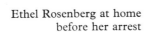

Ethel Rosenberg at home before her arrest

Julius Rosenberg being arrested

(*Left to right*) Morton Sobell, Julius Rosenberg and his wife Ethel. They are being driven from the court during the trial

Harry Gold, code name Raymond, who acted as intermediary between Fuchs and Anatoli Yakovlev, Soviet Vice-Consul in New York in charge of espionage. Besides testifying against the Rosenbergs, Gold was tried and sentenced to 30 years

David Greenglass, Ethel Rosenberg's brother, who in return for his testimony against his brother-in-law and sister, received the lighter sentence of 15 years

Ruth Greenglass, David's wife, who was accorded immunity from prosecution in consideration of her testimony

The three chief prosecution witnesses in the trial of the Rosenbergs

The Rosenberg children, Robert (*right*) and Michael (*left*), leaving the Death House at Sing Sing after a last visit to their parents with the defence attorney, Emanuel Bloch

A unique picture of the last moments of a woman (not Ethel Rosenberg) in the electric chair at Sing Sing as a current of 4,000 volts passed through her body. The picture was taken by a reporter with a secret camera in the death chamber

fortunate than the unlucky Mr Whitson with whom Philby expressed understandable sympathy. Clegg, whom I remember from my own wartime Washington days, was a good-natured genial G-man, while Bob Lamphere, described by Philby as 'a nice puddingy native of Ohio,' had been mainly responsible with Whitson for the analysis of the case from the American side. There was some opposition in Parliament when the news got out that two of Hoover's agents were to be allowed to question Fuchs in prison. It was suggested that Fuchs should be legally represented during the interrogation, and some MPs demanded that reputable British scientists should also be present, and others thought that MI5 and Scotland Yard officers were capable of interviewing Fuchs and getting from him, if he was prepared to volunteer it, the information which the Americans were seeking. Finally the Home Secretary stilled the critics by assuring them that 'in the exceptional circumstances of this case the FBI's request had been granted' and that 'in accordance with the usual practice the visit will take place in the presence of a prison officer and will be subject to the usual conditions governing the interviewing of prisoners.'

Since the time of Fuchs's arrest, the FBI had been trying to identify his American contact and their suspicions had been narrowed to Harry Gold, who the Bureau was convinced must be their man after they had talked to Fuchs's sister Kristel in Cambridge, Massachusetts. On 22 May, they searched his apartment and discovered the map of Santa Fé he had bought there, although he had previously sworn that he had never been west of the Mississippi. Gold then broke down and confessed, and a few hours after his arrest word came from England that Fuchs, whom the FBI agents had begun to question on 20 May, had identified him from some recently taken motion pictures, although he had previously rejected a still photograph of Gold, saying he had never seen him before. At all events it was officially announced in Washington late in the evening of 23 May that Gold had been arrested earlier the same day in Philadelphia 'on espionage charges based on information supplied by Dr Fuchs.' According to a joint statement by the Attorney General J. H. McGrath, and the Director of the FBI, J. Edgar Hoover, the accused had 'admitted his contacts with Dr Fuchs and . . . given a detailed account of his activities.'*

From a memorandum dictated by Hoover from his office in the Justice Department about 5.30 p.m. on 23 May, it appeared that there had been a 'leak' possibly from the White House which resulted in Gold's premature arrest, although Hoover had not told the President; but he had naturally informed the Attorney General.

---

* According to a later FBI report, dated Philadelphia, 5 September 1950, 'Harry Gold on 22 May 1950, admitted he received A-bomb infromation from Emil Julius Fuchs in 1945 for transmission to the Soviet Union.' After his arrest Gold furnished this and other information on his espionage activities to FBI Special Agents T. Scott Miller and Richard E. Brennan: FBI archives, file no. 65–4337 VFH.

I stated this whole thing was very secret because I wanted Clegg and Lamphere to work on Fuchs for 2 or 3 days and simultaneously we were working on Gold here. Of course I said it took me some time to develop the identity of the man whom Fuchs contacted here in this country because Fuchs only knew him by a code-name and it was only by various descriptions, size, appearance, occasions, etc., that we finally narrowed it down to about five people and finally narrowed it down to two and on Sunday (19 May) we got it down to one.

I stated this was only known to about six people in the Bureau and to Mr Clegg and Mr Lamphere in London, because we were afraid there might be some leak as Gold has given us a wealth of material involving a lot of other people he had contacted as he had been working as a Soviet agent back in the Thirties. I stated that we have been anxious to run down these leads and Gold has been entirely willing to co-operate and now with a leak of this kind the only safe move we can make is an arrest; but the case is practically lost from the point of view of developing a large espionage ring.[17]

The interrogation at Wormwood Scrubs lasted intermittently for eleven days and amounted in all to some twenty hours; it was conducted in the solicitors' interview room in the prison, where the FBI surveillance film of Gold, taken without his knowledge, was also shown. The only other individual present besides the two interrogators was William Skardon from MI5, although there was a warder stationed outside the glass panel in the door within sight but out of hearing of those inside.

The following has been extracted from the hitherto unpublished report of the interrogation by Clegg and Lamphere:

> The first substantive matter taken up with Dr Fuchs during the initial interview on 20 May 1950, was the exhibition to him of four photographs of Harry Gold. The first of these photographs was the identification picture of Gold which had previously been shown to Fuchs and rejected. The other three photographs were surveillance photographs of Gold, two of which had been prepared from the motion picture photographs taken by special agents of the Philadelphia Office on 18 May 1950. These four photographs were shown to Fuchs, in company with ten or twelve other photographs. Fuchs quickly rejected all other photographs, including the identification picture of Harry Gold, leaving only the surveillance pictures of Harry Gold. After studying these photographs for some time, Fuchs stated: 'I cannot reject them.' He, however, did not identify these photographs with any degree of certainty, stating they were not clear enough for identification, but still maintaining that there was enough similarity so that he could not reject them . . .
>
> On the morning of Monday, 22 May 1950, motion picture film

depicting Harry Gold was shown to Fuchs. These movies were the film taken under surveillance conditions by the Philadelphia Office. Dr Fuchs viewed three repeat showings of this motion picture film of Harry Gold, and stated at the end of the first viewing, 'I cannot be absolutely positive, but I think it is very likely him. There are certain mannerisms I seem to recognize, such as the too obvious way he has of looking around and looking back.' A moment or two later, Dr Fuchs stated, in answer to a question that there was something that did not quite fit but that might be explained by the passage of time. He then requested a second showing of the film and it was again projected. At that time Fuchs stated, in answer to a question, that there was nothing in the physical appearance of the man shown which was dissimilar to his recollection of the physical appearance of his American espionage contact. He advised that the countenance of the person in the moving pictures was in a serious vein, and that practically always, when he was contacted by his contact, he observed he was in a happier frame of mind, as if he were pleased with the importance of his assignment, and, although not exactly bombastic, this word almost described his pleased countenance and demeanour. The projection machine was then moved further away from the screen in order to enlarge the projection, and at the conclusion of this third projection, Fuchs stated that the identification was 'very likely'.

Apparently this information was sufficient to enable the authorities in Washington to arrest Gold, which, as has been seen, was done on the evening of 23 May in Philadelphia, although it was not until the following day that Fuchs positively identified Gold, and not until two days later according to the FBI report that the identification was confirmed in writing.

On 24 May 1950, shortly after 4.00 pm, still photographs and motion picture photographs taken of Harry Gold, and which he apparently had posed for, were received during the course of the interview with Fuchs at Wormwood Prison. Fuchs viewed the still photographs of Gold, and after examining them he stated, 'Yes, that is my American contact.' There were then projected the motion pictures of Gold, and after viewing them the first time Fuchs said, 'That is him, my American contact.' Fuchs, on 26 May 1950, wrote the following in his own handwriting on the back of each of two of these photographs: 'I identify this photograph as the likeness of the man whom I knew under the name of Raymond—Klaus Fuchs—26 May 1950.

The remainder of this long report set out in meticulous detail the story of Fuchs's espionage activities and contacts, the substance of which has already been related in these pages. Several of the final paragraphs on the bomb and his own activities are worth quoting:

Fuchs stated that, generally, information of a technical type was given to Raymond in writing. He maintains that at no time did he have any other contact, nor was he associated with anyone else, in the United States directly or indirectly in espionage activities. His American contact, Raymond (he later identified his photograph as Harry Gold), would not be able to understand technical information furnished orally; thus, to a considerable extent, and generally, the oral information dealt with personalities, the identities of scientists, facts of the test explosion at Alamogordo, and things that were within the scope of comprehension of his contact. He advised that Raymond never took notes at any meeting.

He stated that his best estimate is that the information furnished by him speeded up by several years the production of an A-Bomb by Russia because it did permit them to start on the development of the explosion and have this ready by the time the fissionable material was ready. His estimate of 'several years' is based on a speculation as to how good the Russian scientists are and how far advanced the Russian development was at the time. His conclusion is that the Russian scientists are as good as the scientists in England and in the United States, but there are fewer good scientists in Russia than in the United States and England. He gave his Russian espionage contacts nothing which would speed up their production of plutonium, and he estimates that if he had given the same data, which he gave to the Russians, to the United States, as of the date of his arrival in the United States, he would have speeded up the American production of an A-Bomb very slightly. He did pass on to his espionage contact what he learned concerning the production of plutonium during the final period of his work at Los Alamos. Upon further reflection, he stated that the information furnished by him alone could have speeded up the production of an A-Bomb by Russia by one year at least. He advised that if Russia got no information on the plutonium process from any other source, his data, as furnished them, could not have been of material assistance on this plutonium phase.

Fuchs claims to have furnished no information to his Russian contacts concerning the H-Bomb while he was in America. As far as information furnished by him on this subject is concerned, he referred to a statement obtained from him by Mr Michael Perrin who is a British Consultant in Atomic Energy Development and who interviewed him at the request of American authorities, and a report has been submitted by Perrin.*

During the last period of his work in Los Alamos, Fuchs said he did some research work on the H-Bomb including hydro-dynamics as involved in the US work. He was arguing with himself about this time

---

* Perrin was not such a Consultant and he interviewed Fuchs at the request of the British and not the American authorities: see above, p. 103.

concerning working on the H-Bomb, and although he subsequently passed on to his espionage contacts in England what he had learned in the United States, he was then nevertheless possessed of some doubts as to the wisdom or propriety of his action.*

Fuchs stated that he engaged in no Communist Party activities at any time while in the United States. He advised that he knew of no other scientist engaged in espionage or Communist Party work while he was in the USA. He stated he never talked to Dr Peierls about his Communist or espionage activities, and Dr Peierls did not know about Fuchs's Communist activities in England prior to coming to the United States. He advised that some people may have thought that Fuchs was a Communist, but no one knew it definitely. He stated repeatedly that he knew of no one who was engaged in espionage activities in the United States at any time other than himself and his contact, 'Raymond' (Harry Gold).[18]

The question whether Fuchs indeed identified Gold has been disputed. In a television documentary entitled *The Unquiet Death of Julius and Ethel Rosenberg* produced by Alvin H. Goldstein for the American National Public Affairs Center for Television, and shown in the United States and in Britain (by the BBC) in 1974, two of the participants were the FBI agent Robert Lamphere and an American lawyer named Marshal Perlin, who had been allowed to visit Fuchs some years after Lamphere with another American lawyer and a British Member of Parliament.

'We took this film to the prison, set it up and ran it for Dr Fuchs,' Lamphere repeated, 'and as it was being shown I watched him and not the film; and he was expressionless, made no comment until the film was concluded and the lights went back on, and I turned to him and said, "Can you identify that man?" And Klaus said: "Yes, that was my American contact".'

To which Perlin retorted, 'One of the prime questions was, "Was Gold the courier?" Did Fuchs ever identify Gold as the courier? And the clear and unequivocal evidence that came out of Fuchs's mouth was, "No, he never identified Gold as the courier, either to the FBI, British Intelligence, or to his attorney".'

'That is absolutely not what happened,' said Lamphere. 'There was a

---

* According to Chapman Pincher, chief defence correspondent of Beaverbrook Newspapers, when the FBI interrogated Fuchs in prison, 'he admitted giving the Russians information on the H-bomb from 1947 onwards, including some of the theoretical mechanics of triggering off the heavy-hydrogen charge, and while claiming that they would still have to do most of the work for themselves, thought they would make one in three to five years': *see* Chapman Pincher *Inside Story* (1978), p. 71. Fuchs's estimate was relatively accurate since the first Soviet H-bomb was exploded in August 1953 on Wrangel Island in the Arctic Circle. Unlike the first American device, which had been exploded in the Marshall Islands nine months previously, it was a compact deliverable bomb, whereas the American bomb was not deliverable by rocket or plane. Consequently for a time this was to give the Soviet Union potential nuclear military superiority over the Americans.

representative of MI5 there (William Skardon), there was an assistant director of the FBI (Hugh Clegg), and I was there. And what happened is what I related to you.'

But Marshall Perlin would have none of it.

He [Fuchs] told us how they kept importuning him to identify him, saying 'For God's sake, say he's the man—Gold insists he is.' British intelligence said the same thing. And in substance Fuchs said, if he insists he's the guy, he's the guy, and if he wants to identify himself as the guy, let him be the person. But Fuchs said to us that he never identified Gold.

Although there was no move on the part of any members of the public to seek to have his sentence reduced, Fuchs was not deserted by his friends in prison. However, his conduct must have harmed other refugee scientists like Professor Peierls by directing suspicion towards them, since Lord Goddard in passing sentence had implied that it would be difficult to trust aliens after this case. A particular friend whom Fuchs had betrayed but who did not let him down was Henry Arnold, the security officer at Harwell, for whom he had deep regard. As Alan Moorehead has pointed out in *The Traitors*, the relationship between the two men is, indeed, an interesting study in the field of counter-espionage.

Arnold from the first had a general reservation in his mind about Fuchs. It hardly amounted to a suspicion: he simply felt that if anyone at Harwell was betraying secrets then it was more likely to be Fuchs than anyone else. So from 1946 onwards he deliberately cultivated Fuchs's friendship. At first Fuchs did not respond very eagerly, and it was Arnold who had to make all the approaches. Then, little by little, Fuchs began to come round, and by 1949 a genuine intimacy had grown up between them. It was the kind of intimacy—perhaps trust is the better word—that exists between opponents who see that they are implacably committed to a duel against each other. Such relationships can be more lucid and enduring than those based upon emotional liking; and the familiar enemy becomes at least more trustworthy than the temperamental friends.

By 1949 Fuchs found himself in a hopeless position, for by then he wanted to give up the struggle; he wanted to accept Arnold's friendship *in toto* and come over to Arnold's side. But he could not bring himself to make an open avowal to his friend of the appalling things he had done. This was the point where Arnold, having to some extent prepared Fuchs for his conversion and confession, handed him over to Skardon; and

Fuchs, no doubt, found it a good deal easier to confess to a stranger whom he had not personally betrayed over a period of time.[19]

To his surprise, now that it was all over, Fuchs found that Arnold bore him no ill-will, as a less charitably minded man might have done in the circumstances. It was Arnold who wound up Fuchs's estate at Harwell, selling his saloon MG car, which he had bought from Professor Skinner. Arnold also disposed of Fuchs's furniture, clothes and books, settled his debts and lodged the balance, something between £300 and £400 to his credit with his bank. One thing, however, Arnold could not bring himself to dispose of or keep, and that was the prisoner's internee uniform with a patch on the back which Fuchs had worn in Canada and which he later kept in a trunk under his bed. Arnold wrote to Fuchs in prison and told him that he proposed to burn it. 'Fuchs indifferently agreed and that was one more bit of the past that was gone for good.'

Finally, the question of Fuchs's naturalisation had to be considered. It came before the Deprivation of Citizenship Committee in December 1950. Fuchs did not exercise his right to appear before the committee nor was he legally represented. However he composed a letter which was placed before the members in which he argued that there could be little doubt where his loyalties now lay. He had made his confession, he wrote, of his own free will after Sir John Cockcroft had asked him to resign from Harwell but had offered to retain his services as a consultant. He had co-operated loyally with MI5 and the FBI since his arrest, and he had done this without any threat or promise having been made to him. The fact was that Fuchs very much wanted to retain his British citizenship, and it seemed clear that it was here in England that his loyalties had at last become fixed. Surely to distrust him now was to go against the facts? But the Committee was not impressed. In any event they were bound by the law as it applied to his case, and in these circumstances Fuchs decided to drop the matter. On 12 February 1951, Dr Emil Julius Klaus Fuchs was formally deprived of his British nationality by order of the Home Secretary 'on grounds of disloyalty', and the order was subsequently published in the *London Gazette*. Fuchs let it be known that the decision distressed him very much.

The first part of his sentence was served at Wormwood Scrubs, after which he was transferred to Stafford and finally to Wakefield. At first he was employed in sewing canvas mail bags, but was later put in charge of the prison library, which no doubt he found a more congenial occupation. According to accounts by fellow prisoners he was generally liked, being generous in sharing his cigarettes and other perquisites with them. He was released from Wakefield prison on 22 June 1959, having served nine years of his sentence and earned full remission. He could have remained in England, had he wished, since as a stateless person he could not have been deported, since there was nowhere legally to deport him to, and doubtless he could have found employment in some form of laboratory work. However, he preferred to go to East Germany, where his father was now living in retirement. On the same day as his release he was taken under police escort to London airport and placed on board a Polish airliner bound for East Berlin, where he duly arrived and was reunited with his father. He immediately held a press conference which belied his former protestations of love for the English way of life, since he proudly announced that he was still a Marxist and intended to become an East German citizen and 'work for the new society.' His application to become a national of the German Democratic Republic was granted a few days later.

At the end of August 1959 the East German authorities announced that Dr Klaus Fuchs had been appointed deputy director of the East German Central Institute for Nuclear Physics at Rossendorf, near Dresden, where the first East German nuclear reactor became operational in 1957. At the same time it was stated that his position would be equivalent to that formerly held by him at Harwell. In fact it was rather more in material terms, his salary being equivalent to £12,000 a year, with two cars and a house of his own—rare at that time in East Germany. Soon afterwards he married his childhood sweetheart and possibly one-time mistress, Greta Keilson. In the words of Dame Rebecca West in *The Meaning of Treason* 'it was the end of a polished performance; and if some credulous people had been deceived for some time into thinking him what he was not, it added nothing to the real injury he had done them.'[20]

But was it the end? Perhaps not altogether. About two years after Fuchs had settled in East Germany, a British scientist who prefers to remain anonymous, went to a conference in West Berlin. While he was there, the scientist who had visited Fuchs in prison, knew that a physics conference was being held in East Berlin and he thought that Fuchs might possibly be attending it. So he got into touch with the conference organisers and sure enough Fuchs was there. What is more, when he received a message from the scientist Fuchs suggested with some enthusiasm that they should meet for lunch. 'I had a very pleasant lunch with him,' the scientist later recalled. He found that Fuchs had changed very little during the ten years that they had not met. 'We had a chat and we talked a little bit about the present-day politics in East Germany and East Berlin,' the scientist went on. 'I expressed some criticism about what was going on there and he in a very friendly way tried to explain to me why he thought these unfortunate things were necessary.' He told the scientist quite spontaneously, that 'one thing that really shook him'—he may even have used the word 'hurt'—was that all his English friends and colleagues at Harwell with many of whom he was really friendly, turned against him and never had anything good or kind to say of him 'He never heard anything but reproaches'—except for one man.

'The one man who throughout all these years was utterly kind, considerate and helpful to me,' said Fuchs, 'was Henry Arnold, the chief security officer at Harwell. When you see Henry Arnold please give him my regards and tell him how I appreciated his personal attitude to me.' And yet it was Arnold, who, to quote the scientist, 'by slowly working on him and becoming almost his personal friend, got all the information out of him which really led to his arrest.'[21]

The director of the East German Institute of Nuclear Physics at this time, and so Fuchs's chief, was forty-eight-year old Professor Heinz Harwich, East Germany's leading nuclear physicist and a Stalin prize winner. On 11 September 1964, news reached the West that Professor Harwich had defected and been granted political asylum by the United States. What could be more natural than that Dr Klaus Fuchs should take over his former chief's post? And who could be better qualified not only as a nuclear physicist but as a defector himself?

[5]

Looking back at the Fuchs case ten years or so after the trial, Attlee was asked by his former public relations adviser Francis Williams whether he did not think that the case had set back British co-operation with the Americans on atomic energy even more than the passing of the McMahon Act. 'To a certain extent,' Attlee agreed, 'although a short time afterwards they were gunning for Oppenheimer* and their own people instead. But I don't think you can put their attitude down to Fuchs. They were extremely cagey before that.'

When asked why the post-war Labour Government had decided to

---

* Dr J. Robert Oppenheimer was the physicist in charge of the Anglo-American civilian team of scientists at Los Alamos during the war when the first atom bomb test took place. In 1949 he appeared before the Congressional Joint Atomic Energy Committe presided over by Senator McMahon in Washington to defend the nomaination of Mr David Lilienthal, a civilian whose appointment as Chairman of the US Atomic Energy Commission set up under the McMahon Act had been strongly attacked on the ground of suspected disloyalty. Oppenheimer was chairman of the Committee's General Advisory Committee at the time. In 1954, Oppenheimer's own loyalty was investigated and he was eventually dismissed as adviser to the commission. 'The 992 pages of the Hearings will remain for the historian of our time a unique document. Here we find high politics and military strategy, nuclear physics and technology, bitter individual rivalries and high personal drama . . . The major overt issue of the Hearings in 1954 was, of course, Oppenheimer's initial opposition to the H-Bomb programme.' P. M. S. Blackett, *Atomic Weapons and East-West Relations* (1956) p. 72 *et seq.*

manufacture a British bomb, the former Prime Minister replied that it had become essential. 'We had to hold our position vis-à-vis the Americans,' Attlee went on. 'We couldn't allow ourselves to be wholly in their hands, and their position wasn't awfully clear sometimes.'

'In what way?' queried Williams.

'Well,' said Attlee, 'we had to bear in mind that there was always the possibility of their withdrawing and becoming isolationist once again. The manufacture of a British bomb was therefore at that time essential to our defence.' He continued:

> You must remember that this was all prior to NATO. NATO has altered things. But at that time, although we were doing our best to make the Americans understand the realities of the European situation—the world situation—we couldn't be sure we'd succeed. In the end we did. But we couldn't take risks with British security in the meantime.
>
> We had worked from the start for international control of the bomb. We wanted it completely under the United Nations. That was the best way. But it was obviously going to take a long time. Meanwhile we had to face the world as it was. We had to look to our defence—and to our industrial future. We could not agree that only America should have atomic energy.[22]

The decision to make the bomb was taken by Attlee and five of his ministerial colleagues in the Cabinet, including the ministers of defence and supply, in conditions of extreme secrecy at the beginning of 1947. The carrying out of the necessary work in similar conditions of secrecy was in the charge of Dr (later Lord) William Penney, Chief Superintendent of Armaments Research in the Supply Ministry and later chairman of the United Kingdom Atomic Energy Authority. The principal weapons establishment was located at Aldermaston, like Harwell in Berkshire, although in the earlier stages the work proceeded at other venues, Fort Halstead, near Sevenoaks in Kent, and Woolwich. During 1948 the Chiefs of Staff tabled their requirements as 200 bombs by 1957, so that the establishment had a firm production order. But there was much argument among the individuals concerned whether to concentrate on a known but obsolete weapon such as the plutonium bomb which had been dropped on Nagasaki, or on something newer and more sophisticated such as the hydrogen bomb. Penney was in favour of long-term work and planning, as also, remarkably enough, was Fuchs.

On the other hand, after the first Soviet test had become known in September 1949, Sir Henry Tizard, chairman of the Defence Research Policy Committee, argued that the United Kingdom should abandon production of its bomb and leave development to the United States, where research was far ahead of the British effort. Britain, he concluded, should concentrate on resisting the threat to Western Europe from the Red Army by strengthening its continental land forces. 'How, I ask,' he wrote at the time, 'do we add to the American deterrent effect by letting it be known that we have none but hope to make a few bombs later on?' His suggestion, Sir Henry said later, was greeted 'with the kind of horror one would expect if one had made a disrespectful remark about the King.'[23]

But Tizard found himself in a minority of one in the Whitehall debate which followed on the Soviet A-bomb explosion, as appears from the recently released papers from the British Public Record Office under the thirty-year rule. The Prime Minister, in particular, took a diametrically opposite view. On 20 September 1949—two days after his informative meeting at Chequers with Menzies and Perrin and three days before President Truman's official announcement—Attlee wrote to the ministers concerned with the British bomb project:

> Research and development of the atomic weapon and the means of delivering it . . . are all projects to which I attach the highest importance. Their needs must be considered alongside the needs of the other vital defence research and development but they should be met unless the effort required gravely imperils any of those other projects.

The Prime Minister's view coincided with that of the three service Chiefs of Staff, as appears from a secret telegram from the Foreign Office to the British delegation to the United States which stated a few weeks later, on 22 October:

> In present circumstances and probably for many years to come, we should do nothing to prejudice our right to use the atomic bomb in a war with the Soviet Union which results from Soviet aggression.

In the early stages of research and development, for reasons of secrecy, the work at Aldermaston and the other establishments was known simply as 'High Explosive Research'. But after the first explosion of the British bomb at Monte Bello in Western Australia in October 1952, the secret of what went on at Aldermaston became widely known, and its opponents, the self-styled Committee for Nuclear Disarmament (CND), regularly participated in an annual march of protest to Aldermaston.

Despite the fact that the Russians, thanks in part at least to the activities of Nunn May and Fuchs, were several years ahead of the British in their work on the bomb, they were naturally interested in Britain's progress in the field. If a leading British experimental physicist could be persuaded to transfer himself permanently behind the Iron Curtain, it would have distinct advantages for Soviet physicists. And this was precisely what happened when Bruno Pontecorvo with his wife and children failed to return to England from a continental holiday in the summer of 1950, a few months after Fuchs had gone to prison. It was a precedent to be followed by the diplomatists Guy Burgess and Donald Maclean, and the journalist and ex-Secret Intelligence Service officer Kim Philby, although Pontecorvo was the only scientist to go over to the Soviet side in this manner.[24]

Pontecorvo had only been at Harwell for eighteen months, having come from the Canadian heavy water plant at Chalk River in February 1949 to take up the post of principal scientific officer, at a grading and a salary (approximately £1300 a year), a little lower than those of Fuchs. However, unlike Fuchs he was very much the extrovert type, gay and light-hearted, quickly becoming one of the most popular men on the station. Dark, of medium height and extremely handsome, he was nicknamed 'Ramon Navarro' by the local girls. His manners were polished, he made friends easily, talked well and flirted with the pretty women he met at cocktail parties, besides playing an excellent game of tennis. On the other hand, although he had a good salary, he was notoriously careless about money and was constantly hard up. He once said that he never counted the notes in his wallet so that he should not worry if he lost it. He was known to everyone at Harwell as Bruno or 'Ponte'. He and his Swedish wife and their three children lived in a sparsely furnished, small semi-detached house on a housing estate in nearby Abingdon, and they entertained very rarely. Soon after his arrival at Harwell, he bought a new Standard Vanguard, in which he would drive every day to Harwell and also explore the Berkshire Downs. At this time he was thirty-six and recently, while still in Canada, had become a naturalised British citizen, the usual security inquiries having revealed nothing 'against' him. Both he and his wife, born Marianne Nordblom, were Jewish.

During a declassification conference at Harwell in January 1950, just before Fuchs's arrest, the station head Sir John Cockcroft learned from a United States delegate that he had heard from an Italian physicist working in America that Pontecorvo and his wife were Communists, or at least had Communist sympathies. Soon afterwards a similar report was received from Sweden, no doubt as the result of an inquiry from MI5, that Marianne was tarred with the Communist brush. Bruno Pontecorvo may possibly have got wind of this. At all events he went to Wing-Commander Henry Arnold, the security officer at Harwell, and told him that he would like to have a private talk with him on the subject of the routine questionnaire about his *curriculum vitae* which was sent to everyone employed at the establishment who had signed the Official Secrets Act. He told Arnold that he had a younger brother named Gilberto who was a Communist. This Gilberto had no connection with Harwell or science, said Bruno—he was an Italian citizen living in Italy and working there for an Italian film company. Still, he felt that 'security ought to know about him'.

A few days later Arnold asked to see Bruno again and put a pertinent question to him. In the previous September Bruno had attended a conference of nuclear physicists at Lake Como. Had he met his brother there? Somewhat taken aback by this question, Bruno admitted that he had. Questioned further about his family background, Bruno admitted that Gilberto had been living in Paris with his French wife Henriette, who was also a Communist, and that in France he had been the representative of a young Communist organisation and acted as correspondent of an Italian left-wing weekly, *Omnibus*, and the Communist daily newspaper, *Milano Sera*, since when he had been mainly based in Italy. His eldest sister Giuliana was likewise a Communist, Bruno went on to admit, as also was her husband Duccio Tabet; they both lived in Rome, where Duccio was a well-known party member and worked for the party as an adviser on agricultural affairs. A younger sister named Laura, who was a nurse working in a hospital in Hampstead, might have Communist sympathies, he added. Bruno also volunteered the information that his cousin Emilio Sereni was a prominent Communist party member, serving on the party's central committee, representing a Naples constituency in the Italian Chamber of Deputies, and having been a Communist minister in two of the post-war coalition governments in Italy. At the same time Bruno emphatically denied that either he or his wife were Communists, although he conceded that, so far as he had any politics, they were Labour.

This information can be usefully supplemented by some further biographical details. Bruno Pontecorvo was born at Pisa on 22 August 1913, being the third or fourth of the eight children born to Massimo and Maria Pontecorvo in a crowded two-storey building behind a high wall close to the famous Leaning Tower. Massimo and his wife were both Jews and the children were all brought up in the Jewish faith. Massimo was a business man with interests in the textile industry, and for a time his affairs prospered until the decline due to anti-Jewish feeling which set in under Mussolini and his Fascisti. Nevertheless the father was able to provide all the sons and daughters with a good education, most of them going on to university after leaving school. Guido, the eldest, became a biologist and genetics specialist; he eventually settled in Scotland, became naturalised and joined the staff of Glasgow University. Another brother Giovanni David, and two sisters, Anna and Laura, also settled in Britain, where the boy became an agriculturalist, and the girls a teacher and hospital nurse respectively. Of the three remaining children, besides Bruno, Gilberto and Giuliana have already been mentioned, while the other brother Paul emigrated to the United States, became an American citizen, and took up radar research work. The Pontecorvo parents remained in Italy, moving to Milan after the children had grown up and left Pisa.

Bruno was unquestionably the ablest of the family. He passed all his school examinations with ease and at the age of sixteen enrolled at Pisa

University. Here he was awarded a certificate in physics and mathematics before going on to Rome University where he obtained his doctorate with honours in physics in 1934. He remained there to teach and do research, working under two well-known physicists, Professors Fermi and Amaldi. In 1935, when he was only twenty-two, Bruno was one of the six signatories, which included the two professors, to a paper entitled *Artificial Radioactivity Produced by Neutron Bombardment*, subsequently published in the Proceedings of the Royal Society in London. Then in the following year he was awarded a fellowship which enabled him to travel to Paris and enrol in the Collège de France, shortly afterwards working with Professor Frederic Joliot-Curie at the Paris Institute of Radium. When the war began, he was a research associate at the Laboratory for Nuclear Chemistry in the Collège de France. Many of the students were decidedly left-wing in politics, and Joliot-Curie was himself a Communist, but Bruno does not appear to have participated much if at all in their activities, being at this time more anti-Fascist than pro-Communist. Meanwhile he had travelled a little and seen something of the laboratories in Scandinavia, Belgium, Holland and Switzerland, as well as having spent a week's holiday in England. It was in Paris that he met his future wife Marianne Nordblom, who had also come to Paris to study. She was four years younger than Bruno and they lived together at first, having a son named Gil in July 1938. They did not get married until 9 January 1940. Then after France fell to the Germans, and Italy entered the war, they joined the general flight to the south, according to one account travelling on bicycles, each taking it in turn to carry the baby Gil in the basket below the handlebars. According to another account, only Bruno travelled by bicycle, while Marianne and the baby went by train. At all events they all reached Toulouse, where they were joined by Duccio and Giuliana Tabet. Fortunately they managed to obtain exit visas from the Pétain government. Together they went on through Spain, and thence to Portugal, finally reaching Lisbon. There they were able to secure passages on the *Oranza*, a neutral vessel bound for the United States. On 20 August, two days before Bruno's twenty-seventh birthday, they reached New York. It was probably in the course of his conversations with his Communist brother-in-law Duccio Tabet, when they were thrown together at this period, that Bruno was converted to Marxism.

Shortly after his arrival in America, Bruno, through his academic connections in the scientific field, got a job with the Wells Survey company of Tulsa, Oklahoma, where he was employed as a consultant in radiographic research in mineral oil deposits. It was while he was working in Oklahoma that he developed an improvement in oil-logging and filed an application for a patent for his invention. At the same time he and his fellow scientists who had produced the paper for the Royal Society, as already mentioned, applied for a similar patent and were later to begin a suit against

the United States Government, claiming ten million dollars for infringe-
ment of this patent. Eventually, in 1953, the case was settled, the six
claimants being awarded $60,000 apiece. But by this time Bruno may not
have been in a position to receive it, since he was working in a laboratory in
the Soviet Union. At least it is not known whether he was allowed by his
then employers to do so. Had he known that he was to be awarded such a
comparatively large sum, he might well, with his luxury-loving tastes, have
decided to remain in the West.

Meanwhile, research in atomic energy had been proceeding in the US and
in Canada, and it may well have been through his old teacher Professor
Fermi that in 1943 he was invited to join the Anglo-Canadian research team
in Montreal, although he was technically an enemy alien, since he still held
an Italian passport. However, he had already filed papers for American
naturalisation two years previously, which accorded him interim protection
while his application was being considered.

When work on the Chalk River heavy water pile began at Petawawa in
Ontario, the Pontecorvos moved to the nearby settlement of Deep River,
where they were to remain for the next six years, and where Bruno's pay
enabled them to live in reasonable comfort. They had a house, and as
recreation Bruno played tennis and once won the local singles champion-
ship. Two more children were born to them at this period, both boys, Tito
(evidently called after the Yugoslav partisan leader) in 1944 and Antonio in
the following year. Bruno was well liked by his fellow scientists with his
light-hearted, easy-going ways, though he always proved himself to be an
exceptionally hard worker. Marianne did not fit in so well with the
community, and once, after she discovered that her husband had had an
extra-marital adventure with a girl whom he took on a trip to Boston, she
withdrew $1800 from the bank, probably the whole of the credit balance in
their joint account, and took off with the children on the train for Banff in
the Rockies. However, friends eventually traced her there and persuaded
her to return to Deep River.

When he accepted the appointment in Canada, Bruno was subjected to a
security check, but nothing was recorded to his detriment. After the war
ended he was asked to stay on as a member of the British Ministry of Supply
team and help in further experimental research at Chalk River. Again,
when he applied for British nationality, as he did in 1948, he was once more
'vetted' by security and was given a complete clearance, so that he became a
British subject, having allowed his American application to lapse. Yet it is
conceivable that he was and for some time past had been working for the
Russians, although he was not positively identified in the Report of the
Royal Commission in Ottawa.

In a notebook kept by Colonel Zabotin, subsequently removed with the
rest of the secret espionage documents by Gouzenko from the Soviet

Embassy in Ottawa, some particulars were recorded of the espionage organisation as it had previously existed under Major Sokolov, the Commercial Counsellor, who had originally taken his instructions from an officer named Mikhailov in the Soviet Consulate in New York. The particulars mentioned a group in Montreal described as 'activists', which was directed by Fred Rose and included Professor Boyer. There followed some notes on an 'auxiliary group' as follows:

1. *Gini—(Jew)*　　　　　　　*Auxiliary group*
Owner of a drug store. He provided a place for photography. He has a photo-laboratory.
　　There are working at his place:
　　(a) Golia, a young artist, works in the photographic studio[25]

In the Military Attache's notes, 'Gini' was originally described as a 'Photographer', but this was deleted and 'Owner of a drugstore' substituted. Neither 'Gini' or 'Golia' was identified by Gouzenko or any other witness at the hearings before the Royal Commission. However, as has already been noted, at the time of Fuchs's arrest 'Golia' was identified by French sources of uncertain reliability as being the code-name for Klaus Fuchs, while 'Gini' was 'an associate of Fuchs at Harwell.' If that is true, then 'Gini' more than likely was Bruno Pontecorvo, which may appear fantastic, but then Bruno Pontecorvo was in many ways a fantastic character, and his story certainly possesses a fantastic quality.

[6]

Although he agreed to stay on in Canada after the war, Pontecorvo had no shortage of offers of work, the initiative usually, if not invariably, coming from him—an associate professorship at a radiation laboratory in Massachusetts at $6000 a year, a full professorship at the University of Ann Arbor, Michigan, at $5000 a year, and tentative offers from the General Electric Company at Schenectady, New York, and the radiation laboratory at Berkeley, California. In 1947, he received two more offers, the chair of experimental physics at the Hebrew University, Jerusalem, and an associate professorship at Cornell University at $7000. At the same time he would make regular trips at six-monthly intervals across the border to the United States so that he could establish his residence there in case he should wish to become an American citizen. However, the pull of Europe was stronger for both Marianne and himself, so he decided not to go on with his application for American citizenship but to become a naturalised British subject.
　　In December 1947, he made a trip alone to Europe and stayed at

Abingdon with some old friends from his wartime days at Chalk River, Dr Henry and Mrs Seligman. At Harwell where he called, he was told that a post was available for him if he was interested, so he renewed his contract with the British Ministry of Supply. He then flew to Milan where he saw his parents, and planned to return to North America by the *Aquitania* on 4 January 1948. However, he lingered too long in Paris, looking up old acquaintances, possibly Communist contacts, with the result that he missed the boat and had to fly back instead. In the following month, he became a naturalised British subject, and having accepted the post at Harwell the whole family left Canada in January 1949. At Harwell they stayed first with the Seligmans until they found a house in Abingdon. Marianne was now able to visit her parents in Sweden, the children were accommodated in English schools and the family seemed to be on the verge of finally settling down. Yet a strange restlessness characterised Bruno.

In May of the same year he lectured in Paris at Joliot-Curie's invitation, went on to Brussels for some unknown purpose, and took on some work for the Anglo-Iranian Oil Company. In September, he went off with some other Harwell scientists to a conference at Lake Como, where he met his Communist brother Gilberto. Meanwhile he continued to angle for other jobs. At this time there were two university chairs in experimental physics vacant in Italy—one in Rome and the other in his native Pisa. He actually applied for the latter, but his application arrived too late, and he dropped his application for the Rome chair when pressure was put on him, as will be seen, to accept an offer from the University of Liverpool.

Following his conversations with Wing-Commander Arnold at the time of the Fuchs case, it was now felt at Harwell that Bruno Pontecorvo was a potential security risk, since he had failed to disclose his family's Communist connections in the questionnaire which he had filled in when he was appointed. On the other hand, Cockcroft felt that his knowledge and abilities could be put to good use in an academic post where he did not have access to secret information as he had at Harwell. With Cockcroft's encouragement, if not actually at his instigation, Liverpool University offered him such a post where he would work with Fuchs's old friend Professor Herbert Skinner, who had been at Harwell and had recently become Lyon Jones Professor of Physics at Liverpool. Bruno Pontecorvo made a trip with Marianne and the children to Liverpool, where he was greatly impressed by the university laboratories and the new cyclotron which was being built there for atomic research. Nevertheless, he hesitated about accepting the offer. Marianne was worried about the cold in the north, and Bruno was uncertain whether he really wished to work in Liverpool. Eventually, after Skinner had written to him officially, he accepted and it was arranged that he should move to Liverpool in time to take up the appointment in January 1951. Meanwhile he planned to leave

England for his continental holiday towards the end of July, taking with them his unmarried sister Anna, who had graduated from Glasgow University and was now teaching in England.

Arnold and his security colleagues were aware of the planned holiday trip abroad, but they had no power to prevent it, since nothing definitely detrimental had been proved against Bruno, and as a naturalised British subject he was free to move about in the same way as any other British citizen. In preparing to leave, Bruno bought some expensive camping equipment, refusing an offer from friends to lend him all the canvas beds and tents they would need. Another friend, who had some French francs in a bank in France, asked Bruno to collect them for him. The friend was not sure of the exact amount and he suggested that they should settle up when the Pontecorvos returned for an open scientific conference which had been arranged to begin at Harwell on 7 September. But Bruno brushed this suggestion aside and insisted on giving the owner of the francs a blank cheque. Another curious remark by Bruno was to be recalled later. A few days before the family set off, he had a final game of tennis with Mrs Seligman, and as they came off the court, he looked serious for a moment and said, 'We'll play again some day.' Afterwards the Seligmans gave a small farewell party for Bruno and Marianne in their house at Abingdon, which was only a few doors away from the Pontecorvos. During the party Marianne went off into a corner by herself and appeared to be reading a copy of *Vogue*. On noticing this Mrs Seligman went over, and saw that she was not reading but had buried her face in the magazine. When Marianne looked up, she was in tears. Bruno seemed to be annoyed by this display of emotion, but the incident passed off and he then took his wife home.

Next day the family set off for the Continent—it was a tight squeeze in the Vanguard with three adults and three children, besides the baggage, camping equipment and Gil's bicycle, which were strapped together on the roof. Otherwise they travelled light, as Bruno and Marianne left all their heavy clothes and most of their other possessions behind in Abingdon.

They reached the coast in the afternoon of 25 July, in time to catch the Dunkirk ferry with the car. On disembarking, they took a leisurely route through Arras and Dijon. Bruno was not the man to make careful arrangements for hotel accommodation in France, and anyhow it was the height of the holiday season, and so they camped out at most of the places at which they stopped. From Dijon they travelled by road across Switzerland via Neuchâtel, taking three days to reach Menaggio on Lake Como, which they did on the 31st. Here they camped until 4 August, when Anna left them to take the boat down the lake to see her parents in Milan. At Menaggio Bruno struck up an acquaintance with a Professor Caldirola, a scientist of Padua University. Bruno invited the Professor to come to the conference at Harwell on 7 September, since it was unrestricted, and the

Professor accepted. Then, on the spur of the moment, Bruno decided to spend a couple of days in the Dolomites, and so they crossed into Austria. At Landeck in the Vorarlberg, Marianne sent a postcard to a friend in Canada, saying they were having a wonderful time and would be away for 'another two or three weeks before returning'—presumably to England.

Next the family drove south to Milan, where they saw Bruno's parents, before going on by easy stages to Ladispoli, a small seaside village near Rome, which they reached on 17 August and where they had arranged to meet Duccio and Giuliana Tabet and their children. The Tabets, who had returned from America some time previously, had taken a house at Ladispoli for the summer. After a few days together, Bruno and Marianne decided to drive south in search of a part of the coast where Bruno could indulge his passion for submarine fishing, with a snorkel and submarine gun. They left Antonio, the youngest child, with Giuliana Tabet but took the other two children along until after another seventy miles or so they found an ideal place for Bruno's purpose at Circeo, just south of Anzio.

Before leaving England, Bruno had planned to spend a few days at Chamonix on the homeward journey, since his parents had arranged to spend their holidays there. There was also an international scientific laboratory in Chamonix, which specialised in cosmic rays that were also Bruno's speciality. Dr Bretscher, Bruno's chief at Harwell, who knew that he was going there to meet his parents, now sent him a telegram suggesting he should call in at the laboratory. The telegram was duplicated, one copy being addressed care of Bruno's parents in Milan and the other to Professor Amaldi, Bruno's old teacher in Rome. The telegram was despatched on 20 August and it was forwarded to Bruno in Circeo a few days later.

On 22 August, Gilberto and Henriette arrived in Circeo from Rome, bringing Anna who had come on from Milan after she had seen her parents. The occasion for the family reunion at Circeo was no doubt Bruno's birthday, since Gilberto, Henriette and Anna all returned to Rome next day, leaving Bruno, Marianne and the two elder children still camping. This date seems to have been a turning-point in Bruno's affairs. Hitherto the holiday had been a happy-go-lucky affair where everything went off well and everyone enjoyed themselves. Thereafter things began to go wrong, and Bruno's movements became erratic.

First, Bruno collided with a cyclist in his car. It was not a serious accident, the kind that often happens on the Italian roads in summer. No one was hurt, but Bruno seemed to think that the car needed some repairs and so he drove it up to Rome, a journey of one or two hours at the most. On his return to Circeo, Marianne greeted him with the news that the children had gone down with sunstroke. Bruno thereupon telegraphed his parents, saying he was sorry but owing to the accident to the car and the childrens' illness he would not be able to join them in Chamonix. Almost immediately afterwards he got a postcard from his parents saying they had already left Milan. Bruno then wrote to them: 'As soon as the children are well enough, we shall return to England. It is not possible to come to Chamonix as we shall have no time and it would tire the children.' This letter was posted from Rome on 25 August, presumably when Bruno was on his way to Ladispoli to collect Antonio. He returned to Rome with Antonio and the Tabets on 27 August, and they all stayed at the latter's small house, 40 Via Gabi, near St John Lateran. Here, in addition to Duccio and Giuliana and their family, there were Gilberto and Henriette, Anna, Bruno and Marianne and their three children. Since there was no room for him in the house, Bruno, who had collected his car from the garage where it was repaired, spent the next few nights on the back seat of the Vanguard, somewhat uncomfortably, since he was cramped for space and the heat in Rome in August can be well-nigh unbearable. This did not improve his temper and he became noticeably irritable. By this time Antonio was also suffering a heat stroke, and the noise and confusion in the house with six children and as many adults was indescribable. It was during this stay with the Tabets that Bruno took a dramatic step which was to change the whole of his future career.

[7]

On Tuesday, 29 August, Bruno and Marianne went to the booking office of Scandinavia Airlines and asked about the fares and departure times for Stockholm. On being given the information, Bruno proceeded to book five single tickets, his own being in the name of Pontecorvo and the other four for Marianne and the three children in the name of Nordblom-Pontecorvo. While he was doing this, Marianne pulled him aside, out of earshot of the booking clerk, and they had a short conversation. Bruno then went back to the counter and asked that his own ticket should be changed to a return. The other tickets were to remain single and Marianne and the children would travel on her Swedish papers, since she had kept her Swedish passport, while Bruno would travel on his British passport. Bruno said that he would pick up the tickets next day, although he was told by the booking clerk that it was customary for reservations to be confirmed and paid for on the same day. He appeared quite unconcerned while making these arrangements.

Next day Bruno returned to the airline office, bringing with him the amount of the fares in Italian lire. However on proffering this money, he was informed that foreigners who had less than six months' residence in Italy had to pay air fares in American dollars, which in this case amounted to over $600. Bruno was surprised and annoyed by this, but had no choice but to agree. He went away and came back several hours later with the cash, which he paid out in one hundred-dollar bills, an unusual denominaton rarely used except by American tourists in hotels. On this occasion, his second visit to the booking office, Bruno was alone.

Next day, 31 August, Bruno wrote a postcard to Harwell, which was received there five days later. It was unquestionably in his handwriting and was sent after he had made up his mind not to return there. It read:

> Had a lot of fun with submarine fishing but I had plenty of car trouble. I will have to postpone my arrival until first day of conference. Can you tell E. Bretscher? Hope everybody has prepared his talk and done good work at Chamonix. I am sorry I have missed Chamonix but I could not make it.
>
> Bruno

The family left Rome by SAS plane on 1 September, the route being via Munich and Copenhagen. They reached Stockholm at 20.50 hours the same day. At the airport, Bruno made inquiries about hotel accommodation for the night. On telephoning two hotels in the town, he was told that accommodation was available in both, and he left his name with each. But he and the family did not show up at either of them. It is not known for certain where they spent the night, but it is believed that they did so in a house belonging to the Soviet Embassy in Stockholm. Significantly, it was not with Marianne's parents who lived close by the airport and had no idea that they had arrived there.

Next day they turned up at the airport and took a plane to Helsinki, apparently having enough dollars to buy the tickets. On disembarking about 11 a.m. they passed through the Finnish Immigration and Customs control, where Bruno filled up the usual form, giving the reason for his visit as 'tourism' and stating that the length of the family's stay would be about a week. For his place of residence there appeared the single word 'Hotel'. According to a Customs official at the airport, who was questioned later, a man and a woman drove up in a car just before the plane landed and asked that the Pontecorvos' luggage should be put in their car and not in the airways coach. This was done, after which the family got into the car and were driven off. That was the last that was to be seen of any of them for a long time. However, when their absence became known, and the story of their disappearance appeared in the world press six weeks later, a fellow passenger on the flight from Stockholm to Helsinki recalled that Antonio, the youngest Pontecorvo boy, had announced during the flight that they were going to Russia and kept looking out of the window and asking, 'Is that Russia?' According to another report, one of the passengers on the Helsinki flight was the Finnish Minister of the Interior, Johannes Virulainen, who was travelling with his wife. On their arrival, Bruno, who recognised the minister, handed him his British passport, saying that he had no further use for it. Mrs Virulainen is also said to have remarked that Marianne Pontecorvo was 'conspicuously nervous, pale and haggard.'

Exactly how the Pontecorvos reached the Soviet Union has never been definitely ascertained, since the Finnish authorities have no record of their departure. It may have been by Russian Embassy car, which would not have been challenged when it crossed the border at Abo. On the other hand, there was a Soviet vessel, the *Byelostrov*, lying at anchor in Helsinki harbour. She was due to sail for Leningrad that morning, but her departure was delayed until the afternoon, which would have given the Pontecorvos time to have a meal with their Soviet hosts and go aboard in the afternoon. The *Byelostrov* sailed about five o'clock and arrived in Leningrad on 5 September.

Back in Harwell there was at first no great concern when Bruno failed to appear for the opening of the conference, since he had the reputation of being late, particularly when he had been on holiday. However, Professor Caldirola arrived, and after he had failed to find any trace of the missing scientist he left a note at his home and returned to Italy. Meanwhile, mail kept being dropped through the letter-box of the house at Abingdon by the postman, mostly bills and circulars. But there were several letters from Marianne's parents, saying they had been writing with greetings for one of the boys' birthdays and were puzzled at getting no response. Bruno's parents also wrote saying that they were worried at getting no news and asking for a reply. It was not until 21 September that the authorities first felt anxiety about the Pontecorvo family's failure to return to England, and official inquiries began to be made.

In Rome, Bruno's sister Signora Talbet said that as far as she could remember the family had stayed with her until 6 September, when they had left early in the morning, saying that they were returning to England by easy stages. However, towards the middle of September, Giuliana continued, she had had a letter from her brother which gave her the impression that he was still in Rome. In it Bruno asked her to pay the garage expenses for the Standard Vanguard and to send it back to England. If she received such a letter, it was in all probability sent from Russia in a Soviet diplomatic bag to the Embassy in Rome for posting there. However, Giuliana seems to have taken no action to comply with Bruno's request, since the vehicle was subsequently discovered by the police in a garage in the Piazza Verde in Rome. The licence, log book and other papers were missing.

Giuliana could throw no light on what had happened to the family. According to her, Bruno had seemed quite normal when he stayed in the Via Gabi with her, and he never mentioned to her or to anyone else she knew of that he had any plans other than to return with Marianne and the three boys to England. Nor could the other sister Anna, the teacher, help.

She had last seen her brother and the others at Giuliana's house on 28 August, the day before she returned by train to England, and she noticed nothing amiss with Bruno. On the other hand, Laura, the nurse who was slightly older than Anna and was thought to have some sympathy for the Communist cause, also disappeared about this time. One of the letters found in Abingdon was dated 11 September and purported to come from Laura in Rome saying that she was negotiating for a post in Italy. Giuliana had added a postscript to this letter in which she asked what she should do with the property the family left at her house, including Gil's bicycle—keep it until they returned to Rome, or send it back to England? It seems reasonable to assume that at the date this letter was written, both Laura and Giuliana thought that the family were back in Abingdon, whereas in fact they were in Russia. Incidentally, Laura never returned to resume her hospital work in England.

One night early in October, Inspector W. Rydon of the Berkshire constabulary, accompanied by several security officers from MI5, arrived at the Pontecorvos' house in Abingdon. The police inspector opened the front door with a skeleton or duplicate key, and he had to push the door in since the floor was piled high with unopened mail. After switching on the lights and drawing the curtains, the visitors removed all the books from the bookcase in the living room and examined each one carefully for any clue to the missing scientist's disappearance. The letters, postcards and magazines were also meticulously gone through, but in neither instance did they discover anything of consequence. They left with three brief-cases crammed with papers they had found in the house.

At the same time, neighbours who were interviewed recalled some curious incidents which occurred before the family's departure. First, there was Bruno's cryptic remark to Mrs Seligman after their last game of tennis. Then, Marianne Pontecorvo told the wife of another Harwell scientist on the night before they left that even if her husband did not return to Abingdon she would be back with the children. She also gave two ducks to a neighbour, saying, 'Take care of them or kill them. You never know when we may come back.'

For the next few weeks the British authorities kept quiet in the hopes that some definite information about the missing family's whereabouts would be discovered. Eventually, on 20 October 1950, the story broke in the Italian press, when every Rome newspaper, with the exception of the Communist journals, headlined the disappearance of Bruno Pontecorvo and the efforts which the British authorities had been making to trace him and his wife and children. This news led to a welter of speculation. Some commentators thought he had been kidnapped, others that he had become insane, and some deduced that he had been lured to the Soviet Union on the bogus pretext that he could serve as an intermediary between scientists in the East and in the West. There was no hard evidence to support these views. Nor could any newspaper reporter put on to the story discover anything conclusive, although the speculation continued. Then there was the question as to why the story should have broken when it did. To this there are two possible answers. Either the British authorities asked the Italian police to let them have any information they had on Bruno Pontecorvo, and the Italian police 'leaked' the fact of his disappearance to the Italian press. A possible, though perhaps less likely explanation, is that the Russians through their local Tass agency gave the story to the non-Communist newspapers, while saying nothing about it in their own press, so as to prolong the interest in the mystery in the West.

Meanwhile, in the British House of Commons, Mr George Straus, the Minister of Supply responsible for Harwell, had to face a barrage of embarrassing questions. When had the inquiries begun? Why was it not known all along that Bruno Pontecorvo was a Communist? How come that he should have been naturalised and allowed access to atomic secrets, having later defected to Russia? But the Minister had practically nothing to say in his replies. He could not even positively state that the family were in fact in Russia.

It is difficult to believe that, despite Marianne's depression and tears, when Bruno left Abingdon with his wife and children on 25 July he had no intention of returning. There were the clothes and furniture and books and papers in the house, the newspaper boy and the milkman were told to discontinue deliveries until further notice, Bruno had £165 in his English bank account and $1714 in his Canadian account at Deep River, Ontario, while Marianne had £52 in a Post Office savings account in Abingdon. The departure and the next few weeks had all the characteristics of a genuine holiday, swimming, snorkelling, underwater fishing and so on. Also it seems inconceivable that Bruno, who was deeply attached to his parents, should have been so inconsiderate as to arrange a rendezvous with them at Chamonix which he had no intention of keeping. As we know, Marianne did not relish the idea of going to Liverpool, and Bruno may, in his usual way—it had happened before—have decided to look round for a post in an Italian university or institute, returning to England before taking it up, to collect the family's belongings left behind in Abingdon.

It is fairly clear that Bruno only decided not to go back to Abingdon after he had seen his brother Gilberto at his birthday reunion on 22 August, and that something happened between that date and his boarding the plane for Stockholm to make him change his plans. The present writer's view is that he had been doing some spying for the Russians while he was at Chalk River, that he was the unidentified 'Gino—a Jew' in Zabotin's notebook, and that through his family's Communist connections he met Russian intelligence agents in Rome who invited him to go to Russia, pointing out that he would be of no further use to them in England, since he was already under suspicion in Harwell and had accepted an academic post in Liverpool solely concerned with non-secret work. It may conceivably have been hinted to him that if he refused he would be exposed to the British and suffer the same fate as Nunn May and Fuchs. His agreement presumably followed, and thus there was no problem in his acquiring sufficient American dollars from the Russians in Rome to pay the family's fares to Helsinki. The fact that when making the reservations at the SAS office, he changed his own ticket from a single to a return may have been a deliberate ploy to put the airline off the scent in the event of inquiries being made to SAS about him.

The question remains, what was his potential value to the Russians at this particular time? Admittedly he was familiar with the heavy water pile at Chalk River where he had worked, and he also had knowledge of the plutonium piles in the United States, as well as the recent researches into plutonium and its uses at Harwell, though these seem to have had little to do with the atomic bomb. In any event the Russians were almost certainly in possession of this information already, since they had made their first nuclear explosion nearly a year before the Pontecorvos' flight.

'My impression,' said Bruno's old teacher Professor Fermi shortly after his disappearance, 'is that if he went to Russia he may not be able to contribute to their work by the things he had learned during his connection with the Canadian and the English projects, but rather through his general scientific competence.' Certainly his specialised knowledge of cosmic rays and the use of radio-active methods in prospecting for uranium and oil might be of considerable value to the Russians. And that is more or less how it turned out to be.

[8]

A long official silence followed in the Soviet Union. Not that there were not plenty of rumours which emanated from outside Russia's frontiers. One of them, which may have had some truth, was ostensibly based on Swedish intelligence sources and expressed by an American columnist, Victor Riesel, on 16 April 1951, to the effect that Bruno Pontecorvo was working on the development of an air defence system based on cosmic rays and designed to prevent the United States from being able to deliver atomic or hydrogen bombs. Other rumours had him working on atomic projects in Moscow, the Urals and even in far-off Sinkiang in China. However, the latter possibility was dismissed by American authorities as ruled out by the lack of supplies and machinery not to mention communications in that area. Then in November 1951, two Rome newspapers, *Il Tempo* and *Momento*

Sera came out with the astonishing news, based on unidentified Russian sources, that Bruno had been surreptitiously sending secret atomic information to President Truman and had been arrested as an American spy. 'It is intriguing,' commented a Ministry of Supply spokesman in London, 'that such news, if true should have percolated through the Iron Curtain.' This highly improbable report was not confirmed by any of the reliable intelligence outposts in Scandinavia or elsewhere. Nor did any leading Italian Communists such as Togliatti and Sereni, who visited Russia at this time, have anything to say; if they knew anything, they certainly kept silent about it. So did the French Communist Professor Joliot-Curie, who was a regular visitor to Moscow. Meanwhile, Bruno's parents visited England in the hopes of finding out something, however slight, which might help them to trace their missing son, but they drew a complete blank.

In fact, Comrade Bruno Maximovich Pontecorvo, to give him his Russian-style patronymic, was working in the newly established Institute of Nuclear Physics of the Soviet Academy of Sciences, situated with its laboratories at a new town named Dubna about eighty miles from Moscow on a site near the junction of the Moscow-Volga Canal and the River Volga. The spirit pervading the establishment, to which Comrade Bruno and his colleagues were expected to conform on danger of being branded as dangerous revisionists, was expressed in the concluding passage of the article on the atom in the 1950 edition of the *Great Soviet Encyclopedia* as follows: 'The continued development of the theory of the atom on the basis of dialectical materialism, on the basis of the teachings of Lenin and Stalin, is the foremost task of Soviet physicists.' Bruno Maximovich seems to have carried out whatever assignments were allotted to him in this context, since only four years after his arrival in the Soviet Union he was awarded the Stalin Prize Second Class for his research in the field of high energy physics.

Early in 1955 the Soviet authorities decided that the time had come for Bruno Maximovich to be allowed to reveal publicly where he was and the nature of his work. On 5 March he held a press conference in the ballroom of what used to be the Tsar's Summer Palace in Moscow and which now belonged to the Soviet Academy of Sciences.

Wearing a grey Russian suit, a blue shirt and a red tie, Pontecorvo began by holding up his Soviet identity card and happily declaring that he had become a Soviet citizen in 1952. Speaking of his arrival in the USSR, he said: 'I was offered several fields in the application of atomic energy for peaceful purposes. Since I was interested in the physics of high energy, I chose that field. I have never worked in the field of military application of atomic energy.' He added that he had chosen his new country freely and of his own accord because he was convinced that in the Soviet Union 'scientific knowledge was employed in the service solely of human progress and not for war'.

Asked how he could be sure that the results of his research would never be used by the Soviet Union for warlike purposes, he showed some annoyance and replied testily: 'It is a question of direction. After the war the Soviet Union lagged behind somewhat, but still managed to build the first atomic power station. I think this answers the question of direction. The Soviet Union no longer lags behind in this field'.*

Meanwhile Bruno Maximovich went on living with Marianne and the children in a plain, yellow-washed, two-storey house in the scientists' housing complex at Dubna, where the staff had now increased to 1200, of whom about 300 were scientists. Shortly afterwards Khrushchev, who was not so obsessed with secrecy as Stalin had been, transformed Dubna into an open town, to which approved foreign scientists were admitted.

Following a conference of Communist bloc states in Moscow in March 1956, it was decided to convert the Institute into an international organisation. The original intention was to call it The Eastern Institute of Nuclear Research, but Mao Tse-Tung's China objected on the ground that the Chinese were the only true exponents of the Eastern outlook and were unwilling to share this label with such westerners as the Russians. Hence the place became officially known as the Joint Institute of Nuclear Research or the International Centre of Research in the Peaceful Use of Atomic Energy, to which ten states contributed besides the USSR, although the Institute remained predominantly Russian. Pontecorvo continued his work under the new dispensation, and on 21 April 1963, he was awarded the Order of Lenin for 'great services in physics,' a prize worth 7500 roubles (about $6000 or £3000). A few months later he was further honoured by being elected a full member of the Soviet Academy of Sciences. About the same time he and his family moved into a six-roomed house on the banks of the Volga.

In 1978, a convention was held in Rome to honour Bruno's old teacher, the veteran physicist, Professor Enrico Amaldi. Bruno Maximovich was invited to attend and the Soviet authorities unexpectedly granted him a temporary exit visa. He accepted the invitation and arrived at Fiumicino airport on 6 September, almost twenty-eight years to the day since his

---

* Without giving a specific date, the Soviets claimed to have built the first atomic pile or reactor in Europe, probably at the beginning of 1947 and some months before the British pile: see George A. Modelski, *Atomic Energy in the Communist Bloc* (1959) p. 36 *et seq.* The reactor and accompanying industrial complexes, used to produce the first Soviet atomic bomb, were built with slave labour supplied by the secret police chief Beria in a 'picturesque town' in the Cheliabinsk region of the South Urals. Towards the end of 1947 the reactor became operative under the direction of Igor Kurchatov, the 'father' of the Soviet bomb. Later, during the winter of 1957–58, after the first bomb had been detonated, the area was the scene of a terrible nuclear disaster in the shape of an explosion of nuclear waste which was stored in underground shelters, causing hundreds of casualties and covering towns and villages over a thousand square miles with radio-active dust. The disaster was kept a closely guarded secret for twenty years until it was revealed by the emigré Russian scientist Zhores A. Medvedev: see his *Soviet Science* (1979), pp. 50–51, and p. 232 *et seq.*

dramatic flight to Russia. At the age of sixty-five, he looked remarkably fit and well. To the crowd of reporters who plied him with questions, he answered the inevitable one: *'Non ho mai lavorato alla bomba.'**

After the convention was over, Comrade Bruno Maximovich Pontecorvo returned to Moscow, a distinguished expatriate Soviet physicist and pensioner. In October 1979 he was reported as having visited his native Pisa as the guest of the Italian–USSR Association. A short time before this the US Treasury 'unfroze' his account in Washington and paid him about $2000, the total due amounting to some $15,000, presumably being his share of the sum in the patent suit which he had been awarded by the American Government in 1953.†

---

* 'I have never worked on the bomb.'   † See above, pp. 125–30.

CHAPTER FOUR

On To The Rosenbergs

[1]

At this time there were two bodies in the United States that were concerned
with domestic espionage, one administrative and one political. The first was
the Federal Bureau of Investigation, the official law enforcement agency,
nominally a branch of the Justice Department but a virtually independent
organisation under the omnipotent direction of Mr J. Edgar Hoover. The
second was the House Committee on Un-American Activities, a
Congressional Committee which had come into being as a result of a
resolution put forward in 1937 by a popular young Texan Democrat
Representative, Martin Dies, with the object of investigating subversive
and un-American 'propaganda' and incidentally of counteracting the
Senate's Civil Liberties Committee, which had the blessing of President
Roosevelt and was headed by the liberal Senator Robert La Follette. At first
known as the Dies Committee when Dies was its chairman, by 1940 the
Committee had an annual appropriation of $235,000, the largest amount
ever appropriated to a special investigating committee. The House Committee's object was to expose Nazi, Fascist and Communist activities, and
suspect aliens generally, particularly those employed in defence plants,
which could be and in fact on occasion were subject to acts of sabotage. In
1944 Dies resigned on grounds of ill-health, but neither under Dies nor his
immediate successors could the Committee really be said to justify the large
sums of money which it spent on its investigations and hearings both
private and public, although before and during the war it did alert the
public to German activities, especially in Latin America. After the war the
Committee concentrated on Communist and Soviet subversion, the motion
picture industry in Hollywood being singled out as an alleged hot-bed of
'Commies.' It was inevitable, after Drew Pearson's broadcast and the
appointment of the Canadian Royal Commission, that the Committee
should turn its attention to atomic espionage; in fact it uncovered little if
anything which was not already known to the security authorities. For
example, all its spokesman could say when a Russian naval lieutenant was
arrested in Portland, Oregon, in March 1946 was that 'it seemed to him that

the fellow might be a courier.' Representative John Rankin from Mississippi, the acting chairman, announced from time to time in the press that 'there were spies in this country trying to steal the secrets of the atom bomb.' But neither at that time nor afterwards was he able to produce any evidence to substantiate this charge.[1]

And so it went on, the technique of the smear, exemplified in the action of the Republican Chairman J. Parnell Thomas in publicly endorsing an adverse report on the loyalty of Dr Edward Condon, a distinguished American physicist, who had been closely involved with the development of the atomic bomb since 1939 as 'one of the weakest links in our atomic security,' a baseless charge which seems to have been inspired by the fact that his wife was of Czechoslovak descent, and in also stating that in March 1946 that America ought to welcome Russian scientists to its laboratories, adding that he did so because the Soviet Union was 'right now the target of attack by those irresponsibles who think she would be a suitable adversary in the next world war.' A Committee investigator managed to gain a sight of the FBI file on Condon which contained a letter from Hoover himself, stating that as late as 1947 Condon had been in contact with an individual alleged 'by a self-confessed Soviet espionage agent, to have been engaged in espionage activities with the Russians in Washington, DC, from 1941 to 1944.' The self-confessed agent turned out to be Elizabeth Bentley, who had defected from the Communists, while the alleged spy was one Nathan Gregory Silvermaster, a government economist whom Miss Bentley had named as heading a Soviet spy group in Washington during the war. However, one crucial sentence from Hoover's letter was omitted from the Committee's report, although it was subsequently 'leaked' by the Commerce Department then headed by Mr Averell Harriman. It was this: 'There is no evidence to show that contacts between this individual [Silvermaster] and Dr Condon were related to this individual's espionage activities.' Shortly afterwards the Atomic Energy Commission, having read the whole file including the FBI reports of Condon's associations, announced that the physicist's 'continued clearance' was considered to be 'in the best interests of the atomic energy programme.'

During the run-up to the Presidential campaign in 1948, committees in both houses of Congress denounced executive departments for laxity in failing to ferret out Reds and prosecute spies, and even the Republican presidential candidate Thomas Dewey accused the Truman administration of 'Communist coddling.'

In the immediate pre-election months, the House Committee under Thomas's chairmanship, having managed to obtain reports of security investigations from the days of the Manhattan project, turned its attention specifically to scientists who had worked on the development of the atom bomb. Open hearings were ruled out on security grounds, but Thomas promised revelations which would 'shock the public by showing that Presidents Roosevelt and Truman and Attorney General Thomas C. Clark had had the facts regarding a spy-ring that obtained A-bomb secrets and had done nothing about them.' Representative Richard Nixon from California, who had by this time become an enthusiastic member of the House Un-American Activities Committee, went so far as to charge Truman with preventing Edgar Hoover from testifying because he was 'afraid of the political consequences.' The Committee also undertook to reveal what it described as 'a shocking chapter in Communist espionage in the atomic field.'[2]

Truman was not slow to counter-attack in his presidential campaign. For example, he took the opportunity at a meeting in Constitution Hall in Washington of the American Association for the Advancement of Science to shake hands with Dr Condon and give him a friendly greeting, going on to issue a warning that *'scientific work may be made impossible by the creation of an atmosphere in which no man feels safe against the public airing of unfounded rumours, gossip and vilification.'* (Author's italics). Later, in Nixon's home state, Truman remarked, in the knowledge that what he said would receive appropriate publicity, that the House Committee was 'more un-American than the activities it is investigating'. He also predicted, with remarkable accuracy, that Chariman Thomas would not be sitting in the House for very much longer.*

Meanwhile, on 28 September 1948, a few weeks before the election, the House Committee issued its report, which it likened to the Report of the Canadian Royal Commission, to which in fact it bore little resemblance due to its avowedly partisan character. 'It has been established,' it said, 'that certain vital information was actually transmitted to the Russian government and that this information has been and will be of assistance to the Russians in their development of the atomic bomb.' That some information had reached the Russians from the sources indicated by the Committee is quite likely, but it is questionable, to say the least, whether it was correct to describe any of it as 'vital,' or that it had been of much help to the Russians in developing their bomb. The House report specified three incidents, to all of which it attributed considerably exaggerated importance.

The first concerned Steve Nelson, a native of Yugoslavia whose real name was Stafab Mesarosh and who ran the Communist Party branch in western Pennsylvania. He had now transferred to the West Coast. He was said to have been visited late at night—in 1943—at his home in Berkeley by an anonymous individual referred to as 'Scientist X', who worked in the radiation laboratories of the University of California at Berkeley. The

---

* Thomas was subsequently charged with bribery and corruption, tried and convicted, with the result that he resigned from Congress in January 1950.

scientist's name was withheld because of his emphatic denials in the Committee's executive sessions, which were held in secret. Shortly afterwards Nelson allegedly met Peter Ivanov, the Soviet Vice–Consul in San Francisco and handed him an envelope. Some time later Vassili Zubulin, the third secretary in the Soviet embassy in Washington, appeared in San Francisco on a visit. He later called on Nelson at his home and handed him ten dollar bills of unknown denomination. Nelson refused to give any information to the Committee which he described as 'a gathering of political pyromaniacs.'

Secondly, it was alleged that in 1944 a Manhattan project scientist from Canada named Dr Martin Kamen, who had been working in the radiation laboratory at the University of Berkeley, had dinner with two Russian officials, Gregory Keifets, a Soviet Vice–Consul, and his successor, Gregory Kasperov, at Bernstein's Fish Grotto in San Francisco, where they 'discussed some phases of atomic research.' Whether the Russians were given any information that they should not have had remained a moot question. Two FBI men occupied the adjoining booth with a sound-amplifying device. Unfortunately the Fish Grotto was very noisy and the reception was poor, although the names of Niels Bohr and Santa Fé were picked up, as also was a reference to the dangers of radio-activity in handling atomic piles.

It seems that Dr Kamen had only met Vice–Consul Keifets once, at a cocktail party in San Francisco, but this was sufficient to justify the Vice–Consul asking Kamen if he could procure some radio-active phosphorus to treat a Soviet consular official in Seattle who was seriously ill with leukaemia. There was nothing secret about the use of phosphorus for this purpose, and Dr Kamen was able to oblige. The object of the dinner, which took place on 2 July 1944, and lasted for two hours and forty minutes, not an unusual length of time for a Russian dinner with drinks, was to thank Kamen for his courtesy and to introduce him to Kasperov 'in case you ever have any business you want to discuss with the Russian Consulate.' Afterwards, Kamen, whose parents came from Russia and who seems to have been regarded as a vague fellow-traveller, conceded that he might have been indiscreet, but not disloyal. In fact, the Russians apparently sounded out the scientist as to his willingness to share atomic secrets. However, when pressed by his hosts Kamen argued that the sharing should be a two-way affair, and he chose the occasion to mention that when the Americans had recently landed in Normandy many of them were badly shot up by the Germans who were using stolen Russian anti-tank guns, the details of which the Russians had kept secret from their allies. Nevertheless, ten days after the dinner, Dr Kamen was suspended for his indiscretion without any chance of being heard in his own defence, and he went off to work in a shipyard.

The third case, also in 1944, concerned a young physicist, Clarence

Francis Hiskey who had been working with the Manhattan project on the gaseous diffusion process in Chicago before he was called up for military service on the recommendation of security officers who used this means of getting rid of him, for he was reported to have been an active Communist since at least 1942. Before he left for the army, Hiskey asked a chemical engineer, J. H. Chapin, employed in the Metallurgical Project in Chicago and later in Cleveland, if he would like to meet a veteran Soviet agent named Arthur Alexandrovich Adams so as to continue the flow of information when he (Hiskey) was removed from the scene. The meeting took place, but proved abortive since Chapin got cold feet and refused to co-operate in any way. Adams later fled the country, while Hiskey refused to testify before the Committee, pleading the Constitution's Fifth Amendment to avoid self-incrimination.

The Committee admitted that all of its information, apparently obtained from US army counter-intelligence sources, had been known to the government for some years, and it bluntly charged the Truman administration with a 'completely inexcusable lack of action' in these cases and called for the impeachment of the Attorney-General. The Justice Department replied that the Committee was indulging in 'political activity in the field of espionage' in an election year. 'There is absolutely no competent proof here,' an official departmental spokesman stated, 'of the actual or attempted communication, delivery or transmittal of information relating to the national defence to a foreign government or to one of its representatives' within the meaning of the Espionage Act. Meanwhile Thomas refused to suspend the Committee's activities until after the election. 'As far as I am concerned, the election has nothing to do with it,' he declared, 'nor has the election ever had anything to do with our investigations.'

Neither the Committee's hearings nor its report added anything to what was already known to the FBI. As for the alleged 'completely inexcusable' lack of action, Thomas and his colleagues on the Committee were unable to produce any concrete evidence to support this charge. They gave the impression that they had uncovered a nest of traitors to the great detriment of the nation's security, whereas in reality they had done no more than draw attention to the possibility of a few scientists during the war having inadvertently or otherwise revealed information of little or no use to the Russians in the atomic field.

The Committee's hearings in this vintage year of the 80th Congress were also marked by the appearance of the ex-Communists Elizabeth Bentley and Whittaker Chambers, whose testimony was designed to compromise Harry Dexter White, Alger Hiss and about two dozen others in government employ as being aiders and abettors of Communism if not being actually party members. According to Mackenzie King, Gouzenko had specifically implicated Harry Dexter White and Alger Hiss, as well as underlining

Elizabeth Bentley's role as a Soviet agent before she turned informer. All of these charges were either strenuously denied by the individuals concerned when they were called before the Committee, or else the witnesses took refuge in the Fifth Amendment. In any event there was no suggestion that any of these suspected Communists or Communist sympathisers passed any atomic information to the Russians.

[2]

During the first months of the 81st Congress, after President Truman's return to the White House, the House Committee under the chairmanship of a Democrat from Georgia, John S. Wood, who appeared a more gentlemanly character than the Republican Parnell Thomas he had replaced, was relatively inactive. After the arrest of an employee of the Justice Department named Judith Coplon for passing information concerning foreign agents, diplomats and American Communists to the Russians, Representative Richard Nixon demanded an investigation on the ground that the case showed that the department might be 'unfit and unqualified to carry out the responsibility of protecting the national security against Communist infiltration,' but no investigation ensued in spite of Judith Coplon's conviction and imprisonment.*

The greater part of the Committee's time in 1949 was devoted to going over the wartime espionage cases which had been made public in the previous year. In particular, the mysterious Scientist 'X' was identified as Dr Joseph W. Weinberg, an assistant professor of physics in his early thirties at the University of Minnesota, who had been employed in the University of California's radiation laboratory at Berkeley in the war and was alleged to have passed information to Steve Nelson for transmission to the Russians. The other principal suspect involved in the Manhattan project was Clarence Hiskey, who was shown by an informer to have been a Communist Party member from before the war. Hiskey, who was an analytical chemist now teaching at the Brooklyn Polytechnic Institute, denied that he had been in any way disloyal, but again pleaded the Fifth Amendment to all questions relating to the American Communist Party, Arthur Adams, John Chapin, and the like.

However, a member of the Army Counter–Intelligence Corps, who was detailed to keep an eye on Hiskey while he was on his way to Alaska in the course of his military assignment, searched his belongings and discovered a notebook full of data on nuclear fission, which he promptly seized. Security

---

* Coplon was entrapped by means of a bogus letter purporting to come from Hoover to the US Attorney General about Russian commercial interest in geophones used for measuring blast pressure and manufactured in connection with the original atomic tests.

regulations of the Manhattan District project required that the loss of any restricted material should be immediately reported, but Hiskey never made any such report, and it was surmised that Hiskey had a rendezvous with a Soviet agent for the purpose of disclosing this material. Eventually Hiskey was indicted for contempt of Congress in that he had consistently refused to answer the questions put to him by the Committee, and the Brooklyn Polytechnic suspended him from teaching. Nevertheless, a federal judge in Washington quashed the indictment, ruling that he was within his rights in declining to answer questions which might possibly incriminate him. Hiskey was thereupon reinstated in his teaching post in Brooklyn on full pay, backdated to the beginning of his suspension.

Weinberg, on the other hand, emphatically denied all the charges. However, the Committee, which had in its possession a report from an FBI agent who had according to his own account listened in to a meeting at Weinberg's apartment in August 1943, attended by Steve Nelson and four allegedly Communist scientists, doubted his testimony and later publicly accused him of lying under oath when he denied that he had ever been a Party member or that he ever knew Steve Nelson or Nelson's secretary, Bernadette Doyle. Weinberg was subsequently indicted for perjury, tried and acquitted, although the Republican Representative Harold H. Velde, a newcomer from Illinois who had been an FBI agent during the war and was to succeed Wood as Committee Chairman during the 83rd Congress in 1953, when the appalling Senator Joseph McCarthy was fulminating on the subject of 'Reds', declared that there was 'a complete and indictable case against so-called Scientist 'X' ', adding that 'Soviet espionage agents are still highly active in the continental United States.' When the news broke late in 1949 that the Russians had exploded their first atomic bomb, Velde went on to state publicly that the Russians had 'undoubtedly gained from three to five years' in producing their weapon 'because of a soft official attitude.'

The Committee's claims of the existence of A-bomb conspiracies, stimulated by the atom bomb's development by the Russians and following the announcement of Harry Gold's arrest in May 1949 after he had been identified by Fuchs as his contact with Moscow, amounted to little more than was generally known, namely that the Russians had been most interested in the activities of American radiation laboratories in the early nineteen-forties, and had done what they could to tap friendly sources among atomic scientists working on the Manhattan project. Yet, although the Committee had upwards of a million names on its files of suspects, unlike the FBI files, they did not include the name of the obscure Philadelphia chemist who formed the vital link in Soviet atomic espionage in the United States.

With the exception of Hiskey and Weinberg, the university scientists who had been examined before the House Committee and pleaded the Fifth Amendment, were exposed in public session as ex-Communists and for this they had to resign their teaching and research posts. One of them, an associate professor at Fisk University, was subsequently traced by a reporter to Oklahoma City, where he was working as a labourer for a utility company at $1.20 an hour; he climbed to the top of a high water-tower to avoid being questioned. On the other hand, Robert Oppenheimer's brother Frank and his wife, who both admitted to having been Communists, did not take advantage of the Fifth Amendment, although they refused to answer certain questions on the detail of their past associations. 'Questions about political affiliations or sympathies or actions,' said Frank, 'seem to me not matters which I can talk about here, because the people whom I have known throughout my life have been decent and well-meaning people. I know of no instance where they have taught, discussed or said anything which was inimical to the purposes of the Constitution or the laws of the United States.' By refusing to answer questions of this kind, Frank Oppenheimer and his wife laid themselves open to the charge of contempt, but the chairman Representative John Wood would not agree to this being brought in their case. 'I am not in favour of contempt action,' he said, 'except in cases where a witness withholds information that is vital to Committee investigation.' However, he did not say why it was necessary to question them in public session at all, since they now tended to be suspect although their loyalty was really never in doubt.

Incidentally, it is worth noting that Peter Ivanov, the Soviet Vice–Consul in San Francisco, asked George Eltenton, a physicist working for the Shell Corporation in 1942, in the words of a Congressional committee report, 'to secure information concerning some highly secret work pertaining to the atomic bomb which was being carried on at the Radiation Laboratory', on the grounds that 'since Russia and the United States were allies, Soviet Russia should be entitled to any technical data which might be of assistance to that nation.' Eltenton, who was offered money for his co-operation, contacted the Professor of French at the University, Chevalier, and Chevalier in turn spoke to Robert Oppenheimer, which he did at Eltenton's request. Oppenheimer, deeply shocked, told Chevalier that he considered such efforts to secure secret information to be treasonable, and he reported the circumstances of the approach to General Groves, the military head of the Manhattan project. Groves, who trusted Robert Oppenheimer implicitly, appointed him scientific head of Los Alamos, and on the elder Oppenheimer giving an assurance of his brother's loyalty, Frank was also appointed to a post there under his brother's direction. It is also worth noting that at the end of the war Frank Oppenheimer received special commendation from General Groves for 'patriotic and useful service.'

It only remains to mention the most sensational topic aired at the

Committee's hearings during this Congress, namely the shipment of atomic material to the Soviet Union during World War II.[3] It was initially highlighted by a former major in the American Air Force named G. Racey Jordan, who had been a lend-lease inspector at the Great Falls airport in Montana, a stopping place for aircraft en route to the USSR. According to Major Jordan, in an interview with the popular right-wing radio commentator Fulton Lewis, several shipments of uranium and heavy water and numbers of suitcases containing State Department documents labelled 'Manhattan Engineering District', 'Uranium 92' and the like had been consigned to Russia via the Montana base. Jordan also stated that in the spring of 1944 he had received instructions from the late Harry Hopkins, President Roosevelt's confidential adviser, to expedite a particular shipment and not inform his superiors anything about it. In a folder marked 'Oak Ridge', he said he found a memorandum from Hopkins, then lend-lease administrator, to the Soviet Deputy Prime Minister Anastas Mikoyan, which read 'Had a hell of a time getting these away from Groves.' As a result the Washington *Herald* ran the interview under the following banner headlines:

HOPKINS ACCUSED OF GIVING REDS A-SECRETS

Vice-President Henry Wallace was also said to have overruled Groves in order to get the uranium shipments to Russia.

After Jordan had repeated his story before the Democratic members of the Committee—the Republicans were out of town—General Groves conceded when questioned that he had approved two relatively small shipments to the Russians in an effort to discover their sources of uranium, and to avoid enlightening them of the uses to which the American scientists were putting the material. The General added that the Committee had been informed of these shipments some months previously, but he doubted whether they contained any heavy water, which he compared in value to diamonds. He had never been pressurised by the Russians, he had never met Harry Hopkins or talked to any member of his staff, and he had had very little to do with Wallace, whom incidentally he seems to have regarded as something of a security risk in his position.

Nixon and Velde and another Republican member of the Committee who had been absent now entered a strong protest at what they called the 'whitewash' which had been perpetrated in their absence. They concentrated on the only large shipment of uranium which had been made to Russia during the war, namely one thousand pounds from a Canadian firm. But despite Nixon's energetic endeavours to pin responsibility on the US lend-lease officials, no irregularities could be proved against Hopkins or anyone else. 'No pressure from any source was used or indeed necessary,' said the New York broker for the shipment, 'at a time when we were rushing all available supplies to our then allies.' Wallace, who also came before the Committee, pointed out that his wartime Board of Economic Warfare exercised no effective supervision over lend-lease.

Jordan also charged that a huge mass of documents also went to Russia, many through diplomatic pouches, among them some from Hiss and Sayre, the latter being Hiss's superior in the State Department. What Jordan's accusations boiled down to was that there was a conspiracy by New Deal officials to send atomic materials and other secret matter to Russia. But they were not substantiated by any evidence other than a diary of dubious authenticity which Jordan claimed to have kept in 1944. That the Russians did receive several shipments of uranium under lend-lease is beyond dispute, but there was no credible evidence implicating Hopkins or Wallace or any other New Dealer in conspiracy. As for the mass of documents most of them were technical manuals and road maps which ranked as unclassified material and were generally available to the public at large. Once the attempt to smear Hopkins and Wallace had failed, the Committee dropped the subject of atomic espionage and turned to other fields of investigation, once more including alleged Communist front organisations and the motion picture industry in Hollywood. There we may leave this illiberal and partisan, but by no means enfeebled, Congressional body.

[3]

We must now return to the case of Harry Gold, who, it will be recalled, was arrested in Philadelphia on 23 May 1950, 'on espionage charges based on information supplied by Dr Fuchs.' It was not the first time that Gold had come to the attention of the FBI. Three years previously, a certain Abraham Brothman, a chemical engineer in New York City, and his secretary and business manager Miriam Moskowitz, a thirty-one-year-old college graduate, were being investigated as Communists and possible Soviet agents on the basis of information furnished by the informer Elizabeth Bentley. It appeared that during the summer and autumn of 1940, Brothman had furnished Miss Bentley with blueprints of various chemical processes, which she had passed to her lover, the Soviet spymaster Jacob Golos. For some reason Golos became dissatisfied with Brothman and he told his mistress, whom Brothman knew only as 'Helen', that he was transferring him to another courier. This was Harry Gold, who in 1947 was working in Brothman's Long Island laboratory. Thus, when Gold was interviewed by the FBI, he freely admitted that he had been introduced to Golos at a meeting of the American Chemical Society at the Franklin Institute in Philadelphia. After the meeting Golos confided in Gold that he had connections with Abe Brothman, who occasionally turned over to him certain types of blueprints in the chemical field. Golos proposed that Gold should pick up these blueprints from Brothman and analyse them from a chemist's point of view. Gold told the FBI that he agreed to meet Brothman, who did hand over a good deal of information about chemical processes. However, said Gold, Golos never bothered to pick them up and Gold later claimed that he had destroyed the relevant papers. Both Gold and Brothman insisted that these were all simple and legitimate transactions, and since by this time Golos was dead there was no one to contradict the story.

Later in 1947 Gold and Brothman had both been subpoenaed before the Special Federal Grand Jury in the Southern District of New York, called to hear evidence of possible violations of espionage and other federal statutes by persons implicated by Elizabeth Bentley. Both denied any knowledge of Golos's spying activities, Brothman stating that Golos had come to him as a representative of Amtorg, the official Soviet purchasing agency in the United States, with the object of buying rights in a mixing apparatus which Brothman had invented and offered for sale through a trade journal. The Grand Jury accepted their testimony and returned a 'no bill', since the information passed did not come within the definition of the espionage statutes. Thus, although neither Gold nor Brothman was indicted, the FBI had acquired some extremely useful information, particularly about Gold. 'We knew that *some* chemist had worked with Dr Fuchs,' Edgar Hoover wrote afterwards. 'And Harry Gold was a chemist who seemed to fit the general pattern in many other particulars.'

On 29 July 1950, a few days after Gold had been arraigned and pleaded guilty, Abe Brothman and Miriam Moskowitz were arrested and charged with conspiring to obstruct the course of justice by misleading the Grand Jury which was investigating subversion in 1947, a charge in effect amounting to one of espionage. The two chief prosecution witnesses were Elizabeth Bentley and Harry Gold, who admitted that they both had worked for the Russians and incriminated the two defendants in their espionage activities. Neither defendant elected to testify and both were convicted. On 29 November 1950, Brothman was sentenced to seven years' imprisonment and fined $15,000, the maximum sentence in the circumstances.[4]

'What I do not understand and simply cannot fathom,' said the trial judge, Irving Kaufman, in passing sentence, 'is why people seek to undermine the country which gave them every opportunity—opportunity for education, opportunity for livelihood, and an opportunity for a fair trial such as they have received here.'

This trial set the scene for another trial on substantive espionage charges which was to take place a few months later before the same judge and with Harry Gold and Elizabeth Bentley as key witnesses for the prosecution— the trial of Julius and Ethel Rosenberg.

Harry Gold, whom the public prosecutor in the Rosenberg trial described as the 'necessary link' with the Russians in that case, was an untrustworthy witness who lived, like Walter Mitty, in a world of fantasy. At the Brothman trial it was disclosed that over a period of years Gold had told numerous persons what purported to be elaborate details of his personal life—that he had married and had had children, that he had been divorced and following his divorce he would travel to Philadelphia to watch his children play, but that he could not bring himself to speak to them. He was also said to have told people that he had had a brother who died in the war.

The truth was that Gold had never married, had no children, had never travelled to Philadelphia to watch children play, and had no brother who died in the war. Furthermore the judge and prosecutors in the Brothman trial were the same as those in the Rosenberg trial. Yet neither the judge nor the prosecutors saw fit to bring to the notice of the Rosenbergs' defence counsel Gold's appearance at the earlier trial and the patent unreliability of the statement he had made about his personal life.

Meanwhile Harry Gold had been arraigned before Judge James P. McGranery in the Federal Court in Philadelphia. 'I think it is important for me to say that there has been some view that has gone forth abroad that this case was first exposed by Fuchs,' the judge observed at the outset. 'This is not true. This matter was uncovered by the Federal Bureau, and Fuchs, as a matter of fact, as I understand it, had never co-operated in any way, shape or form until after the arrest of Harry Gold. Am I correct in that?'

'I think the statement is, Your Honour,' Mr Scott Miller replied for the FBI, 'that the identification of Harry Gold's picture was not made until after Gold signed a confession.'

'The point I make is that Fuchs had never co-operated with the Federal Bureau,' the judge went on. 'I am told that by both the Attorney-General and Mr Hoover.'

'That is correct,' the FBI man agreed.[5]

Why Judge McGranery should have made this statement remains something of a mystery, particularly as Mr Hoover, the FBI Director, in a signed article in the *Reader's Digest* a year later (June 1951) clearly stated that pictures of Gold had been sent to Fuchs in Wormwood Scrubs prison *before* Gold's arrest, although they had not been positively identified until afterwards. Other pictures had been sent to Fuchs, and certainly it cannot be truly said that he did not co-operate with the Bureau, as indeed is confirmed by the FBI archives.

Furthermore, the judge, who was subsequently to become Attorney General himself, was possibly trying to ingratiate himself with the Government, who may have wished at that time to 'play down' Fuchs's part in Gold's incrimination. At the same time, in view of Gold's plea and the 'publicity' which had attended his case, the judge made it clear that he could not pass a 'just' sentence unless the prosecution presented 'sufficient supporting evidence.' This the prosecution was unwilling to do, because there was certain information which it did not wish to make public. 'Of course, the same information,' the federal prosecutor went on, 'if he pleaded not guilty, we would probably have to make public at a trial, but in view of the fact that he has entered a guilty plea, it may very well be that the Government does not wish to make public certain things that it has learned, for security reasons.' In the event the judge did not press the matter further, after the defence counsel had indicated on his client's behalf that he would be perfectly willing to accept any statement of the crime that the prosecution might make 'without supporting evidence.'

Harry Gold was eventually brought up for sentencing on 9 December 1950. Asked if he had anything to say before sentence was passed, Gold admitted that he had made a 'terrible mistake.' 'There is a puny inadequacy about any words telling how deep and horrible is my remorse,' he declared, after thanking the Court for 'the most scrupulously fair trial' and commending the FBI and other agencies of the Department of Justice and the prison authorities for the good treatment he had been accorded. 'Most certainly,' he declared, 'this could never have happened in the Soviet Union or in any of the countries dominated by it.'

The Attorney-General, J. H. McGrath, had meanwhile recommended that the sentence on Gold should be limited to twenty-five years, long enough in all conscience. But Judge McGranery, who was determined to make an example, in view of 'the need to deter others in the future', disregarded this recommendation and passed the maximum sentence of thirty years. By this date he was aware that President Truman was going to appoint him to succeed McGrath, and no doubt he was conscious that he was addressing the nation as the future head of the Department of Justice.[6]

The period which elapsed between Gold's arraignment and sentencing, over four months, was unusually long. The reason soon became apparent. He was removed from Philadelphia to the notorious eleventh floor of the Tombs prison in New York, familiarly known as the 'Singing Quarters', where prisoners awaiting sentence were particularly well treated, enjoying special food and other privileges in return for their co-operation with the law-enforcement authorities. Among the admissions he made was that in May 1945 'John' (otherwise Anatoli Yakovlev, Soviet Vice-Consul in New York and local spy chief) had instructed him to go to Santa Fé and obtain atomic energy data from Klaus Fuchs. Gold also confirmed that he was ordered to contact an American soldier in Albuquerque to pick up similar data on the Los Alamos project. Gold described the soldier as sturdily built, about five feet seven inches in height, with dark hair. He thought the soldier was a native of New York City and he recalled that they had discussed the possibility of a second meeting in New York during the coming Christmas holidays.

On 3 June 1950, FBI agents paid another visit to Gold's comfortable quarters in the Tombs. A list of twenty names was read to him. Gold eliminated all but two of the names as that of the soldier he had contacted in Albuquerque. Next day the agents showed him a number of photographs and from this collection Gold picked out one of David Greenglass as most nearly resembling the Los Alamos spy. 'But if this is the same man,' he added, 'he has put on some weight since I saw him in 1945.' Greenglass had in fact grown noticeably heavier since his honourable discharge from the United States Army. Now aged twenty-eight, he was employed by a Brooklyn engineering firm along with his brother in-law, whose name was Julius Rosenberg. David was now living with his wife Ruth and their children in a New York City apartment. The Greenglasses were already under investigation for their Communist associations, and the FBI was also interested in David because of thefts of government property, usually taken as souvenirs, at Los Alamos when David was working there during and after the war. However, he denied all knowledge of the thefts when visited by FBI agents shortly after Gold's arrest. The agents told Greenglass that they were checking on property stolen from or misplaced at Los Alamos, and asked if they could look round the apartment. David and his wife agreed, and during the search the agents found a collection of recent snapshots of the Greenglasses. David allowed the agents to borrow them in response to their request, and it was from one of these that Gold was able to identify David Greenglass. As far as his Communist associations went, David's sister Ethel, who was married to Julius Rosenberg, had been known as a Communist sympathiser for some years, as also had her husband Julius. When the news of Gold's arrest broke in May, Julius Rosenberg was said by his brother-in-law to have advised him and Ruth to seek refuge in Mexico and offered him money. But David Greenglass could not bring himself to go; he and his wife wished to bring up their children in America. In the result David Greenglass was arrested on 16 June 1950. But Ruth remained free.

According to the FBI records now available, David Greenglass was interrogated by Assistant US Attorney Myles Lane in New York, on 4 August 1950, while he was in custody, on the subject of his conversations with Julius Rosenberg when Greenglass was on leave from Los Alamos in September 1945.[7] 'When we were alone he brought this subject up,' said Greenglass. 'Of course I gave him that description I gave you.'

'Of the bomb?' queried Lane.

'Of the bomb,' Greenglass agreed.

'Did he write it down?'

'I wrote it down.'

'And gave it to him?'

'And gave it to him,' Greenglass again agreed.

'In Manhattan?'

'Yes. I gave him a complete description of what I knew with sketches.'*

'Did he say what he was doing with them?'

'I knew he was giving them to the Russians.'

'Did he say he was giving them to the Russians?' Lane went on.

'Oh, yes,' answered Greenglass, 'he said to me originally he was asking for information to give the Russians. It was obviously to give it to the Russians that he originally recruited me to that plan.'

'I am trying to get to the actual fact that he was again, in the fall of 1945, giving it to the Russians?' the Assistant US Attorney persisted.

'He said, "I'm giving this to my friends".'

'Was Ethel present on any of these occasions?' Lane asked.

'Never,' said Greenglass.

'Did Ethel talk to you about it?'

'Never spoke to me about it, and that's a fact,' replied Greenglass, confidently. 'Aside from trying to protect my sister, believe me that's a fact!'

'Did you tell the Rosenbergs in the fall of 1945 that you were anticipating getting out of the army?'

'Yes.'

'What did he say?'

'He said, "It's all right, but can you get a job there as a civilian?" I said yes. He said, "Stay there". I said, "I'm coming home".'

'Did he say why he wanted you to stay there?'

'Yes, so he could get more information.'

'You were discharged shortly after that?'

'The last day of February, 1946.'

Greenglass went on to deny giving his brother-in-law any further information after his release from the army and later when they were working together in business. Finally, Greenglass was asked about his discussion with Julius Rosenberg on the possibility of he and his wife going to Mexico.

'Tell me why he wanted you to leave the US?'

'Well,' answered Greenglass, 'the reason that he wanted me to leave the US is because Fuchs, he told me, was the contact man, was contacted by Gold, and Gold was Fuchs's contact to give information. He did not mention Gold by name—he said, "The same man, you remember, that man out in Albuquerque." I thought and then I remembered.'

On the subject of Fuchs and Gold, there is also a note in the FBI files to

---

* In a signed statement made by Greenglass on 17 July 1950, he said: 'Almost as soon as I got to New York City, Julius Rosenberg got in touch with me and I met him in the street somewhere in the city. At that time I furnished Julius Rosenberg with an unsealed envelope containing the information I had been able to gather concerning the atomic bomb, as well as a couple of the sketches of the moulds which make up the bomb.'

the effect that on 13 June 1950, Hamburg Radio in West Germany had broadcast a news item to the effect that the Berlin Reuter's correspondent John Peet had asked for sanctuary in the Soviet zone, and that he had done so presumably to avoid arrest since he had been known to have collaborated with Fuchs and Gold 'in an organisation engaged in spying on atomic secrets.' There is no further evidence to substantiate this charge except that Peet was in fact granted asylum and for many years edited an English language propaganda news sheet in East Berlin.[8]

Julius Rosenberg was interviewed on the same day as his brother-in-law was arrested, and he stoutly denied that he had any connection with spying. He admitted that Ruth Greenglass had told him that David was working on the Los Alamos project but added, 'I didn't know anything about the atomic bomb until it was dropped on Japan.' He was arrested next day and his wife Ethel was taken into custody on 11 August. A college class-mate of Julius named Morton Sobell, who was employed by a New York instrument manufacturing company and had, as the result of the FBI's researches, supplied a reel of 35 mm film to Rosenberg, fled with his family to Mexico, whence he was allegedly deported. He was picked up in Laredo, Texas, on 18 August.

David Greenglass, the two Rosenbergs, Morton Sobell, Harry Gold and Anatoli Yakovlev were all indicted following appearances before a Federal Grand Jury on charges of conspiracy to commit acts of espionage. Gold and Greenglass both pleaded guilty, but Yakovlev managed to escape back to the Soviet Union before he could be apprehended. Both the Rosenbergs and Sobell pleaded not guilty.

Shortly before this Hoover had written to the Attorney-General J. Howard McGrath: 'There is no question that if Julius Rosenberg would furnish the details of his extensive espionage activities, it would be possible to proceed against other individuals.' Furthermore, he added, 'proceeding against his wife might serve as a lever in this matter.' Hence her arrest as a co-conspirator barely two months after that of her husband. However, the trouble from the Government's point of view, was that the FBI's only source of information on Ethel Rosenberg was from the Greenglasses and at the time of her arrest and for some time afterwards the Greenglasses proffered no evidence of any overt act on her part. It was not until ten days before the trial opened that the Greenglasses completely changed their story about the extent of Ethel's involvement—specifically as typing information on the atom bomb for her husband.

[4]

About 155,000 out of a total of 250,000 documents on the Rosenberg case have now been released by the FBI, largely as the result of the persistence of the two Rosenberg sons and a number of academics. They throw novel and interesting light on several important features which were not disclosed at the trial. These include the true rôle of David and Ruth Greenglass as revealed by their correspondence, the alleged post-war activities of Julius Rosenberg, information furnished to the FBI by a fellow prisoner about Julius Rosenberg while awaiting trial, the actual measure of participation by Ethel Rosenberg in the alleged espionage conspiracy, and the questionable conduct of the trial judge in the case. These new revelations have come to light to a considerable extent through the researches of two American students of the case, Sol Stern, a journalist, who formerly edited *Ramparts* magazine, and Ronald Radosh, Professor of History in the University of New York.[9]

First, David Greenglass and his wife Ruth. On the day of David's arrest a number of wartime letters between David and Ruth Greenglass were removed by the FBI from their apartment and were never returned. They reveal that the Greenglasses, far from being young innocents lured into the web of espionage, as has been generally supposed, were both dedicated Communists from an early age, being active members of the Young Communist League and Ruth being president of her League chapter at the age of twenty; thus, in the event, they were equal participants in the spying game. 'I am happy to hear you spent a pleasant day with the Rosenbergs,' wrote David to Ruth, on 9 November 1944, from Los Alamos where he was then working with full knowledge of the secret character of his work (contrary to what he later stated in court).

> My darling, I most certainly will be glad to be part of the community project that Julius and his friends have in mind. Count me in, dear, or should I say it has my vote.

On 12 June 1979, Stern and Radosh succeeded in obtaining an interview with David and Ruth Greenglass, who now live under an assumed name and had hitherto refused to be interviewed. They were plainly surprised when confronted with the 9 November letter and had evidently forgotten all about its existence. However, according to Stern and Radosh, David quickly acknowledged that this and other letters indicated that he was trying to alert Julius about his (David's) work on the atomic bomb as early as the summer of 1944. 'I knew Julius would want to be involved with something like that.' He went on to recall, by way of explanation, how he and Julius had been waiting outside the Capital Theatre on Broadway to buy tickets for a show in 1943. According to David, Julius told him he had powerful friends. 'We'll go into business after the war,' said Julius. 'They'll use us as a screen for getting the information.'

Looking at the 9 November letter on the table in front of him, David

Greenglass remarked, 'That fits in with that bit at the Capital Theatre.' Asked if the 'friends' referred to in the letter were the Russians, David replied: 'That's right. There were no other friends.' As to the suggestion that David himself was offering to become a spy of his own accord, he said: 'Well, let's say I was promising co-operation?' Yet the prosecution never made any use of these letters at the trial, although they offered strong corroboration of the existence of an espionage conspiracy. Nor, of course, could the defence have become aware of them. The reason for their being withheld is obvious, Stern and Radosh argue. 'As part of the deal offered the Greenglasses—leniency in exchange for their role as co-operative state witnesses—the government was willing to make it appear that they had been reluctantly lured into espionage by the Rosenbergs.'

During his first interrogation by the FBI, David Greenglass admitted that, as a machinist stationed at the Los Alamos research establishment during the war, he had passed information to Harry Gold. He also implicated his 26-year-old-wife Ruth and his brother-in-law Julius Rosenberg. Immediately after Greenglass's arrest, his attorney O. John Rogge went to see James McInerney, head of the Department's Criminal Division, as soon as he had learned how deeply his client and his wife were involved in espionage. 'I'll give you a couple of witnesses,' said Rogge, in an attempt to strike a bargain. 'However, I want Ruth Greenglass left out of the indictment.' After some haggling, according to Rogge, McInerney agreed not to indict Ruth and also agreed to recommend a three- to five-year sentence for David. Rogge then turned over his client and Ruth to the government authorities for interrogation. The story the Greenglasses told the FBI and the US Attorney has already been indicated; they had been lured into an espionage conspiracy by Julius Rosenberg in 1944, when Julius sent Ruth out to New Mexico to ask David to get information on the atomic bomb from Los Alamos, contact at the same time being established by Julius with Harry Gold while David passed sketches and notes on the bomb to Julius on two occasions while he was on furlough in New York in 1945.

The FBI papers show that the authorities were satisfied that in the main the Greenglasses' testimony was sufficient to convict Julius Rosenberg of espionage during time of war. The Bureau had also collected a considerable amount of information about Julius Rosenberg's post-war espionage activities, although these were not to form a part of the indictment nor were they to figure in the trial. The Bureau's initial discovery was that many of Julius Rosenberg's friends had disappeared during June and July 1950, having left the country via Mexico. For instance, when Julius Rosenberg had advised his brother-in-law and his wife to escape to Mexico and offered David $5000 which David refused, Julius had told him that an old college-mate of his and also of Morton Sobell named Joel Barr had left by this route in January 1948, without difficulty.

Since then the 32-year-old Barr, who held a degree in electrical engineering and had given as his reason for travelling abroad when applying for a passport that he wished to broaden his background by study in Europe, had lived mostly in Paris, although he had also spent short periods in technical schools in Sweden and Holland, ostensibly supporting himself by playing the piano. By the time the FBI had obtained Barr's Paris address, he had departed leaving behind his motor-cycle and other belongings. An American friend of Barr named Samuel Perl told FBI investigators that Barr had said on 2 June he was planning to leave. Asked where he was going, Barr allegedly answered that 'it would be better' if Perl 'did not know his intended destination', adding 'Don't worry, I just won't be around.' Barr has never subsequently been heard of.

The next of Julius Rosenberg's friends to disappear, also a friend of Barr's, was Alfred Sarant, another engineer aged thirty-two. He was the first of Julius's friends whom the FBI contacted after Julius's arrest. At first he seemed co-operative and allowed the Bureau agents to search his apartment. But ten days later, after several further meetings with the FBI, Sarant drove from his home in Ithaca, New York, to New York City where he met a woman named Mrs Carol Dayton, who was a neighbour of Sarant's with her husband in Ithaca. Sarant and Mrs Dayton then drove to Tucson, Arizona, where they obtained false Mexican tourist cards under the names of Mr and Mrs Bruce Dayton. On 9 August, they crossed the Mexican border and vanished like Joel Barr.

Then, four days after Julius Rosenberg's arrest, an unknown man, possibly a Russian courier, called on a former girl friend of Barr's named Vivian Glassman. Without identifying himself but mentioning Barr's name, he gave her $2000 in small bills and told her to go to Cleveland, Ohio, and find an aeronautical engineer whom he presumed she knew, although he did not name him. Glassman understood that the engineer was Samuel Perl's brother William, whose father was Russian and whose mother was Polish, and who had legally changed their name from Mutterperl to Perl. In the event Glassman succeeded in locating William Perl, but Perl refused to accept the money since he had recently been interrogated by the FBI about his association with Julius Rosenberg. Glassman then returned to New York and returned the $2000 to the unknown man when he came to see her again. Incidentally William Perl was later convicted of perjury and sentenced to five years for denying before the Rosenberg grand jury that he knew Rosenberg and Sobell.

The FBI further discovered that Barr, Sarant, William Perl and Glassman each lived in an apartment at 65 Morton Street, Greenwich Village, on various occasions after 1945; also that the apartment had been used for photographic purposes. Another of the Bureau's relevant discoveries was that Barr and Sarant had both been members of the same Communist Party club as Julius Rosenberg, and that after the club was dissolved in 1944 all three transferred to new clubs, but apparently at the same time dropped their party memberships.

Additional corroboration was provided by two Communist party or former party members, James Weinstein, editor of a Chicago socialist newspaper, and by his friend Max Finestone, who was also a friend of Sarant's for whom he used to work in his contracting business in Ithaca, and who lived for a time in the apartment at 65 Morton Street which Sarant had made available to him. During the academic year 1948–9 when Weinstein and Finestone were both seniors at Cornell University, Finestone told Weinstein that he was quitting the party to do 'secret work'. (Finestone later denied this to Stern and Radosh.) Weinstein did not ask for details, but he subsequently met a man to whom he was introduced by Finestone as 'Julius' whom they drove back from Finestone's parents' farm to New York. Later when Weinstein was sharing another apartment with Finestone, there was a knock on the door and there was 'Julius' inquiring for Finestone. Weinstein recognised the caller as Julius Rosenberg when he saw his photograph in the papers at the time of his arrest a fortnight later. Finestone was not at home when 'Julius' called, but when Weinstein later told him of the visit 'Max turned white as a sheet' and blurted out, 'He knows he's not supposed to come here.'

Finally, some credence as to the nature of Julius Rosenberg's clandestine activities after the war has been attributed to his own admissions to a fellow prisoner in the New York Federal House of Detention in Lower Manhattan, when Rosenberg was awaiting trial. The fellow prisoner, with whom Rosenberg struck up an acquaintance in the course of a game of chess, was a young man, Jerome Eugene Tartakow, who was serving a two-year sentence for inter-state automobile theft. During the game Julius Rosenberg began to talk about his youth and activities in the Young Communist League in the 1930s, and then about more contemporary matters. Their conversations continued over a period of six months, during which Rosenberg allegedly revealed details of his recent espionage activities. It may well be asked why he spoke so freely. In the first place they took to each other, since they were both Jewish, with immigrant working-class parents, and both had been members of the Young Communist League in their youth. Above all, Rosenberg may well have trusted Tartakow, since he was highly spoken of by the American Communist Party Secretary, Eugene Dennis, who was also in the House of Detention at this time for contempt of Congress, and Tartakow seems to have acted as a liaison between Dennis and Rosenberg since 'Gene Dennis didn't want the three of us to be seen together at that time.' What neither Dennis nor Rosenberg knew was that Tartakow was acting as an FBI 'stool-pigeon' and relaying everything he had learned from Rosenberg to the Bureau as well as to Dennis.

Asked why he had not fled the country before he was arrested, Rosenberg told Tartakow, according to the latter, that he had to 'take care of some friends', and that if he only had had another week he could have escaped.

Some pertinent extracts from the FBI report dated 3 January 1951, are given below:

Tartakow stated that he discussed with Rosenberg the possibility of his being found guilty, and his possible sentence in that event. Rosenberg told Tartakow that his lawyers have advised him that it was likely that he would be found guilty, and that he would probably be sentenced to thirty years and Ethel would be sentenced to twenty years. Rosenberg's lawyers also advised him that there was a possibility he would get the death penalty. Tartakow stated that Rosenberg told him 'that he had played the game and lost, and would have to take the results.' Tartakow stated that Rosenberg's only concern is that Ethel might break down in the event he got the death penalty, but in Tartakow's opinion neither Julius or Ethel would ever talk.

Tartakow stated that Julius was very agitated on 19 December 1950, when he returned from a conference with his lawyers. He stated that later that night Rosenberg told him that his lawyers found out the doctor whom Julius had questioned about smallpox inoculations had been interviewed by the FBI and would probably testify against him, because this questioning of the doctor was an indication of his possible intention to flee the country . . .

Tartakow stated that he discussed Sobell's arrest with Rosenberg, and that Rosenberg told him Sobell had been taking a vacation in Mexico 'coincidental' with the arrest of his brother-in-law David Greenglass. He told Tartakow that Sobell was accosted in his hotel room, slugged by the police, and carried to the United States border, where he was arrested by Government Agents.

Tartakow advised that Rosenberg told him there were two units operating in this area, and that he headed one, and the other was headed by two men Joel Barr and Alfred Sarant. Regarding these two men, Rosenberg stated that one of them Barr was in Europe at the time of his, Rosenberg's, arrest, and that the other one Sarant had fled one week after Rosenberg's arrest. Tartakow was unable to say where this man had fled from or where he had gone. Rosenberg further stated that the FBI had visited the home of one of these two men and had spoken to his aged mother, who had furnished the FBI with the names of other persons who were friendly with her son.

Tartakow stated Rosenberg said among the names given to the FBI were some persons who were involved in espionage with him, and that a number of these persons were ordered before the Grand Jury but that he was not concerned they would err because 'some cannot and others dare not.' Tartakow also stated Rosenberg had made this statement concerning his activities: 'I have a certain amount of authority in various matters and my friends are responsible on the other end.' Rosenberg also indicated that the first of these two men was still safe in Europe.

Tartakow stated that Rosenberg had questioned him about photography and had told him that they have a way of copying documents on microfilm and then exposing this film to the light. He further stated that there is then a process of redeveloping and bringing back all the exposed material. Tartakow stated that he, Tartakow, is a photographer by profession, but that he had never heard of this process, and that Rosenberg had stated this process was not known in the United States.

Tartakow advised that Rosenberg does not confide completely in his lawyers and that he is desperate to make some contacts outside the prison, the identities of whom are unknown to Tartakow. Rosenberg has also promised Tartakow to put him 'on the right track' when Tartakow is released, and stated that his, Tartakow's, value would be in espionage work . . .

Tartakow advised that Rosenberg is very critical of the present set-up of the American Communist Party stating that it is 'shot through with FBI agents.'

Tartakow stated that with regard to the doctor who furnished Rosenberg with information concerning the smallpox inoculations for travel to Mexico, Rosenberg stated that this doctor had been expelled from the Communist Party. . . .

Julius Rosenberg indicated to Tartakow that he had planned an escape route to be used from New York to Mexico City, and that Caracas, Venezuela, San Juan, Puerto Rico, and Havana, Cuba, were strongholds for revolutionary activities. Rosenberg himself stated that if he could, he would go to Caracas, Venezuela.[10]

According to Stern and Radosh, Tartakow's reports helped to convince the law enforcement authorities that nothing short of the ultimate 'lever' would force Julius Rosenberg to confess. At a secret meeting of the Joint Congressional Committee on Atomic Energy, attended by representatives of the Department of Justice including Assistant US Attorney Myles Lane, the latter stated that Julius Rosenberg was the 'keystone to a lot of other potential agents', including William Perl and Vivian Glassman, who were still at large. The Justice Department believed, Lane told the Committee, that 'the only thing that will break this man Rosenberg is the prospect of a death penalty or getting the chair, plus that if we can convict his wife too, and give her a sentence of 25 or 30 years, that combination may serve to make this fellow disgorge and give us the information on these other individuals. It is about the only weapon you can use as a lever on those people.' At the same time, Lane, who had interrogated both the Green-glasses at length, was obliged to admit that 'the case is not too strong against Mrs Rosenberg.' Nevertheless, he emphasised, 'it is very important that she be convicted too, and given a stiff sentence.'

Unfortunately, from the Justice Department's point of view, the evidence against Ethel was very flimsy, although she had been arrested and charged with conspiracy to commit espionage like her husband. On the other hand, Ruth Greenglass had not been indicted in accordance with the bargain struck by her counsel John Rogge with the prosecution, although she would be admitting from the witness stand that she was deeply implicated in the conspiracy herself.

Then, barely ten days before the trial was due to open, the Greenglasses completely changed their story by alleging that Ethel knew everything about her husband's part in handing over the atomic secrets to the Russians, since she had typed the incriminating material for him. This is merely described in the FBI papers so far released as 'additional informa-tion', whereas in fact it was in complete contradiction to what David Greenglass had stated about his meeting with Julius in September 1945 and his handing over the details and sketches of the atomic bomb in an unsealed envelope, as previously mentioned. Now, according to Ruth Greenglass, the material was handed over in the Rosenbergs' living room.

> Julius took the information into the bathroom and read it and when he came out he called Ethel and told her she had to type this information immediately. Ethel then sat down at the typewriter which he had placed on a bridge table in the living room and proceeded to type the information which David had given to Julius.

The reason why Ethel had to be called in to type the atom bomb material, so Greenglass told the FBI, was because his handwriting was very difficult to understand, and Ruth was to testify to this effect at the trial. Yet there were hundreds of David's letters to his wife in the FBI files, all of which are completely legible.[11]

Years later, when Stern and Radosh met the Greenglasses and pointed out that they never mentioned the incident of Ethel's typing until shortly before the trial, both expressed astonishment. 'You mean that was the first mention of it?' asked Ruth, while David exclaimed, 'Is that a fact?' At first David offered the explanation that at first he was trying to keep his sister out of the case. When asked how he eventually came to implicate her, he recalled that at one point the FBI men said to him: 'You came to Julius's apartment and you discussed all this stuff. Where was Ethel?' 'Yeah, she must have been around,' Greenglass told the agents, adding for the benefit of Stern and Radosh 'because obviously she was.'

Ruth was unable to remember any of the details of Ethel's typing. She knew they were told to the interrogators, but when she could not recall. 'I can't remember when I told them a particular thing.' Nor could she remember going over to the Rosenbergs' house for dinner in September 1945 when the atomic bomb sketches were supposedly handed over. 'I remember David bringing something and giving it in his [Julius's] house.' But whether it was in September 1945 again she could not remember. According to David's recollection, he [David] had already given Julius the sketches, and what he thought happened was that Julius later told him he should come over to his house, saying 'It's got to be typed.' As will be seen, this version was contrary to the account given by David in his trial testimony.

Finally both Greenglasses denied, at their interview with Stern and Radosh, that the law enforcement authorities had put any pressure on them to change their original story about Ethel's involvement in the conspiracy. But afterwards David made a significant admission to the effect that it was a choice between his wife and his sister, he would take his wife 'any day'. That was the choice he thought he had, he said. 'It was all in my mind,' he added. 'Nobody put pressure on me.'

The trial judge's questionable behaviour in his relations with the prosecution will be touched upon in their proper place.

[5]

The trial of the two Rosenbergs, husband and wife, and Morton Sobell on charges of conspiracy to commit acts of espionage contrary to the Espionage Act of 1917, for which the maximum penalty was death or imprisonment for a period not exceeding thirty years, opened in the Federal Court House in Foley Square, New York City, on 6 March 1951.[12] The presiding judge was the Hon. Irving R. Kaufman, a Jew, and one of the district judges for the Southern District of New York, who had recently tried Abraham Brothman and Miriam Moskowitz. He was known as 'the boy judge' since he was only thirty-nine when he had been appointed to the federal bench two years previously, having given up a remarkably successful law practice in which he was reputed to have been earning $100,000 a year. His father had been a manufacturer of tobacco humidifiers, and for some unknown reason which can only be surmised he sent him to Fordham, a Catholic university. He was reputed to live a quiet and even austere family life with his wife and three children in their Park Avenue apartment and he attended the local synagogue regularly. The prosecution was led by Irving H. Saypol, US Attorney for the Southern District, and he had with him five assistant US Attorneys, of whom one was Roy H. Cohn, who was to achieve an unenviable reputation as a Communist witch-hunter during the 'McCarthy era.' For the defence, Emanuel H. Bloch appeared for Julius Rosenberg and Bloch's father Alexander represented Ethel Rosenberg, while Morton Sobell was defended by Harold M. Phillips and Edward Kuntz. O. John Rogge held a watching brief for David Greenglass and his wife Ruth, who were both expected to testify for the prosecution. David had pleaded guilty but not yet come up for sentence, while Ruth had not been indicted and in fact never was.

A day and a half was devoted to selecting the jury, whose members were chosen from a panel of two hundred. All prospective jurors, twenty-nine in all, who were peremptorily challenged by the defence, were ordered to stand down. In the event the jury as empanelled consisted of eleven men and one woman, who were all approved in open court by the defence attorneys as being 'satisfactory'. Five prospective jurors with identifiably Jewish names asked to be excused from serving and their requests were granted in each instance by the Court.

After the three defendants had formally pleaded not guilty, the District Attorney opened the case for the prosecution. 'The significance of a conspiracy to commit espionage,' he said, speaking in deadly earnest tones, 'takes an added meaning here where the defendants are charged with having participated in a conspiracy against our country at the most critical hour in its history, in a time of war. . . . .'

The evidence will reveal to you how the Rosenbergs persuaded David Greenglass . . . to play the treacherous role of a modern Benedict Arnold while wearing the uniform of the United States Army. We will prove that the Rosenbergs devised and put into operation with the aid of Soviet nationals and Soviet agents in this country an elaborate scheme which enabled them, through Greenglass, to steal the one weapon which might well hold the key to the survival of this nation and the peace of the world—the atomic bomb.

The District Attorney gave due credit to the FBI for breaking the spy ring. At the same time he made it clear that this could not have been done had it not been for the information revealed by Klaus Fuchs, whom agents of the Bureau had been allowed by the British authorities to question in prison after his conviction. Fuchs had later been able to identify Harry Gold, whom he knew as 'Raymond', as his contact with the absent defendant Anatoli Yakovlev.

'What is the evidence of Sobell's participation here?' Saypol went on to ask, and proceeded to supply the answer to this rhetorical question. 'The evidence is that Sobell had been an associate of Julius Rosenberg since City College days. They were joined by the common bond of Communism and devotion to the Soviet Union . . . It is the Communist ideology which teaches worship and devotion to the Soviet Union over our own government

. . . to serve the interests of a foreign power which today seeks to wipe us off the face of the earth.'

On the defence lawyers protesting strongly at the District Attorney's dragging in the issue of Communism, as a result of which the jury might be misled or prejudiced against the defendants, the judge intervened to underline the real issue. 'The charge here is espionage,' he said to the jury. 'It is not that they are members of the Communist Party or that they had any interest in Communism. However, if the Government [i.e. the prosecution] intends to establish that they did have an interest in Communism, for the purpose of establishing a motive for what they were doing, I will, in due course, when that question arises, rule on that point.'

The first of the prosecution witnesses to be called to the stand was Max Elitcher, an electronics engineer who had worked in the US Navy Bureau of Ordnance between 1938 and 1948. Elitcher admitted to being a Communist and to have become a member of a 'cell' at Sobell's solicitation. It was also through Sobell, said the witness, that he had met the Rosenbergs and learned that they were active party members and secret Soviet agents. Julius Rosenberg, the witness went on, invited him to participate in the transmission of secret information from the ordnance office files. Elitcher swore that he pretended to do so, but in fact he had never given Rosenberg any information classified as secret. Under cross-examination, the witness admitted that he had lied when he took the loyalty oath, but he firmly insisted that 'ever since the FBI got hold of him he had told the entire truth.' Finally, Elitcher admitted that he had regularly acted as a courier between Sobell and Julius Rosenberg. But the only action which overtly suggested espionage was when Elitcher took a 35 mm reel or can of film from Sobell's house and they drove to a point near the Rosenbergs' house, where Sobell took the reel out of the glove compartment of the car and apparently delivered it to Rosenberg. Elitcher had not seen the contents of the can and he could not say what the film consisted of. During the previous four years when Elitcher had conversations with Sobell and Rosenberg, the subject was not more specific than 'this espionage business', or that Rosenberg 'needed somebody to work in the Navy Department for this espionage purpose.'

Elitcher was followed on the witness stand by David Greenglass, who with his wife Ruth was to be the principal prosecution witness, although they were self-confessed accomplices of the Rosenbergs. David's direct examination (examination-in-chief) was conducted by the twenty-four-year-old Assistant Attorney Roy Cohn. The latter began by questioning him about his early life and background and in particular his sister Ethel's marriage to Julius Rosenberg in 1939.

'You were seventeen years old at the time they were married? Is that correct?'

'That is correct.'

'Now did you have any discussion with Ethel and Julius concerning the relative method of our form of government and that of the Soviet Union?'

Upon the defence promptly objecting, Roy Cohn replied by citing the case of a convicted Nazi spy named Haupt. 'The Supreme Court held in sustaining a treason conviction, they held that the statements by the defendant showing sympathy with Germany and with Hitler and hostility to the United States were admissible as competent testimony.'

'What you are trying to bring out from the witness,' Judge Kaufman broke in helpfully, 'is that the defendants expressed some form of favourtism to Russia in their discussions?'

'Exactly, your Honour.'

'I believe it is relevant,' the judge ruled.

This ruling was unfortunate and ill-judged, as were others of Judge Kaufman's, since they tended to create the impression in the minds of the jury that the defendants were being tried for treason, though they lacked the constitutional safeguards in accusations of such a grave kind.

'I think you said these discussions with your sister began in 1935?' Cohn went on.

'I did,' replied the witness.

'When did they begin as far as the defendant Julius Rosenberg was concerned?'

'About 1937.'

'How frequently would they express their views regarding the relative merits of the two countries?'

'I would say two or three times a week.'

Thus it will be seen that, when the witness claimed to have had these discussions with his sister, he was only thirteen years old, and again the jury was asked to believe that Julius and Ethel, who were sweethearts, indulged in discussions of this kind with a fifteen-year-old boy several times a week.

'Talking about Socialism over Capitalism,' Cohn continued, 'did they specifically talk about Socialism as it existed in the Soviet Union and Capitalism as it existed here?'

'They did.'

'Which did they like better?' Cohn persisted. 'Did they tell you?'

Upon the defendants' counsel again protesting that this was a leading question and suggestive of a particular answer, the judge again came to the young Assistant Attorney's rescue. 'I will sustain the objection on that ground, which they like better,' said Judge Kaufman, who put the question himself to the witness. 'You tell us whether or not on any occasion they told you that they preferred one over another.'

'They preferred Socialism to Capitalism,' the witness replied.

'Which type of Socialism?' the judge went on to make it quite clear.

'Russian Socialism.'

Questioned about his time at Los Alamos, Greenglass stated that at first he did not know the nature of the atomic bomb project when he was posted there in 1944. All he knew was that, as a machinist, he was working on 'a secret device of some kind.' It was not until January 1945, after he had supplied the names of important scientists working on the project and given details of security measures in force at the plant, supplemented with a sketch of a high explosive lens mould, that the witness, then on leave in New York, first learned from Julius Rosenberg of the true nature of the project—'fissionable material at one end of a tube and on the other end a sliding mechanism with fissionable material, and when the two were brought together under tremendous pressure nuclear reaction was accomplished.' As far as it went, this description fitted the uranium bomb which was dropped on Hiroshima eight months later. It was allegedly typed out by Ethel Rosenberg.

A few days later, according to Greenglass, Julius Rosenberg introduced him to a Mrs Ann Sidorovich, who was expected to visit New Mexico to receive further atomic information. Because there was some doubt as to whether Mrs Sidorovich could undertake this assignment, a yellow Jello box-top was torn in half and one half given to David Greenglass, the idea being that the contact whom the courier was to meet in New Mexico would be given the other half, so that the two halves would eventually be seen to match.

In the following September, the witness and his wife, who was now living with her husband in Albuquerque, made a trip to New York. There the witness met Julius Rosenberg in the Rosenbergs' apartment, he said, and handed him a sketch of the atom bomb and a ten-page analysis which Ethel again typed out. 'This is *very* good,' said Julius when he read it. These particulars, according to David Greenglass, related to the plutonium bomb which was dropped on Nagasaki. The witness's testimony in this regard revealed so much expert knowledge that Judge Kaufman ordered the court to be cleared except for the press, and directed the newspaper reporters present 'to exercise discretion in what they printed.' Whether or not the witness's technical evidence was understood by the jury, it clearly established that on his own admission David Greenglass had been an effective spy. According to the witness, Julius also mentioned former espionage activities including a stolen proximity fuse, and he added later that he had transmitted other information to Russia, had subsidised college education for promising young contacts and engaged generally in espionage activities. After the war the witness together with Julius and two other partners had been engaged in an unsuccessful business venture.

The tension created in the court room by this witness's long recital of treachery was relieved by a small touch of humour at the close of his testimony. Asked in cross-examination whether, when looking at the Jello box-top, he had noticed the flavour, he promptly replied, 'Yes, raspberry.' This answer raised the only laugh throughout these sombre proceedings.

Ruth Greenglass, born Ruth Printz of a Hungarian father and a Polish mother, followed her husband on the witness stand. Besides generally corroborating her husband's testimony, Ruth described how in the autumn of 1944 Julius Rosenberg asked her to go to Los Alamos and obtain classified information from her husband, who was then working on the Los Alamos project. At first she demurred, she said, but Julius assured her that her husband would be willing to co-operate. Russia was an ally of the US, Julius argued, and as such deserved information about the atomic bomb, but the Soviet authorities were not getting the information they should. Eventually, said Ruth, she agreed to make the trip as her second wedding anniversary was coming up and she wished to spend it with her husband. Julius gave her $150 for her trip, saying the money came from 'his friends the Russians.'

According to the witness, her husband was at first reluctant to co-operate, but next morning he agreed to give her 'the general layout of the Los Alamos project', together with the number of employees, the experiments being conducted and the names of the scientists working there. Ruth Greenglass carefully memorised this information, she said, and duly passed it on to Julius Rosenberg on her return to New York. Ruth Greenglass went on to describe the alleged meeting with her husband when on leave in January 1945 with Mrs Sidorovich and the two Rosenbergs in the latter's apartment, when Julius produced the Jello box-top which was torn in half. She remembered, when her husband commented on the simplicity and cleverness of this device as a means of identification, that Julius Rosenberg remarked, 'The simplest things are always the cleverest.' She then described the contact made in Albuquerque in June 1945 when a man called early one morning and, producing the matching piece of the Jello top, said, 'I come from Julius.' Ruth Greenglass identified him as Harry Gold, adding that he gave her husband $500, which he handed over to her.

By May 1950, the witness continued, she and her husband, who had been discharged from the army, were back in New York, and their relations with the Rosenbergs were closer than ever, particularly as Julius and David were in business together. On 24 May, according to Ruth Greenglass, Julius Rosenberg burst into her apartment brandishing a copy of the New York *Herald Tribune*, which carried a picture of Harry Gold on the front page accompanied by the news of his arrest as a Soviet spy. 'You will be next,' said Julius and urged her and David to escape at once to Mexico. Ruth did not think their ten-month-old baby could stand the trip, but Julius Rosenberg brushed her doubts aside and left $1000 with her and her husband to cover preliminary expenses, telling her to have passport photographs taken and to be inoculated against smallpox. But in spite of these warnings the Greenglasses stayed in New York and on 15 June David was arrested.

In cross-examination Julius Rosenberg's counsel Emanuel Bloch tried to bring out that the witness knew she had committed a crime and that the evidence she had just given had been influenced by fear of the FBI. 'Weren't you frightened of the FBI?'

'Everyone is frightened of the FBI,' Ruth Greenglass replied, 'but it was not because I realised it was a crime that I was frightened. I didn't think the FBI wanted my husband. I thought they wanted someone my husband would lead them to, someone much more important than he and much more deeply involved.'

The next prosecution witness was Harry Gold. He told how he had been working for the Russians as far back as 1935, and how in 1944 he acted as a go-between for Russian agents and persons who procured information for them. At that time, he said, his Soviet superior was Anatoli Yakovlev, but the witness only knew him as 'John'. (He identified him from a photograph admitted in evidence.) It was at Yakovlev's instruction that in June 1944 the witness first met Dr Fuchs, who promised to give him information 'relating to the application of nuclear fission to the production of a military weapon.' At a subsequent meeting in Cambridge, Mass., early in 1945, Fuchs told the witness that he was working on the atomic bomb with other scientists in Los Alamos, which he described, particularly mentioning a lens which was one of its essential parts. It was agreed between them that Gold should visit Los Alamos in June, when Fuchs hoped to have more information about the bomb and its lens.

When Gold told Yakovlev of this, the Soviet master spy intimated that he had another very 'vital' job for him in New Mexico, namely to contact Greenglass in Albuquerque. At first the witness objected, he said, but when Yakovlev insisted he agreed, since he took this to be an order. After he had seen Fuchs and obtained a sealed envelope from him, Gold went on to Albuquerque where he met the Greenglasses as already described and received another envelope from them. A few days later, he reported to Yakovlev in Brooklyn, handing over the two envelopes which the Soviet Vice-Consul later told him 'contained extremely excellent and very valuable information.' The witness's last meeting with Yakovlev took place at the end of 1946, the day before Yakovlev sailed for Europe with his family.

Yet at the Brothman trial nine months previously Gold had testified that Yakovlev had not attached much importance to what Greenglass had given him. 'I turned the information over to John,' he said. 'John never mentioned anything about it, and on the one occasion that I did mention this man [Greenglass] in the late fall of 1945, John said that we should forget all about him, that there wasn't much point in getting in touch with him. And I got from the manner in which he made the remark, that

apparently the information received had not been of very much consequence at all.'

At the same trial Gold gave a different version of the password which he
used when he met the Greenglasses in Albuquerque. 'I believe,' he said on
that occasion, 'that it involved the name of a man and was something of the
order of 'Bob sent me', or 'Benny sent me' or 'John sent me', or something
like that.'

It may be asked, how did the names Bob or Benny or John evolve into
Julius? The answer was subsequently supplied by an FBI agent named
Richard Brennan when he recalled an interview he had with Harry Gold
before the Rosenberg trial came on, no doubt in the 'Singing Quarters' of
the Tombs prison in New York:

> He used the expression 'Benny sent me', which was the best he could
> recall at the time. Subsequently, when the trial of Greenglass led to
> Rosenberg, we asked him—Miller and myself or one of the
> others—'Could it have been Julie sent or Julius sent me?' And imm-
> ediately he brightened up with a great light. 'Yes, that is it. It wasn't
> Benny, it was Julius sent me.'

In the Rosenberg trial Gold was not cross-examined. These were good
tactics on the part of Sobell's attorneys, since Gold's testimony had not
implicated their client in any way. As for the Rosenbergs' counsel, they may
well have decided not to cross-examine, because Gold had shown himself
eager to help the Government in any way he could, and his answers elicited
in cross-examination might only have made matters worse for the two
Rosenbergs.

Several other material witnesses testified to the value of the information
imparted by Greenglass as being of 'inestimable value to a nation which did
not possess the secret of nuclear fission.' If the Rosenbergs and Sobell had
committed the crime they were charged with, they said, their actions
seriously jeopardised the security of the United States. One of the expert
witnesses was Walter Koski, a physical chemist who had worked at Los
Alamos in secret research on implosion. Shown three prosecution exhibits-
—replicas recently drawn by Greenglass from memory of lens mould
sketches he allegedly had turned over to Rosenberg and Gold in January
and June 1945, Koski agreed with the District Attorney that the replicas
were 'reasonably accurate.' In cross-examination by Emanuel Bloch, he also
agreed that Greenglass was 'a plain, ordinary machinist.' The sketches were
'rough', he said, but they did 'illustrate the important principle involved.'
Asked by Judge Kaufman if the substance of his testimony was that, while
the sketches might omit some details useful to a foreign nation, they did
reveal to an expert what was going on at Los Alamos, the witness again
agreed.

It was unfortunate that the defence did not (or possibly could not) call any expert evidence in rebuttal. Many years later, a reporter on the London *Sunday Times* showed reproductions of both the bomb and lens mould sketches to two distinguished American scientists, George Kistiakovsky, Professor Emeritus of Chemistry at Harvard, and Victor Weisskopf, Professor of Physics at the Massachusetts Institute of Technology. Weisskopf described the bomb sketch as 'ridiculous, a baby drawing, it doesn't tell you anything.' Kistiakovsky described the same sketch as 'uselessly crude', and at the same time added that the value of the lens mould sketches would have been 'almost nil' to the Russians.

The last of the non-formal witnesses was the notorious Communist informer Elizabeth Bentley. She swore that, while she was working for the Communists, one of the contacts who often telephoned her, was a man whose only identification was 'Julius.' She did not know who he was, and in cross-examination admitted that she could not identify the caller's voice as that of Julius Rosenberg.

Although over one hundred witnesses were subpoenaed by the prosecution, including Dr J. Robert Oppenheimer and Dr Harold C. Urey, the two American scientists most responsible for the Los Alamos project, only eighteen witnesses were actually called and they did not include either Oppenheimer or Urey. The final Government witness was the Immigration Officer at Laredo, Texas, who had admitted Sobell and his wife to the US and had noted on the relevant paper 'Deported from Mexico.' This statement was quite untrue, since the Sobells had been kidnapped in Mexico City, probably by the FBI or their agents and forcibly transported across the border. Nevertheless the judge admitted the paper with its significant notation as an exhibit in evidence.

It was at this dramatic point in the record, that the chief prosecutor announced: 'The Government rests, if the Court please.'

[6]

Emanuel Bloch opened the defence by calling Julius Rosenberg to the witness stand. Answering his attorney, Rosenberg admitted that he was a first-generation American of Russian parents who had migrated to New York City. He was a Bachelor of Science, having graduated from New York City College. He told how he married Ethel Greenglass and in 1940 became a junior engineer in the US Signals Corps, from which he was dismissed five years later.

'Did you ever have any conversation with Ruth Greenglass about November 1944 with respect to getting information from David Greenglass at the place where he was working?'

'I did not.'

'Did you know in the middle of 1944 where David Greenglass was stationed?'

'I did not.'

'Did you know in the middle of 1944 that there was such a project known as the Los Alamos project?'

'I did not.'

'Did you ever give Ruth Greenglass $150, or any other sum for her to go out to visit her husband at Los Alamos for the purpose of trying to enlist him in espionage work?'

'I did not.'

Julius Rosenberg denied everything. Shown the sketch of the atomic bomb that David Greenglass had made, the witness denied that his brother-in-law had ever delivered such a sketch to him. 'I never saw this sketch before.' Apart from what he had heard in court, he could not describe the bomb. Nor had he ever taken a course in nuclear or advanced physics. He also denied all knowledge of the Jello box-top; he had never introduced David Greenglass to a Mrs Sidorovich; he had never met Elizabeth Bentley and had never spoken to her on the telephone. Nor had he tried to induce the Greenglasses to leave the country and he had not provided them with money for their trip. Finally he denied that he and his wife had ever contemplated fleeing the country themselves.

Asked in cross-examination by Saypol whether he had been discharged from his job in the Signals Corps because he was suspected of being a Communist and thus belonging to an illegal organisation, he was obliged to admit that this was so.

'Were you a member of the Communist party?' the District Attorney asked bluntly.

Rosenberg paused for a few moments before deciding to invoke the Fifth Amendment. 'I refuse to answer,' he replied, 'on the grounds that it might tend to incriminate me.'

He repeated this reply when confronted with a statement he had signed on joining the Signals Corps to the effect that he was not then and never had been a member of the Communist party. The Court sustained the witness's objection to tendentiously incriminating questions and ruled that he was not required to answer them.

In her evidence Ruth Greenglass had sworn that on the night the Jello box was cut up Ethel Rosenberg had told her that Julius was running around 'a good deal' and using up his energy 'in this thing' (espionage work). She added that 'he had to make a good impression; that sometimes it cost him as much as $50 to $75 an evening to entertain his friends.'

The District Attorney took this point up in his cross-examination of Julius by asking him how many night clubs and 'high class restaurants' the witness had made 'a habit of going to.' Yes, Julius agreed, he had been to a night club.

'What night club?' asked Attorney Saypol.

'Well,' said Julius, 'the Federation of Architects had a dinner party at Café Society.'

'Was that the only night club you were ever at?'

'That is the only night club I ever attended.'

'Did you ever go to restaurants where the prices were expensive?' the District Attorney went on.

'Yes, I did.'

'How many?'

'Well, once when I was taking my wife out, to a place near Emerson Radio called Pappas, and on another occasion I have eaten at a place called Nicholaus on Second Avenue.' He had also eaten at a place called Manny Wolf's about ten years ago when he was working for a radio company and the management invited him and other employees to that establishment 'for dinner and for a show.'

That was the height of the Rosenbergs' expensive dining out, and the prosecution made no attempt to contradict it, seeing that Julius Rosenberg's earnings in the Signal Corps amounted to $52.75 a week, and he paid a month's rent of $45.75 for his three-room apartment. The 'best piece of furniture' was a second-hand book case which an executive of the Jefferson Radio Company had given Julius for $5, the cost of transporting it to the little apartment in Knickerbocker Village. Julius's only overcoat, bought ten years before the trial, had cost $55, while none of the few suits he possessed cost more than $26. During the ten years of his marriage, his wife Ethel's clothes cost around $300, including an $80 'fur coat'. In fact, though they were very happy, their home life frequently bordered on poverty, and it must have riled them to hear the prosecution depicting Julius as directing a criminal espionage conspiracy, financed by a seemingly endless supply of Moscow gold.

At the same time, in answer to further questions in cross-examination, Julius protested his loyalty to the United States. 'I will fight for this country if it were engaged in war with any other country,' he declared. On the other hand, he admitted that he felt some admiration for the achievements of the Russians, particularly in improving the lot of the underdog. 'I felt and still feel,' he added, 'that they contributed a major share in destroying the Hitler beast who killed six million of my co-religionists, and I feel emotional about that thing.'

Judge Kaufman intervened at this point to ask the witness a couple of questions which Julius understandably tried to evade, since the judge had now decided to admit questions about the defendant's Communist associations, even asking them himself.

'Did you approve the Communist system of Russia over the Capitalist system of this country?'

'I am not an expert in these things, your Honour, and I did not make any such statement.'

'Did you ever belong to any group that discussed the system of Russia?'

Again the witness took refuge behind the protective constitutional amendment. 'Well, your Honour,' he said, 'I feel at this time that I refuse to answer a question which might tend to incriminate me.'

Julius Rosenberg was also asked in cross-examination about Vivian Glassman. She had been introduced to him and his wife, he said, by Joel Barr, whose 'sweetheart' she was. After Barr went to Europe she had continued to visit the Rosenbergs' home, as she was a social worker and was being consulted about the emotional problems of the elder Rosenberg son. As a result of their talks, the boy had been given treatment by the Jewish Board of Guardians, with which Miss Glassman worked.

'What else did you talk to Vivian Glassman about?' asked prosecuting counsel.

'I had nothing else to talk to her about but that,' replied the witness.

'Did you ever give her any money?'

'No, sir, never did.'

'Did you ever send her on a trip to Cleveland?'

'No, sir, never did,' the witness repeated.

'Isn't it the fact that you gave her $2000 to take out to somebody in Cleveland?'

'That is not the fact, Mr Saypol.'

The prosecutor continued this line of questioning. Yet Miss Glassman, oddly enough, was not called to testify about the alleged incident, although she was listed as a witness.

Julius Rosenberg was also questioned about Alfred Sarant.

'Where did you first meet him?'

'I met him when he was introduced to me by his friend Joel Barr. I met him in an apartment they were using in Greenwich Village.'

'Where was that?'

'I don't recall the exact name of the street. It begins with an M.'

'65 Morton Street, isn't it?' Saypol suggested.

'Morton,' Julius agreed. 'That is the place. Morton Street'

Asked about Sarant's present whereabouts, Julius replied, 'In Ithaca.'

'How do you know he is in Ithaca now?'

'Well, I saw the name of his wife on the witness list, and the address is given as Ithaca.'

'You have no other knowledge of his whereabouts, is that it?'

'I have no way of knowing.'

'Don't you know that he is in Mexico?' asked the District Attorney.

This question brought an immediate objection from the defence. One of Sobell's attorneys pointed out that the cross-examination was 'deliberately prejudicial' because Sarant 'was never mentioned in this case' and all through the trial the word 'Mexico' had implied flight.

By this means the prosecution succeeded in connecting five of Julius Rosenberg's friends and former class-mates—Mrs Sidorovich, Barr, Glassman, William Perl and Sarant—with the alleged espionage ring, particularly in the context of the premises at 65 Morton Street. Yet not a single one of the five was indicted, named as a co-conspirator or even called as a witness.

'The identity of some of the other traitors who sold their country down the river along with Rosenberg and Sobell remains undisclosed,' the prosecuting attorney added in his closing speech. 'We know that such people exist because of Rosenberg's boasting to Greenglass of the extent of his espionage activities. . . . We know of these other henchmen of Rosenberg . . . We don't know all the details, because the only living people who can supply the details are the defendants.'

Ethel Rosenberg, Julius's wife and co-defendant, corroborated her husband's evidence generally. Asked by her counsel about her life-style, this was the reverse of luxurious, she said, and apart from one brief period when she had some domestic help, following the birth of her children and when she was ill, she did all the chores of a housewife, cooking, washing, cleaning, darning and scrubbing. She blandly asserted that she was a loyal citizen of the United States and had never engaged in espionage. Everything her brother and sister-in-law had testified to was false, she declared emphatically. She admitted that she did some typing for her husband, business letters as well as his reinstatement appeal to the Signal Corps following his dismissal, but she was quite positive that she had never at any time typed anything relating to national defence.

At this point the judge took a hand. 'Did you know,' he asked her, 'anything about the charges that had been levelled against your husband by the Government [the Signal Corps] in 1945?'

'Well,' Ethel replied, 'it was alleged that he was a member of the Communist Party.'

'Now, you typed the reply from him,' Judge Kaufman went on. 'Is that right?'

'Yes.'

'And the reply that you typed for him denied that he was a Communist? Is that correct?'

'That is correct.'

'And was that true?'

The witness hesitated for a moment or two, as if playing for time, and then asked the judge 'Was what true?'

'The statement that you typed,' the judge repeated, 'that he is not a Communist?'

'I refuse to answer on the ground of self-incrimination,' the witness declared firmly.

'All right,' said the judge. It was little wonder that Judge Kaufman gave vent to this expression of satisfaction, since by this time pleading the Fifth Amendment had become tantamount to an admission of Communist membership or at least to being a fellow traveller.

The judge's assumed rôle of prosecutor was taken up by District Attorney Saypol who concentrated in his cross-examination upon Ethel Rosenberg's admission before the Grand Jury that she signed a petition in 1941 nominating a Communist Party candiate for City Councilman. Although this had no possible bearing on espionage, the petition was admitted by the court as a prosecution exhibit.

'Let me ask you this,' the judge again intervened. 'Did you tell the Grand Jury the entire truth when you testified?'

'Yes.'

Finally the District Attorney asked the witness whether she had discussed 'any other crime' with her defending counsel.

'No crime that I could have committed,' was her courageous concluding answer, 'because I didn't commit any.'

This concluded the case for the defence, since on his attorney's advice Morton Sobell did not testify. The only evidence against him came from the self-admitted perjurer Elitcher, and furthermore Sobell had not been charged with atomic espionage. He would have been better advised to have taken the stand and firmly denied Elitcher's accusations, even though the onus was not upon him to establish his innocence. But such a line would probably have made a favourable impression upon the jury.

The prosecution now called two witnesses in rebuttal. The first was Mrs Evelyn Cox, a Negro maid, who had worked as a domestic help and cleaner for Ethel Rosenberg in 1944 and 1945. Her role was to confirm the testimony given by the Greenglasses that a certain console table which originally came from Macy's store had been given to her husband by the Russians. But all she could say was that she understood that it had been a gift from 'a friend'. The maid never looked under the table, she said, and had never noticed anything unusual about it. Nor could she confirm Ruth Greenglass's charge that the table had a hollowed-out portion for concealing microfilms, although Mrs Cox must have cleaned the table from time to time. Shortly after first seeing the table she noticed that it had been put in a closet in the Rosenberg apartment. She asked Ethel Rosenberg why the table was in the closet and if she could put it back in the living room. Mrs Rosenberg told her to leave the table in the closet 'as it was too large for the living room.' She thought that was a curious statement since the table was no larger than three and a half feet by one and a half feet. However, she added, since it was Mrs Rosenberg's table, she did not press the matter further.

The other rebuttal witness was a commercial photographer, Bob Schneider, whose shop at 99 Park Row was in Knickerbocker Village, where the Rosenbergs lived. His name did not figure among the names of the 102 persons whom the prosecution originally announced they might call. This was contrary to the statute that all Government witnesses must be named before the start of a trial for the information of the defence. Attorney Saypol's excuse was that the prosecution was unaware of Schneider's existence until the day before he testified. On that day, he said, two FBI agents had come to his shop and shown him photographs of the Rosenbergs. He told the FBI, he went on, that he was positive the Rosenbergs had come to his shop with their two children one Saturday in May or June 1950 and had ordered three dozen passport photos at a cost of nine dollars. According to this witness, Julius had told him they were going to France to look at some property which Mrs Rosenberg had been left there. As the Rosenberg children were 'sort of unruly' and the witness was afraid they would 'spoil or mess something up', the witness told them all to come back in twenty minutes to half an hour.

'Did you then deliver the photos to Mr Rosenberg?' asked Saypol.

'Yes, sir,' the witness replied.

'And that is the last time you saw him before today?'

'That's right.'

'Now when the agents came to visit you yesterday, did they show you photographs?'

'They did.'

'Was it from those photographs that you picked him [Rosenberg] out?'

'That's right.'

'And is it seeing him here with his wife that recalls to your memory that they were the persons who came in?'

'That's right,' the photographer agreed. 'That's right.'

It subsequently transpired that Schneider's statement to the effect that he had not seen Julius Rosenberg between the day he came to his shop five years previously and the day the photographer testified was untrue. The truth was revealed, probably inadvertently by Saypol's confidential press agent, Oliver Pilat, in a book he wrote two years after the trial. The crucial passage was as follows:

> *While Julius was still on the stand, an FBI agent brought into the courtroom a photographer* from a shop hardly a block away who recalled somebody resembling the description of Rosenberg, with two wild kids, coming in for passport photos. He wanted to look at Rosenberg *to be sure*, and when he took the look, he nodded. [Author's italics.][13]

Unfortunately, Emanuel Bloch did not discover this until Pilat's book appeared. Nevertheless, he did underline what his client had stated in direct testimony that during his walks with his children he had often visited photographers' shops to have their pictures taken which he would keep in albums, and this accounted for the considerable number of such pictures seized by the FBI when the Rosenbergs' apartment was searched. Furthermore, in his direct evidence the photographer claimed that he remembered the Rosenbergs' visit clearly since it was on a Saturday when he did not usually keep his shop open. Yet he flatly contradicted this under cross-examination when he admitted that he kept his shop open every Saturday for at least ten weeks in the year including May and June.

Again, when asked by the District Attorney: 'What do you do mainly?' the witness replied: 'Passport photographs and identification photographs.' And yet, in cross-examination, on being asked by Julius Rosenberg's counsel to describe the signs outside the shop, the witness answered: 'I have a display in the window, marked 'Photographs, signs and photostats.' '

'Do you have in your window pictures of weddings?' asked Emanuel Bloch.'

'That's right.'

'Do you have pictures of brides and grooms?'

'That's right.'

'That is your advertising?'

'Yes, that's right,' the witness again agreed.

'Do you have signs in front of your store, in red, with white lettering, called 'Photos'?' counsel went on.

'That's right.'

'Do you have any large sign on the outside, saying 'Passport photos'?'

'Well, no,' Mr Schneider admitted. 'I haven't got that.'

Thus Julius Rosenberg's counsel was able to demonstrate clearly that Schneider's claim to specialise in passport photographs was belied by the fact that no one passing his shop would normally choose it for such a purpose.

In his closing speech to the jury on behalf of the Rosenbergs, Emanuel Bloch concentrated on the unreliability of Ruth and David Greenglass as witnesses. 'Don't you think that the Greenglasses put it over on the Government when Ruth Greenglass was not even indicted?' he asked the jurors. 'She walked out and put Greenglass's sister in. David Greenglass was willing to bury his sister and her husband to save his life. Not only are the Greenglasses self-confessed spies, but they are mercenary spies. They'll do anything for money . . . Any man who will testify against his own flesh and blood, his own sister, is repulsive, revolting, and is violating any code of civilisation that ever existed. He is lower than the lowest animal I have ever seen.'

'The Greenglasses have told the truth,' said District Attorney Saypol in winding up for the prosecution. 'They have tried to make amends for the hurt which has been done to our nation and to the world.' As for the other major prosecution witness, Harry Gold, said the prosecutor, he could gain nothing by testifying as he did except the inward relief of having told the truth. 'Harry Gold forged the link that points indisputably to the guilt of the Rosenbergs, and he was not even asked one question in cross-examination.' In reality, the DA continued, the unreliable testimony came from the Rosenbergs, who had denied planning to leave the country, in spite of the testimony about the passport photographs. 'The Rosenbergs have magnified their treachery by lying here.' Furthermore they were linked with Sobell in their espionage activities, since Sobell had flown to Mexico with his family in the same month that Greenglass had been paid by the Russians through Rosenberg to do likewise. 'Sobell's conduct fits the pattern of membership in this conspiracy and flight from an American jury when the day of reckoning had come.'

Regrettably the judge's charge to the jury, which now followed, was partial and unfair. For example, he devoted three times as much time to dealing with the prosecution's case as he did to that of the defence, dismissing the latter with the words: 'You have heard their summation and therefore I will not discuss their contentions further.' His explanation of the Greenglasses' principal motive was frankly prejudicial, when he told the jury that the Greenglasses' testimony against the Rosenbergs was 'due to the trouble they had with the Greenglasses while in business together, or for some other unknown reason.' Yet over and over again defence counsel had urged the judge to instruct the jury that the Greenglasses were alleged accomplices and co-conspirators, and that therefore their credibility must be scrutinised with 'the utmost care, caution and suspicion.'

'It is not sufficient,' the judge was reminded in the words of a recent judgment, 'that an instruction be so drawn that a jury may reach the right conclusion, but it is required that it be framed in such a way that a jury may not draw the wrong conclusion therefrom.' However, the judge flatly refused to charge the jury in the language that Emanuel Bloch had asked for. In fact only a brief mention was made of the testimony of the accomplices, Gold and the Greenglasses. Indeed Judge Kaufman virtually approved of their evidence when he stated:

> In the Federal Court a defendant can be convicted upon the uncorroborated testimony of an accomplice whose testimony satisfies the jury of the defendants' guilt beyond a reasonable doubt.

The judge neglected to warn the jury, as he should have done, of the danger of convicting on such uncorroborated testimony, which they should accept carefully and warily, and he did not even mention the defence's major contention that the Greenglasses had lied in order to save their own skins.

When the judge had finished, Bloch walked up to the Bench and out of the jury's hearing asked him to make the point about corroboration clear to the jury, but Judge Kaufman refused to add anything to his summing up. He was in a hurry, he said. 'I want to send the jury out right away.'

The jury retired at 4.53 p.m. on 28 March, and after spending the night under lock and key in a hotel they came back to court at eleven o'clock next morning, when they pronounced all three defendants guilty.

'This case is important,' said the judge in expressing his 'deepest gratitude' to the jury for their verdict and the time they had spent in arriving at it. 'It is important to the Government of the United States . . . The thought that citizens of our country would lend themselves to the destruction of their own country by the most destructive weapon known to man is so shocking that I can't find words to describe this loathsome offence.' Finally the FBI got a big pat on the back. 'Again I say a great tribute is due to the FBI and Mr Hoover for the splendid job that they have done in this case.' And to the jury he gave a final benediction: 'You have shown your recognition of your duty as citizens . . . God bless you all!'

The three defendants were thereupon removed by the deputy marshals to come up for sentencing, the date being set for a week later.

During this week the trial judge conferred with a member of the prosecution team, namely Assistant US Attorney Roy Cohn. This is confirmed by a memorandum dated 3 April from Edgar Hoover to one of his principal aides, Mr D. M. Ladd, in the recently released FBI papers. According to Cohn when he saw the judge, Hoover stated, 'Judge Kaufman personally favoured sentencing Julius and Ethel Rosenberg to death and that he would give a prison term to Morton Sobell.' The memorandum goes on:

> Assistant United States Attorney Cohn reportedly indicated to Judge Kaufman that he thought the death penalty for the Rosenbergs and Morton Sobell was in order, but at the same time he was of the opinion that if Mrs Rosenberg was sentenced to a prison term there was a possibility that she would talk and additional prosecutions could be had on the basis of her evidence. Cohn also indicated that he favoured sentencing Greenglass to fifteen years' imprisonment. Kaufman replied that it was his intention to add five years to any sentence which was recommended by the Government concerning Greenglass.

Some weeks previously, on 16 March, the day after the trial opened, A. H. Belmont, another top agent of the Bureau, was talking about the case to Mr Ray Whearty, a senior official in the Department of Justice, when Whearty commented that if Julius Rosenberg was convicted he thought Kaufman would send Rosenberg to the electric chair. Asked why he thought Kaufman would impose the death penalty, Whearty replied: 'I know he will if he does not change his mind.' This would suggest that the judge had consulted the Justice Department before the case began. It is confirmed by a statement from Mr Gordon Dean, Chairman of the Atomic Energy Commission, to the effect that on 7 February 1951, Mr James McInerney, Assistant Attorney General in charge of the Criminal Division of the Justice Department, had informed Mr Dean that he had talked to Judge Kaufman and that the judge had indicated that he was prepared to impose the death sentence 'if the evidence warrants.'

Yet, when it came to the sentencing, the judge prefaced his remarks with the following:

> Because of the seriousness of this case and the lack of precedents, I have refrained from asking the Government for a recommendation. The responsibility is so great that I believe the Court alone should assume this responsibility.

This statement requires some qualification if we can accept what the prosecutor Irving Saypol wrote many years later to Mr Clarence Kelley, Hoover's successor as Director of the FBI, on 13 March 1975, rebutting the statement which had recently been made on the opening of some of the FBI files on the case that 'prosecutors in the Rosenberg case originally opposed asking for the death penalty but were overruled by Truman Administration officials in Washington.'[14]

'I was never overruled by anybody,' Saypol, by that date a New York state judge, assured Mr Kelley. 'No one in Justice or out ever directed me, let alone overruled me in the matter of recommendation of sentence.' Saypol's letter continued:

> I was the only prosecutor in the Rosenberg case. While some of my assistants assisted in preparation for trial and I let four of them examine some of the witnesses, I took the lead. All policy decisions were mine and mine alone. Advice I sought and took, but I repeat, final decision was always mine.
>
> On the matter of the Rosenberg sentences, I had decided to make the recommendations which later were imposed. I made no recommendation at sentence at the direction of the sentencing judge, in these circumstances. The day before sentence he asked for my views. I gave them and he inquired regarding the views of the Department of Justice. I had not solicited any. He asked me to seek these. I flew to Washington, met with the late Deputy Attorney General Peyton Ford and the late Assistant Attorney General in charge of the Criminal Division, James McInerney. They conveyed the views of your predecessor J. Edgar Hoover. There were differences all around among them, but capital punishment for one or both was in not out. I left to return to New York, asked to telephone to

Peyton Ford that night for final verdict on possible reconciliation of their views. I did so but the Washington situation remained at variance. It was at a public function that night that I phoned Mr Ford in the presence of the judge who was attending the same event. Upon narrating to him the Washington division I was then asked by the judge to refrain from making any recommendation for punishment the next day in the course of my closing statement at sentence.

This explains Saypol's silence on the question of sentence next day. On the other hand, contrary to what Judge Kaufman said in his opening remarks, he did seek the views of the Justice Department in Washington, but apparently they were not unanimous. We also know from a memorandum dictated by Hoover on 2 April, three days before the Rosenbergs were due to come up for sentencing, that 'the Attorney General stated that he, personally, felt that they should not ask for the death sentence for Ethel Rosenberg, but he felt it should be asked for Julius Rosenberg.'[15]*

---

* According to David C. Martin of *Newsweek*, intelligence obtained by American cryptanalysts from radio messages between Moscow and New York provided 'convincing evidence' of the guilt of the Rosenbergs, but it was never publicly revealed and used by the prosecution in court to enable the government to protect the secrecy of these coded intercepts. 'The Rosenbergs were identified only by cryptonyms, but the picture that emerged of a husband-and-wife team of agents matched them precisely, even down to the fact that the woman's brother was part of the plot.' See David C. Martin, *Wilderness of Mirrors* (1980), at p. 42. Unfortunately the author does not give the source of this information, nor the text of any of the relevant intercepts, which presumably came from the CIA. The FBI papers on the Rosenberg case so far released which I have seen give no indication of this alleged top-secret source.

CHAPTER FIVE

Were They Guilty?

[1]

'I consider your crime worse than murder,' said Judge Irving Kaufman to the Rosenbergs in passing sentence on 9 April 1951.

> In murder a criminal kills only his victim. Your conduct in putting into the hands of the Russians the A-bomb years before our best scientists predicted Russia would perfect the bomb has already caused, in my opinion, the Communist aggression in Korea, with the resultant casualties exceeding 50,000, and who knows but that millions more of innocent people may pay the price of your treason. Indeed by your betrayal you have altered the course of history to the disadvantage of our country. We have evidence of your treachery all around us every day—for the civilian activities throughout the nation are aimed at preparing us for an atom bomb attack.[1]

The judge went on to describe Julius Rosenberg as 'the prime mover in this conspiracy', as clearly indicated by the evidence. 'However, let no mistake be made about the rôle his wife Ethel Rosenberg played in this conspiracy,' he added. 'Instead of deterring him from pursuing his ignoble course, she encouraged and assisted the cause. She was a mature woman—almost three years older than her husband and almost seven years older than her younger brother. She was a full-pledged partner in this crime.'

Particularly severe as well as patently unjust was the judge's remark that the two Rosenbergs were unworthy parents. 'Indeed the defendants Julius and Ethel Rosenberg were conscious that they were sacrificing their own children,' Judge Kaufman declared. 'Love for their cause dominated their lives—it was even greater than their love for their children.' On the contrary both parents had made their two boys the focus of their lives—if anything, they were excessively devoted to them, as is borne out by their letters to each other and their concern for the boys' 'precious future.'

> I have deliberated for hours, days and nights [the judge continued] I have carefully weighed the evidence . . . I am convinced beyond any doubt of

your guilt. I have searched the records—I have searched my conscience to find some reason for mercy . . . It is not in my power, Julius and Ethel Rosenberg, to forgive you. Only the Lord can find mercy for what you have done.

'The sentence of the Court upon Julius and Ethel Rosenberg is for the crime for which you have been convicted,' Judge Kaufman concluded. 'You are hereby sentenced to the punishment of death, and it is hereby ordered upon some day within the week beginning with Monday, 21 May you shall be executed according to law.' At that time the death penalty in the state of New York was carried out (as it still is) by electrocution.

Finally it was Sobell's turn. 'I do not for a moment doubt that you were engaged in espionage,' said the judge in sentencing him; 'however the evidence in the case did not point to any activity on your part in connection with the atom bomb project. . . . There isn't any doubt about your guilt, but I must recognise the lesser degree of your implication in this offence.' He accordingly sentenced this defendant to the maximum prison term provided by the statute, namely thirty years, with a recommendation against any parole—in effect a life sentence.

Both the Rosenbergs were then taken down to the courthouse cells, while Sobell was transferred to the Tombs prison. As Julius wondered about Sobell's destination, one of the deputy marshals told him that his office was awaiting instructions from Washington to transfer him and his wife to the death house in Sing Sing prison that every evening. In the belief that this was merely another tactic to break their spirit, Julius called out to his wife through the bars: 'Ethel! Don't be scared if some clown tells you we may be taken to the death house tonight! Everything will be all right—they can't do that.' Sing Sing was, in fact, a state prison, and since the Rosenbergs had been condemned for a federal offence, it would necessarily take a little time before the federal authorities could, if they so wished, make arrangements with the state authorities to borrow the condemned cells and death chamber at Sing Sing, which was located at Ossining, about thirty miles up the Hudson river in New York State.

Ethel Rosenberg, who had once studied singing and had a fine voice, thereupon gave her husband a message of hope from Puccini's opera *Madam Butterfly* by singing the famous aria '*Un Bel Di Vedremo*' (One Fine Day He Shall Return). According to one of the other inmates, she sang it in true pitch and tone without the slightest tremor or quaver. Even the marshal's deputies joined the prisoners when they spontaneously applauded her.

Suddenly her husband's voice was heard again shouting to her, 'Ethel, sing the other aria too!' This, an evident favourite of his, was '*O, Dolce Notte*' from the same opera, and she sang it so beautifully that one of the inmates who heard her thought he was at a concert rather than under lock and key in the courthouse 'bull pen.' One of the deputy marshals who also heard her walked over to Julius's cell and said to him on the spur of the moment: 'Julie, they've marked you upstairs a low-down son-of-a-gun. But down here you're the luckiest man in the world—because no man ever had a woman who loved him that much!'

'Thanks,' Julius replied quietly, but with a touch of bitterness in his voice. 'But look at it this way. I just got the death sentence because I'm supposed to be a big shot in an espionage ring. I pass out $1000 here, $1500 there, toss $5000 to my brother-in-law—but I never had the money to train that voice. I never had the money to do anything for her. Think about that!'

In response to encores from the other prisoners, Ethel sang more songs to keep up their spirits besides satisfying her audience. Eventually Julius joined in, and together they sang 'The Battle Hymn of the Republic', before they were removed to their respective prisons, Ethel to the women's Federal House of Detention on Tenth Street where Julius waved her good-bye from the prison van before going on to the federal detention quarters for men in West Street.[2]

The following afternoon Ethel's brother David Greenglass came up for sentencing. His counsel, John Rogge, stressed the usefulness of his confession, arguing that 'if the Government wants people to come forward and co-operate it must give them a pat on the back,' and he suggested that a three-year sentence would fit the case. However, District Attorney Saypol recommended fifteen years, and this in fact was the sentence which Judge Kaufman passed upon David Greenglass. 'You have at least not added to your sins,' said the judge. 'You repented and you brought to justice those who enlisted you in this cause.' On the other hand, he emphasised, 'justice seeks justice, but you deserve punishment.'

Since no facilities existed in the Women's Federal House of Detention (although there were in the Men's) for the segregation of a condemned prisoner, as required by law, it was necessary to transfer Ethel Rosenberg to Sing Sing a few days later. She arrived there on 11 April. Asked what led her to commit the crime of which she had been convicted, she replied: 'I deny guilt.' The women's dismal but not incommodious section of the death house consisted of three cells, one provided with a shower and toilet facilities, a corridor, and an exercise yard inside a ten-foot-high wall. It had been untenanted since the execution during the previous month of Mrs Martha Beck convicted with her lover of the murder of wealthy victims following a 'lonely hearts' correspondence. The four matrons who had been attending Mrs Beck at $40 a day were rehired to perform the same duties for Ethel Rosenberg.

'As you see, sweetheart,' Ethel wrote in her first letter to Julius from the death house, 'I have already embarked on the next lap of our history-making journey.'

Already there appear the signs of my growing maturity. The bars of my large cell hold several books. The lovely, colourful cards (including your exquisite birthday greeting to me) that I accumulated at the House of Detention line the top ledge of my writing table to please the eye and brighten the spirit. The children's snapshots are taped on to a 'picture frame' made of cardboard and they smile sweetly upon me whenever I so desire. Within me somewhere, I shall find that 'courage, confidence and perspective' I shall need to see me through the days and nights of bottomless horror, of tortured screams I dare not utter, of frenzied, longing I must deny! Julie, dearest, how I wait upon the journey's end and our triumphant return to our precious life from which the foul monsters of our time have sought to drag us!

'Darling, your removal to Sing Sing is a cruel and vindictive action,' her husband replied next day. 'But we agree that the Justice Department will not succeed in its campaign to pressure us physically and emotionally into letting ourselves be used as pawns for political purposes.'

If our lawyers do not succeed in bringing you back to the Women's Detention House at 10th Street, I will move heaven and earth to be sent to Sing Sing to be nearer to you and to be able to see you whenever it is possible . . .

This single document [Ethel's letter] is indelible proof that not only are you a tremendous person but you have the courage, confidence and enlightened perspective to come through this hell and then some with flying colours. My wife, I stand humble beside you, proud and inspired by such a woman . . .

It is impossible to keep the truth and facts of our case hidden from the public. Sooner or later the true picture will become known to all. Many people have already expressed to our lawyers and my family their desire to help us. Take heart and know we are not alone.[3]

The appeal filed by Emanuel ('Manny') Bloch, the first of many appeals, petitions and applications for stays of execution, automatically postponed the date set by Judge Kaufman. The initial appeal to the New York Circuit Court might take many months and, if the case went on further appeal to the United States Supreme Court, possibly years. Of course, no appeal court could alter the sentence—only the trial judge could do that—but it could quash the conviction. However, if the conviction were upheld in the last instance, the trial judge had sixty days to reconsider the case in the light of any change of circumstances. In other words, the door was not finally closed during this period for the prisoners to save their lives, which they could do by confessing.

Bloch's next move, after lodging notice of appeal, was to apply to the court to show cause why the Government should not be required to send Ethel Rosenberg back to New York City. His application was supported by an affidavit in which his client contended that the purpose of the Government in transferring her to the death house was to 'break' her and force a confession. She went on:

> It has long been recognised that the mental and physical pressures of the refined cruelties that man has devised are equal to barbarity of the rack, the thumbscrew and the wheel. It is a living hell to be separated from the warmth, love, affection and strength of my husband, and for him to contemplate my incarceration in this terrible place. It is agony to sit in a cell located not even a stone's throw from the execution chamber.
>
> I am sealed in the grey walls of this prison as if in a tomb. I am alone in an entire building except for the matron who guards me. I see no other human being from morning to night. I have no occupation other than to sit immured in the aching soundlessness of my narrow cell. I have no recreation other than to walk a bare patch of ground surrounded by walls so high that my only view is a bare patch of sky. Sometimes I can see an airplane passing by; sometimes a few birds; sometimes I hear the noise of a train in the distance. Otherwise there is always dead silence . . .

Of course, Ethel was allowed to listen to the radio and on fine days could play a game of handball with one of the friendly matrons, and she also had a selection of magazines and books. But the 'undue and unusual psychological pressures' to which she was subjected must have told upon her health: indeed a psychiatrist who attended her without fee, and talked over the difficult problem of her children's adjustment and her own, asserted that Ethel might become insane if kept for any length of time alone in the death house. Eventually Federal Judge Goddard denied Bloch's application. No evidence had been produced to show any attempt to 'break' the prisoner, he said, and went on to rule that the transfer to Sing Sing was not 'unusual or cruel or inhuman within the meaning of the Eighth Amendment to the Constitution.' Meanwhile Ethel had one consolation. In the middle of May, as a result of press publicity, Julius was moved from the New York Federal House of Detention to Sing Sing, so at least he and his beloved Ethel were under the same roof, even though it was that of the death house.

Asked the routine question on his enrolment at Sing Sing to what he attributed his criminal act, he answered simply: 'Neither I nor my wife is guilty.' The Warden, Wilfred Denno, then explained that he would be allowed to see his wife for one hour a week and to converse across a table divided by a wire mesh screen in the presence of a keeper and a matron.

They could also have consultations with their lawyers in the counsel room. Unlike Ethel, Julius was not alone in the men's wing, since there were seven other condemned criminals there waiting for a summons to the electric chair from their cells in 'death row'. Each man was given two fifteen-minute exercise periods daily. The yard was bounded on one side by the gallery of cells, on the other by the death chamber, and in all was about one hundred and fifty feet in circumference. 'Once in a while I play hand-ball,' Julius wrote to his lawyer in one of his letters, 'but in the main I have an opportunity to walk around the yard and sing the songs I like . . . While I sing it brings back memories, inspires me and makes me think of all the other innocent political prisoners.'

'How sad I was to leave your fond embrace, how loath,' wrote Ethel after their first meeting in their lawyer's presence, 'and how reluctant my step as I approached my cell. It was there waiting for me, silent, inexorable, disdainful, seemingly unaware of its occupant's departure but smug in the knowledge of her eventual return.'

It's only three days ago that my lips clung in desperate hunger to yours and my glance kindled to behold the long-loved, oddly familiar, oddly strange being by whose side I have lain and sweetly slumbered through how many nights. It's only three days by the calendar, yet I am certain that eons have elapsed and that I dreamed our meeting . . . My heart smote me for your pale, drawn face, your pleading eyes, your slender boyish body and your evident suffering.

My dearest husband, what heaven and what hell to welcome you to monotonous days and joyless nights, to endless desire and endless denial. And yet here shall we plight our troth anew, here held fast by brick and concrete and steel shall our love put forth gripping root and tender blossom; here shall we roar defiance, and give battle . . .

At first Manny Bloch was present at these visits, but the Warden, who censored the prisoners' letters, soon came to suspect that they were a pretext for social meetings. 'Your visits to your clients should be confined to strictly legal matters,' the Warden admonished the lawyer. 'Arrangements for personal visits between them will be arranged later.' In fact, as already noted, they were allowed to meet once a week, when a cage was placed opposite Ethel's cell and they had to converse through the bars.

To his wife's first letter Julius replied next day, 21 May:

What you wrote, Ethel, so eloquently expresses our profoundest frustrations our understanding and deep love for each other. The hemmed-in solitude that surrounds us and the oppressive nature of this sombre tomb must not succeed in removing our strong ties to the vibrating and pulsating outside world. We caged here can only protest our innocence and stand up firmly, but it is the task of the American people to stay the executioner's hand and see that justice is done. The hardest thing for me to take is that you, my heart, are also in this Gehenna and only your splendid steadfastness has made it possible for me to stand up . . .

Do not be concerned about my looks as I feel healthy and can take care of myself. . . .

It is tempting to quote from these letters, so pathetic in their poignancy and sexual longing and in the belief that their innocence would ultimately be vindicated. Here is what Ethel wrote to her husband on the twelfth anniversary of their marriage, to make up for being separated, since this was not one of their weekly visiting days, and no exception could be made even for a wedding anniversary.

18 June 1951 . . . It is incredible that after twelve years of the kind of principled, constructive wholesome living together that we did, that I should sit in a cell in Sing Sing awaiting my own legal murder, greeting you in this anguish on what would have been a joyous celebration of two memorable days. Incredible, too, that you should receive felicitations as husband and father in another cell, in which you sit in anticipation of a similar doom.

During this same month, relatives visited the condemned couple to discuss the future of their two sons, Michael aged eight and Robert aged four, who had been kept for almost a year in a Bronx children's shelter, after their maternal grandmother Mrs Tessie Greenglass proved unable to take care of them. Now they could no longer stay in the shelter. Julius's mother, Mrs Sophie Rosenberg and a married sister, Mrs Lena Cohen, with whom the old lady lived, offered to look after the boys, and another sister of Julius, Mrs Ethel Goldberg, promised to help as much as she could. Later in the summer the boys visited Sing Sing and their parents were allowed to see them separately.

Julius wrote to his wife on 9 September:

The children's visit was just perfect. They were in excellent spirits from the time I entered the room, and enjoyed it so much they were disappointed when it was over. Michael said he wants more. Because of the good effect you had on them the atmosphere was like a warm family get-together. . . .

Most of the hour we spent in discussion. It started with the death sentence, which Michael said he had read about in the paper. I told him we were not concerned about it; that we were innocent and we had many avenues of appeal, and that it was not his job to be concerned about it, but to grow up and be well.

He asked me how you die and I told him, and he asked if there is an electric chair here and I said 'Yes'. He kept on asking about the appeals and what if finally we might lose, and death faced us. I kept on reassuring him but I could see he was terribly upset over it. He then looked at the Sergeant [prison guard] and said you'd better watch me for I don't want my mother and father to die for if they do I'll kill Dave [Greenglass]. His determination, sincerity and youthful grave look moved me so.

Another time he said, 'Daddy, the man in the *Guardian* said you are innocent too and I'd like to give him the four dollars I saved in my piggy bank because he's for you.'

He asked many questions on what he had read about money, fingerprints, the action of the FBI and the jury. I explained as well as I could, and Manny helped, and told him on the ride back home he'd go into more detail.

The boy said, 'Daddy, maybe I'll study to be a lawyer and help you in your case,' and I said 'We won't wait that long as we want to be with you while your growing up.' He wants so to help us, to do something, and to be assured that all will be well with us. . . .

The baby and Michael are both frightened and only our early return will heal all the harm done.

During that summer the Circuit Court granted more time for filing amended briefs in the Appeal. At first no journal expressed the opinion that the Rosenbergs and Sobell might be innocent—as they claimed. This apparent consensus as to the guilt of the accused ended with the publication in the *National Guardian*, a Labour-orientated 'progressive' weekly edited by Cedric Belfrage, of a series of seven articles challenging the verdict of the jury by the paper's investigative reporter William A. Reuben, which ran in August and September.[4] 'There was a special political object in making a supreme example of the Rosenbergs because of their left-wing politics,' so ran an editorial announcing the series. 'In police parlance, the 'atomic plot' involved was a 'closed case' before the Rosenbergs were brought into it. All the accused participants had confessed.' As a result of the public interest aroused by these articles, a National Committee to Secure Justice in the Rosenberg Case was formed, with Reuben as acting chairman.

Although the Committee was denounced in right-wing quarters as 'Communist inspired' and at first made little headway except among outspoken opponents of the death penalty, the movement for a review of the case gradually gained momentum. 'From all sides we hear of new support,' Julius wrote to Ethel on 20 January 1952. 'The ball is really rolling now. More and more people are joining the committee, contributing funds, writing letters and increasing thousands of people are being made aware of the facts of our case and its nature . . . But, oh, my wife, how cruel it is to be apart from you and suffer in isolation when we are innocent.' And again a week later:

> Always I keep thinking of what Manny [Bloch] said. 'You are two straws buffeted about by the political winds' and I keep hoping that public opinion will be sufficiently neutralised, that the judge will be able to render a decision based strictly on the legal merits of the trial and not on extraneous issues that stem from the hysterical atmosphere in our land.

At 10 p.m. on 25 February 1952, Julius Rosenberg heard 'the shocking news' that the US Circuit Court of Appeals in New York had rejected the appeal earlier that day. 'I'm still terribly shocked by the horrible and shameless affirmation of our conviction in such apparent haste,' he wrote to his wife twenty-four hours later. 'I hope the clerk of the court sends me a copy of Judge Frank's opinion.'

The judgment of the Court, which consisted of three judges, was delivered by Judge Jerome N. Frank. 'Unless we are to overrule sixty years of undeviating precedents,' the judge declared, 'we must hold that an appellate court has no power to modify a sentence.' Because of these precedents, he said, the Supreme Court alone was in a position to decide whether existing laws gave the courts the right to reduce an otherwise valid sentence, although he appeared to imply that this one was 'unduly harsh.' Had he such a power to change a sentence, Judge Frank added, he might regard 'the quality of the evidence on which the verdict rests' and 'take into consideration' the fact that the evidence of the Rosenbergs' espionage activities 'came almost entirely from accomplices.'[5]

And so the year dragged on slowly and painfully for the condemned. On 8 April, after the Court of Appeals had denied them a rehearing, the defence attorneys announced that they would carry the cases of the Rosenbergs and Sobell to the Supreme Court, which they did six months later. But the Supreme Court denied their motion for *certiorari* which invited the Court to 'certify' that in this case the principles of natural justice had not been complied with. The petition for a rehearing was denied by a vote of eight to one. Only Mr Justice Hugo L. Black dissented. Ethel Rosenberg wrote to Manny Bloch:

> On Monday, 13 October, the Supreme Court, with the praiseworthy exception of Justice Black, used its proud office to write 'justice' off the statute books. By its refusal to review a case that involved two decent young parents and questions of law vital to the democratic well-being of the entire citizenry, they clearly sanctioned the scrapping of due process and the incidental scrapping of human life.
> They also demonstrated all too effectively a creaking make-shift of a

case and a hollow mockery of a trial, thereby revealing a lack of that independence of thought and action we had come to associate with such a venerable body as the United States Supreme Court!

Still the defence attorneys did not give up. They went back to the Supreme Court for a rehearing, but after listening to further argument the Court adhered to its previous denial of *certiorari*. On this occasion Mr Justice Felix Frankfurter filed a memorandum opinion in which he stated that the Supreme Court had no power to change a sentence imposed in a District Court; that it was primarily the responsibility of the Circuit Court of Appeals to review the record of the District Court trial and that the appellate court was 'deeply conscious of its responsibility in this case.'

Four days later, on 21 November, Judge Kaufman signed an order setting the execution date for the week ending 12 January 1953. 'You already know,' wrote Julius to his wife when they brought him this news, 'that the 'honourable' judge has ordered that we remain alive for only fifty-odd more days. I'm sure we'll confound him again for before the ink was dry on his order our lawyer began to fight back. . .'[6]

[2]

On 3 January 1953, the two Rosenberg boys were brought to Sing Sing for what it was thought would be their last visit before their parents' execution. After they had left, Julius wrote to his lawyer:

Today our precious boys came and our own family lived once again for two hours. I could see the trust in little Robbie's eyes, and the warmth and tender feelings of love that passed between us in all that he said and in our play together. I carried the baby on my back, giving him a horseyride. We looked through the barred window at the sea gulls and the tugboat pulling a string of barges on the Hudson. We zoomed through the room pretending to be an airplane as I held him in my arms tightly pressed to my heart. The pictures he drew and the drawings I made for him were interrupted while he kissed my cheeks and circled my neck with his little arms. My son was happy with his daddy. Julie was the big pussy cat chasing the little mousie, Robbie, and we had fun. Our baby got our true feelings.

Michael was troubled, disturbed and the burdens on him were obvious to us, his parents. My darling wife did so well by him. She explained patiently, carefully, firmly, but all the time with a complete acceptance of him and showed such wonderful understanding. It was really a most positive visit for all of us.

I promised to play Michael chess. I hope to someday.

Then they had to go and as I helped Michael on with his coat he suddenly clutched me with his hands and stammered as he lowered his head. 'You must come home. Every day there is a lump in my stomach, even when I go to bed.' I kissed him in a hurry for I was unable to say anything but 'everything will be all right.'

When I was in the solitude of my cell once more and the door clanged behind me, I confess I broke down and cried like a baby because of the children's deep hurt. With my back to the yard, I stood facing the concrete walls that boxed me in on all sides, and I let the pains that tore at my insides flood out in tears. The wretched beastliness and inhumanity of it all. Take heed tyrants, you will answer for your misdeeds.

In another letter the same day to Manny Bloch Julius summarised his sense of injustice and urged his lawyer to further action:

Before God and man I must blazon forth these truths:
    We are completely innocent. Nothing can change this.
    The judge and the district attorney from the very beginning injected the false issue of Communism and political beliefs to obscure and inflame the passions of the jury against us.
    The judge strained every effort to bend the jury to a verdict of guilty with his constant interjections against our interests at every stage that was to our disadvantage. He allowed our rights to be violated and prevented our lawyer from adequately defending us and did not allow the jury to judge the crime, as charged in the indictment, on a fair and impartial basis.
    . . . The world is watching our government's action in this case and the conscience of men of goodwill is outraged by the brutal sentence and the miscarriage of justice in the Rosenberg case.
    Time is short. There are but ten days left to live. I will do my best to crowd in as much work as possible. I am raising a warning for I believe this is a test case of threatening Fascism at home. Don't let them murder us.[7]

One further avenue remained for the defence to explore, namely appeal to the President for the exercise of his prerogative of executive clemency. Consequently Judge Kaufman was obliged to grant a further stay of execution pending the defendants' appeal to the White House.

Meanwhile the Rosenbergs gained two influential individuals to their side, both Nobel Prize Winners, Dr Harold C. Urey, the former head of the Manhattan project at Los Alamos, and Professor Albert Einstein, the world famous German-Swiss physicist, a Jew and refugee from Nazi Germany who had found a haven at the Institute of Advanced Study in Princeton.

On 8 January 1953, the following letter from Harold Urey dated 5 January appeared in *The New York Times*:

After reading the testimony of the Rosenberg case I find that I cannot put to rest my doubts about the verdict and wish to cite the following points:

(1) Max Elitcher's testimony is of doubtful value. He says that he and Julius talked about espionage but never transferred any information for some five years. This doesn't seem probable to me.

(2) No certain conspiracy between Sobell and Rosenberg is established.

(3) The connections to others than Ruth and David Greenglass are not established. Miss Bentley was unable to identify the telephone voice that said, 'This is Julius' with the voice of Julius Rosenberg. If 'Julius' did not refer to him in this case, it probably did not when Harry Gold said, 'I come from Julius' when he met Greenglass in New Mexico. From Gold's testimony it seems that he knew nothing of Rosenberg at all. It seems unbelievable to me that the name of an arch conspirator would be used in such identification phrases.

(4) No contact between the Rosenbergs and Anatoli A. Yakovlev is established.

(5) The Government's case rests on the testimony of Ruth and David Greenglass. He had pleaded guilty but had not been sentenced and hoped for clemency. She has never been charged and tried, obviously it seems as a reward for her testimony. A family feud between the Greenglasses and the Rosenbergs existed because of a business altercation. The Rosenbergs' testimony flatly contradicted that of the Greenglasses.

I found the Rosenbergs' testimony more believable than that of the Greenglasses, although I realise that I have not had the jurors' advantage of hearing and seeing the witnesses. Is it customary for spies to be paid in wrist watches and console tables? Greenglass and Fuchs were paid in cash. The Rosenbergs appear to have been as poor as church mice and the statement that Julius was spending $50 and $75 a night in night clubs seems to me to be a very doubtful one. Had he done this, he would have been obviously and unaccountably rich to all his associates.

However, even if the verdict is correct, I am amazed at the unequal punishment for the same crime. For the very same conspiracy Ruth Greenglass was never brought to trial, though she admitted her guilt on the witness stand; David Greenglass got fifteen years; Morton Sobell and Harry Gold got thirty years, and Ethel and Julius Rosenberg got death. Only the last two took the witness stand and maintained their innocence. If capital punishment is to be given in the future for espionage, I should like to have it introduced in a case for which the evidence rests on the testimony of witnesses who did not stand to profit from their testimony. I do not regard selfconfessed criminals as reliable witnesses.

We are engaged in a cold war with the tyrannical Government of the USSR. We wish to win the approval and loyalty of the good people of the world. Would it not be embarrassing if, after the execution of the Rosenbergs, it could be shown that the United States had executed two innocent people and let a guilty one go completely free? And, remember, somewhere there is a representative of the USSR who knows what the facts are.

Five days later the *New York Times* published the text of a short letter which Professor Einstein had addressed to President Truman. 'My conscience compels me to urge you to commute the death sentence of Julius and Ethel Rosenberg,' he wrote. 'This appeal to you is prompted by the same reasons which were set forth so convincingly by my colleague, Harold C. Urey in his letter. . . .'

By the time the defence lawyers' petition for clemency had reached the White House, Harry Truman had handed over the Presidency to General Dwight Eisenhower, thus leaving the decision on the fate of the Rosenbergs to the new President. Meanwhile Ethel Rosenberg had drafted her own petition, which closely followed that of the lawyers and was despatched on 9 January. It read in part:

> My husband and I testified in our own defence. We denied, generally, and in detail, every part of the evidence introduced by the Government to connect us with a conspiracy to commit espionage. We showed that, during the years in question, we lived a steady normal existence. . . . .
>
> Upon the birth of our two sons, I ceased my outside employment, and discharged the responsibility of mother and housewife. My husband, a graduate engineer, held a regular succession of low-salaried positions until his entrance into the machine shop enterprise with David Greenglass. The modesty of our standard of living, bordering often on poverty, discredits David's depiction of my husband as the pivot and pay-off man of a widespread criminal combination, fed by a seemingly limitless supply of 'Moscow gold.'
>
> Our knowledge of the existence of an atom bomb came with its explosion at Hiroshima, and David's connection with it at Los Alamos, from his revelations to us after his discharge from the Army in 1946.
>
> We knew neither Gold nor Yakovlev, our alleged co-conspirators, nor Bentley—facts which the Government did not controvert.
>
> Our relations with Sobell, our co-defendant, were confined to sporadic social visits. Following a complete six-year break, after graduation from college, our ties with Elitcher assumed similar, but even more tenuous character.

Our relations with the Greenglasses, both during and after the war, were on a purely familial and social level, the cordiality becoming strained to the breaking, however, with the advent of bitter quarrels which arose in the course of our post-war business ties. . . . .

On 19 January, Mrs Tessie Greenglass came to Sing Sing to see her daughter. 'The following transpired which will interest you,' Ethel wrote to Manny Bloch after the old lady had left. 'I am still in a state of stupefaction over its bold-faced immorality.'

I pointed out to her that whatever unfounded fear of reprisal Davy might be harbouring, it was my life that was in peril, not his—and further, if I, while awaiting electrocution, was not afraid to assert my innocence and give the lie to his story, why couldn't he, in a far more advantageous position, be man enough to own up at long last to this lie and help to save my life, instead of letting it be forfeited to save his face!

Our conversation follows, and I quote almost verbatim:

Said she: 'So what would have been so terrible if you had backed up his story?' I guess my mouth kind of fell open. 'What,' I replied, 'and take the blame for a crime I never committed, and allow my name, and my husband's and children's to be slandered to protect him? What, and go along with a story I knew to be untrue, where it involved my husband and me? Wait a minute, maybe I'm not getting you straight. Just what are you driving at?'

Believe it or not, she answered, 'Yes, you get me straight; I mean even if it was a lie, you should have said it was true anyway! You think that way you would have been sent here? No, if you had agreed that what Davy said was so, even if it wasn't, you wouldn't have got this!'

I protested, shocked as I could be. 'But, Ma, would you have had me willingly commit perjury?'

She shrugged her shoulders indifferently and maintained doggedly, 'You wouldn't be here!'

It did not take the new President long to reject the petitions, which he did on 11 February after 'earnest consideration' of the Rosenbergs' case which appeared to have amounted to little more than half an hour. The relevant portion of the prepared statement follows:

The nature of the crime for which they have been found guilty and sentenced far exceeds that of taking the life of another citizen: it involves the deliberate betrayal of the entire nation and could very well result in the death of many, many thousands of innocent citizens. By their act these two individuals have in fact betrayed the cause of freedom for which free men are fighting and dying at this very hour.

We are a nation under law . . . All rights of appeal were exercised and the conviction of the trial court was upheld after four judicial reviews, including that of the highest court in the land.

This last statement about the Supreme Court was, of course, incorrect, since that Court had expressly declined to review the case.

'Just as we had been informed by our lawyer that it would take at least another week for Eisenhower to get the record,' Julius wrote to his wife next day, 'the newspapers let the cat out of the bag and said that the Attorney General [Herbert J. Brownell, Jr] brought over the file to the President's office at 4.00 p.m. and at 5.07 p.m. the prepared statement was read.'

Of course Eisenhower could not have read the record or seen our petition. To cover up this apparent discrepancy, they say that on his own he's been brushing up on the case. Such hypocrisy! He doesn't even make sure that he's accurate in his haste to use shop-worn platitudes —even stating the obvious fallacy that the Supreme Court reviewed our case. He may be successful in that we will be put to death, but he has shocked the conscience of the world.

On 16 February 1953, an order was signed setting the date for the execution for the second week in March. However, next day, on Bloch's application, the New York Court of Appeals granted an indefinite stay of execution to enable the defence again to apply for *certiorari* by the end of March on the ground of new evidence such as the Schneider perjury, so that the execution was again postponed. Meanwhile sympathy for the Rosenbergs was mounting in the European press, particularly in France and Italy, although some of the left-wing Italian journals expressed surprise that the Pope, Pius XII, had not added his voice to the pleas for clemency. Annoyed by this criticism, the official Vatican organ *L'Osservatore Romano* revealed that His Holiness had despatched such a plea through the Apostolic Delegate in Washington, who had passed it on to the Department of Justice, the Pope being said to have acted out of motives of charity 'without being able to enter into the merits of the case.' However the Attorney General had failed to inform the President on the somewhat astonishing ground, as he put it, that 'the matter ended there so far as I was concerned.' *L'Osservatore Romano* afterwards commented: 'There is no doubt that when history returns to this episode, it will seal with a word of highest praise the magnanimous gesture of the Supreme Pontiff.'[8]

On 25 May the Supreme Court vacated the stay of the Court of Appeals and again denied *certiorari*. On 1 June, US Marshal William A. Carroll arrived with another marshal at Sing Sing to serve the Rosenbergs with the papers setting their executions for 11.00 p.m. on 18 June. The date was their fourteenth wedding anniversary. 'My wife and I are to be horribly united in death on the very day of our greatest happiness, our wedding day,' Julius wrote his lawyer shortly afterwards. 'They were very pleasant, but they had a job, a distasteful one at that, to do and they pointedly asked me before they left if they could do anything for me. I said, 'Yes—bring us good news!' Their visit was routine.'

[3]

The eleventh-hour struggle to save the lives of the Rosenbergs began with the visit of Mr James V. Bennett, Federal Director of the Bureau of Prisons, to Sing Sing on the morning of 2 June. He saw Julius first in the counsel room, without the prison Warden or anyone else being present.

'Mr Brownell, the Attorney General, sent me to see you,' Mr Bennett began, 'and he wants you to know that if you want to co-operate with the Government you can do so through me and I will be able to make arrangements to talk with any proper officials. Furthermore, if you, Julius, can convince the officials that you have fully co-operated with the Government, they have a basis to recommend clemency.'

This proposal considerably shocked Julius and he only managed to keep his temper with difficulty. 'You mean to tell me, Mr Bennett,' he said, 'that a great Government like ours is coming to two insignificant people like us and saying 'co-operate or die?' It isn't necessary to beat me with clubs, but such a proposal is like what took place in the Middle Ages. It is equivalent to the screw and the rack. You are putting a tremendous pressure on me.'

James Bennett was fundamentally a decent, kindly man. 'Why,' he said to Julius, 'do you know that I didn't sleep last night when I knew I had to see you and Ethel the next day and talk to you about this matter? I was terribly worried.'

'How do you think we feel, sitting here waiting for death for over two years when we are innocent?' asked Julius. 'My family has gone through great suffering. My sister had a breakdown; my aged, ailing mother is tormented; our children have known much emotional and mental agony. Then you talk to us about this.'

Remember, Mr Bennett, we love our country. It is our home, the land of my children and my family. We do not want its good name to be shamed and in justice and common decency, we should be allowed to live to prove our innocence.

'No—not a new trial,' Bennett replied. 'Only by co-operating will there be a basis to ask for commutation.' Then, after a short pause, he went on,

'Look here, Julius, you didn't deny that you do not know anything about this espionage.'

'I certainly did,' Julius answered heatedly. 'And furthermore, did you read the trial record, sir?'

Bennett said he had not. Then he went on: 'You had dealings with Elizabeth Bentley.'

'I never did,' Julius answered, 'and if you read the record, she said on the witness stand that she did not know me and never met me.'

'But you had dealings with Gold, didn't you?'

'Of course I didn't. Gold also said on the stand he never met me or knew me. You should have read the record to be familiar with the facts.'

'Oh, I read the newspaper accounts of it,' Bennett assured Julius. 'Look, Julius,' he added, 'Gordon Dean, the head of the Atomic Energy Commission, is a very good friend of mine, and if he is convinced that you have co-operated fully and told all you know about espionage, he will see the President and recommend clemency.'

'I don't know anything about espionage since I am innocent,' Julius protested. 'I think you should tell the Attorney General to recommend clemency because it is the just, humane and proper thing to do in this case. Our country has a reputation to maintain in the world and many of its friends are outraged at the barbaric sentence and the lack of justice in this case.'

'Well, Julius, why did your brother-in-law involve you?'

'I believe he did it to save his own skin, also to make himself out to be a minor, innocent dupe dominated by someone else so that he should not be held accountable for his own actions. Besides, the Government had caught the Greenglasses with the goods and they had to find some way to mitigate their own punishment. With my background of being fired for alleged Communism from Government service, because I was a union organiser, and since he was a relative and knew me intimately and there existed personal animosity between us, I was falsely involved. Also the prosecution was a chance to make great political capital out of 'Communist-spy-atom-bomb.' My wife and I became scapegoats and were straws tossed around by the political controversies that raged in the cold war. Why not go to the Greenglasses and get *them* to co-operate to tell the truth about this family?'

You yourself, Mr Bennett, as head of the Prison Bureau, know that Greenglass and Gold were together in the Tombs for nine months, discussing the case, studying notes from a big looseleaf book, rehearsing testimony, talking to FBI agents, the prosecution and their attorney.

You know that Greenglass was coached on the A-bomb sketch testimony, both verbally and from notes. You know the prosecution permitted the Greenglasses to perjure themselves. You know the prosecution caused Schneider [the passport photographer] to perjure himself. You know the Government is preventing my wife's family coming forward with exculpating testimony. You know that the prosecution has exculpating evidence that they are withholding from the court. In short, we did not get a fair trial and we were framed. Now you want us to admit that this big lie is the truth. That we can never do.

'How about the death sentence?' Julius continued. 'Certainly, if the verdict were a true one, which we vehemently deny, we never should have gotten such a severe sentence. The history of our country in freeing war criminals, Nazi and Fascist, in not putting to death traitors and spies, and yet, for the first time, making the Rosenbergs the worst criminals in all our history—you know, as a reasoning man, this is not right. All the facts in the case, the trial record, and the sentence, prove it was a means of coercion. The humane, just and proper action would be for our lives to be spared. . . .'

'Julius, all the courts upheld the conviction many times,' retorted Bennett, 'and all the officials in Washington believe you guilty. Why, most everybody believes you guilty!'

'You know that only the appeal court upheld the verdict of the original trial and the denial of *certiorari* does not pass on the merits of the case,' answered Julius. 'At all other times, we didn't get a hearing, but only the right to file papers. This is the form of the law, not its spirit. Always such haste—because they are afraid we will prove our innocence. Also people like Dr Urey, Professor Einstein, scientists, lawyers, men of letters, have grave doubts about the case after reading the trial record. The Pope, three thousand Christian church leaders, prominent rabbis and millions of people have asked for clemency.'

'No, Julius. The Pope did not ask for clemency.'

'Yes, he did,' snapped Julius. 'And I have the articles from *L'Osservatore Romano* to prove it.'

We had the record printed—the one that records the entire proceedings of the trial and people read it and they come away with grave doubts about the justness of the verdict. . . . The only way to cleanse this damning record is to let us live so that we can prove our innocence.

'Julius,' Mr Bennett persisted, 'the trial not being fair, the sentence being too severe, and all the publicity are not germane to the issue. The *only* way is for you to co-operate and convince the officials in Washington. Then, they will have a basis to ask for clemency.'

After about an hour's fruitless argument, Mr Bennett left Julius and went over to the Women's Wing and announced himself to Ethel. 'I made it short and sweet,' she told Manny Bloch afterwards. 'I was innocent, my husband was innocent, and neither of us knew anything about espionage.'

Gently Mr Bennett prodded her to 'co-operate.' 'Surely you must know something,' he coaxed.

Ethel picked him up quickly. 'Well, now,' she asked, 'how could I when I did not participate in any way? In order to co-operate as you desire, I should have to deliberately concoct a pack of lies and bear false witness against unoffending individuals. Is that what the authorities want me to do—to lie?'

The Prison Bureau Director was horrified at this suggestion. 'Oh, dear, no, of course we don't want you to lie,' he said. 'But now take a family, for example. One member might not be actively engaged in certain activities, but still might have knowledge concerning another member's activities.'

Ethel answered politely but firmly. 'The fact remains that I don't know any more than I knew during the trial. I told the full and complete truth then, and I don't intend to start lying now.'

'I am a perfectly honest individual myself,' said Mr Bennett, trying another tack, 'yet my experience in these matters has shown me that, for one reason or another, a person will sometimes plead innocent, knowing full well that he is guilty. Wouldn't you agree with that?'

'I will be just as frank and grant you that there have been such instances,' answered Ethel. 'Nevertheless, I couldn't concern myself as to the motives involved in such cases. I do, however, know my own mind and heart, and I tell you in all conscience that I continue to maintain my innocence for the sole reason that I am simply not guilty of the charge.'

'Well, the Government claims to have in its possession documents and statements that would dispute that,' Bennett told Ethel, 'so if only you were willing to co-operate, there might be a basis for commutation.'

'I couldn't possibly know nor do I care what they have or don't have,' was Ethel's tart reply. 'If you are persuading me to confess to activities concerning which I have solemnly sworn I have no knowledge, on the basis of evidence with which I was never confronted in court, then obviously the validity of this evidence must be strongly questioned, if in fact it exists at all.'

After about half an hour Julius was brought in at Bennett's request and the argument continued for another half an hour or so, when the Warden appeared to ask what it was all about. After he had been told, Mr Bennett got up, shrugged his shoulders wearily, took his leave and asked the Warden to expedite any messages they might care to send him. He then followed Julius back to his cell where he made one last effort to persuade him to 'co-operate' by letting him 'bring people who were familiar with the case' and 'you would submit to answering questions of what you know about this.' 'Why, that would be like brain washing,' said Julius. Finally,

Bennett asked if he could come and see him again. 'Yes,' replied Julius, 'if you can bring me some good news!' But he never did.

Next day the Rosenbergs issued the following statement to the world press through their attorney:

Yesterday we were offered a deal by the Attorney General of the United States. We were told that if we co-operated with the Government, our lives would be spared.

By asking us to repudiate the truth of our innocence, the Government admits its own doubts concerning our guilt. We will not help to purify the foul record of a fraudulent conviction and a barbaric sentence.

We solemnly declare, now and forever more, that we will not be coerced, even under pain of death, to bear false witness and to yield up to tyranny our rights as free Americans.

Our respect for truth, conscience and human dignity is not for sale. Justice is not some bauble to be sold to the highest bidder.

If we are executed, it will be the murder of innocent people and the shame will be upon the Government of the United States.

History will record, whether we live or not, that we were victims of the most monstrous frame-up in the history of our country.[9]

'Ethel darling,' Julius wrote to his wife on 4 June, 'I think the statement we issued through our attorney is an excellent one and I am very pleased with it. Indeed, I am proud of the fact that the bulk of the words and ideas put into the final draft were a product of your efforts and together this was a joint accomplishment. It is hard for people to realise the very difficult circumstances we are labouring under, and the deep sense of responsibility we felt as we worked out our thoughts to make sure that everyone would know the letter and the full spirit of what we tried to tell the public. . . . Even more important is that the American people should know the truth about our case and also about the reprehensible conduct of the Justice Department officials in this case.'

[4]

Two days later, with the date of the execution only twelve days away, the defence attorneys appealed to the New York District Court on the ground that 'new evidence' which had come to light proved that the principal prosecution witnesses, David and Ruth Greenglass, had lied, and the lawyers asked Judge Kaufman to set aside the convictions and grant the Rosenbergs a new trial.[10] The new evidence consisted of three items—first the missing console table, which had figured in the Greenglasses' testimony as a gift from the Russians and adapted for storing microfilms; secondly, certain confidential pre-trial memoranda which had been apparently abstracted from the office of John Rogge, the Greenglasses' counsel, copied and returned; and thirdly, an affidavit sworn to by David Greenglass's brother Bernard regarding the theft of a sample of uranium from Los Alamos by David.

These revelations aroused considerable interest in the European press. For instance the Paris journal *Le Monde* commented in a front-page editorial that they were too important to be passed over in silence. 'It is up to American justice to evaluate them, check their accuracy, and decide in what measure they call for a new trial.' This new development gave Ethel Rosenberg fresh heart. 'The latest motion for a new trial is beyond any doubt our strongest legal action,' she wrote to her husband on 7 June. 'It contains some devastating stuff that can break this case wide open. . . . I begin to discern the general pattern of the jig-saw plot that was concocted by the Greenglasses to save themselves and frame us . . . I have faith that we will live to be in each other's arms again.'

The console table, which was not produced at the trial, was thought to have been sold with other furniture about the middle of October 1950, when it became clear that the Rosenbergs could not raise bail. In fact, it had been stored with the childrens' toys at the house in Queen's of Julius's mother Mrs Sophie Rosenberg, where it was located by a *National Guardian* reporter in March 1953. Although the District Attorney had tried to discredit the Rosenbergs' assertions at the trial that the table was an inexpensive one, obtainable from Macy's store for not less than $85, Julius had testified that he had bought it for about $21, and an experienced employee of Macy's when shown photographs of the table put its value with sales tax at $20.37, bought about 1944, although unfortunately the firm's records for that period had been destroyed. Affidavits as to the table's authenticity were sworn to by the two defendants, Manny Bloch, three members of Julius's family, and the *National Guardian* reporter.

The Rogge memoranda concerned two interviews given by David Greenglass to the FBI in which Greenglass had allegedly 'made a number of confusing statements in order to confound the FBI and to draw attention from his wife who is in hospital.' Ethel Rosenberg was not mentioned in either of the memoranda. As for Julius, although he was stated to be 'very close to the situation', and to have persuaded Ruth to ask David for information, and to have arranged a meeting for David with a man in a car, there was no indication in the documents as to the kind of information that Julius requested nor any suggestion that he had received any. Nor was there any reference to Julius's alleged receipt from David of atomic bomb information in January and September 1945, or of post-war incidents involving the sky platform and atomic airplane, not to mention the plan for David's escape, giving him $5000 and having passport photographs taken at

Julius's request. Nor was there any mention of the meeting with Gold in Albuquerque or the torn Jello box or the password 'Julius sent me.'

Finally, there was Bernard Greenglass's sworn statement that David had taken a sample of uranium from Los Alamos and that before David's arrest David had told him that he had thrown the uranium into the East River in New York and that this had been confirmed by Ruth.

Giving judgment, Judge Kaufman rejected all the 'new evidence.' He was not satisifed that the console table was the same one that was in the Rosenbergs' apartment, nor had the Government 'knowingly used perjurious testimony.' As for the Rogge memoranda, the judge ruled that David had given as many as six or seven statements to FBI agents and that he had not at the time he gave the earlier statement remembered fully all the details he had supplied at the time of his later ones. Furthermore Ruth Greenglass's statement, made to Rogge, that her husband was inclined to be hysterical and on occasion say untrue things, did not establish that his testimony at this trial was untruthful. Finally he dismissed the defence lawyers' contention that David's theft of uranium indicated he had been involved in espionage independent of the Rosenbergs. 'It is difficult to perceive how a theft and disposal of uranium in the manner described indicates such independent espionage,' he said. 'It is even more difficult to perceive how this espionage would provide a motive for perjury, designed to implicate innocent members of Greenglass's family in this most serious crime.'

Judge Kaufman concluded his written judgment, which it was obvious had been prepared before he had heard counsel's argument on the new evidence:

> It is worthy of re-emphasis that no one Government witness has recanted after all these years. I have said before and I repeat, the guilt of the defendants was established overwhelmingly, and the present alleged new evidence does not in any way diminish the strength of the Government's case. The motions on behalf of the defendants Rosenberg are denied.

Among those in court on this occasion was Professor Harold Urey, who observed the judge's demeanour in court which he had been unable to do before he wrote the letter quoted above to *The New York Times* five months previously. During a recess in the hearing a reporter from the same newspaper asked Urey for his opinion, which the professor gave in forthright terms:

> Now that I see what goes on in Judge Kaufman's court room, I believe that the Rosenbergs are innocent. When I look in that court room I see no Kaufman but McCarthy . . . What appals me most is the rôle the

press is playing. The judge's bias is so obvious. I keep looking over at you newspapermen and there's not a flicker of indignation or concern. When are you going to stop acting like a bunch of sheep?

It is worth noting that the *Times* reported Kaufman's denial of the motion without mentioning a single detail of the new evidence nor quoting Urey's reaction, which it was left to the professor to do himself some weeks later in the *National Guardian* (6 July), the only journal which had publicly championed the Rosenbergs' cause under the outspoken editorship of Cedric Belfrage.

Another professor, Malcolm P. Sharp, who occupied the chair of law at Chicago University and subsequently wrote a perceptive book on the case, *Was Justice Done?* (1956), to which Harold Urey contributed an Introduction, quoted a typical example of 'McCarthyism' at this time. On two occasions, people of unusual intelligence, in response to Professor Sharp's expressions of doubt of the Rosenbergs' guilt, answered: 'Why, they were Communists, weren't they?'—thus equating Communism with a conviction for espionage and the death penalty.[11]

Next day, 9 June, the Rosenberg attorneys appeared before the Court of Appeals to request a stay of execution while they prepared their appeal from Judge Kaufman's decision. Instead, in spite of their objections, they were directed to argue the appeal then and there. This they did as best they could, following it up next day with a list of legal points on which, they said, their research was 'inadequate', and they asked for further time to prepare their case properly. However, on 11 June, the Court of Appeals affirmed Judge Kaufman's decision and denied a stay of execution.

On the following day, 12 June, Bloch and his colleagues appealed to the US Supreme Court for a stay of execution to provide time necessary to print and file a defence petition requesting a review of the motion for a new trial and also several other motions, two of which questioned the legality of the death penalty. The application was considered on Saturday, 13 June, and two days later, Monday, 15 June, the Court announced its decision. The application was denied by a majority of five to four, Justices Black, Frankfurter, Jackson and Douglas voting with the minority. Thereupon, the Supreme Court adjourned for the summer recess. However, Justice Douglas remained in his chambers as vacation judge to meet the defence lawyers, who realised that an approach to an individual judge was the last resort to obtain a reprieve from the Supreme Court.[12]

Meanwhile there was an unexpected development from a completely independent source. A gentleman named Irving Edelman from Tennessee instructed his lawyers, Fyke Farmer and Daniel C. Marshall, to apply for a writ of habeas corpus on the ground that the Rosenbergs had been tried under the wrong law, claiming that the 1917 Espionage Act had been superseded by the Atomic Energy Act of 1946, under which the death sentence could only be imposed if the jury recommended it and the offence was committed with intent to injure the United States. Judge Kaufman, to whom Farmer applied in the first instance, noting that he was acting without the authorisation of the Rosenberg attorneys, rejected the application, describing Farmer as an 'interloper' and 'intruder'. Undaunted by this rebuff, Farmer hastened to Washington where he met Bloch, and in the event Justice Douglas agreed to hear both Bloch and Farmer, the latter as 'next friend' or *amicus curiae*.

Messages pleading for clemency continued to pour in to Washington from all over the country as well as from abroad. 'New evidence makes even more plain what was plain enough before,' Dr Urey cabled the President, 'that the prosecution's case has no logic in it, and that it depends upon the blowing up of patently perjured testimony.' The distinguished scientist, who had tried to see the Attorney-General without success, also requested an interview with President Eisenhower, but received no response. However, on Tuesday, 16 June, the President did agree to see a deputation of four clergymen, representing 2300 ministers who had earlier signed an appeal for executive clemency.[13] The President told the deputation bluntly that he linked the Rosenbergs' espionage activities with the Korean war casualties and that in his view they did what they did for money. The same day the President wrote about the case to his son John who was serving in Korea:

> I must say that it goes against the grain to avoid interfering in the case where a woman is to receive capital punishment. Over against this, however, must be placed one or two facts that have greater significance. The first of these is that in this instance it is the woman who is the strong and recalcitrant character, the man is the weak one. She has obviously been the leader in everything they did in the spy ring. The second thing is that if there would be any commuting of the woman's sentence without the man's then from her on the Soviets would simply recruit their spies from among women.*

On the same morning Manny Bloch brought the Rosenbergs' two sons, Michael, now aged ten and Robert, aged six, to the Death House at Sing Sing for what would in all probability be their last visit to their parents. Emerging two hours later, Bloch waved a paper which he said was a new petition for clemency just signed by Ethel Rosenberg, 'seeking an open and full hearing before President Eisenhower.'

---

* 'It was an attitude worthy of the most pedestrian of United States' Presidents,' was Kim Philby's comment when he learned of this: Philby, *My Silent War*, p. 125. Eisenhower's statement that Ethel Rosenberg was the leader of the spy ring did not accord with Judge Kaufman's expressed view at the trial, when he assigned the major rôle to her husband.

Next morning, 17 June, Mr Justice Douglas granted a stay of execution on the petition of Irving Edelman's lawyers and referred the matter back to the District Court to consider the application of the Atomic Energy Act to the case.

The Attorney-General immediately reacted by applying to Chief Justice Fred Vinson, asking that the Supreme Court should be reconvened to review and vacate the stay of execution granted by Mr Justice Douglas. The Chief Justice assented and ordered the court to reconvene at noon on the following day, 19 June, on which day the Rosenbergs were due to go to the electric chair at 11.00 p.m.

All nine justices were eventually contacted and they duly assembled in the Supreme Court at noon. After hearing arguments from counsel and deliberating among themselves, an official announcement was made shortly after six o'clock that they would adjourn and meet again on the following day at the same hour. This meant that the Rosenbergs would not be executed that night.

The officials at Sing Sing, who were about to prepare the condemned couple for the death chamber, told them as soon as they heard the radio news flash. The Rosenbergs were said to be 'overjoyed.'

[5]

The Cabinet met in the morning of 19 June at the White House. The members included Herbert Brownell, the Attorney-General, who was asked by President Eisenhower to say something about the Rosenberg case. According to a reliable account the Attorney-General told the President that Mr Justice Douglas's action in granting a stay of execution seemed to be 'without foundation,' adding that 'information which corroborated the guilt of the Rosenbergs was in possession of the government . . . but could not have been used at the trial.' This was confirmed by the Presidential speech writer Emmett John Hughes who was also present.

According to Hughes, Brownell said to the President: 'I've always wanted you to look at evidence that wasn't usable in court showing the Rosenbergs were the head and centre of the espionage ring here in *direct* contact with the Russians—the *prime* espionage ring in the country.'* To which the President allegedly replied: 'My only concern is in the area of statecraft—the *effect* of the action.'

At noon the Supreme Court reconvened, having previously conferred in private. Chief Justice Vinson read the majority verdict. The only matter to

---

* Twenty years later, in response to an inquiry, Brownell's secretary stated that 'he had no recollection of the alleged incident, nor does he have any such evidence as referred to therein.' Walter and Miriam Schneir, *Invitation to an Inquest* (1966), p. 245n, p. 441. See also above, p. 187 note.

be decided, he said, was whether the legal point on which the stay had been granted by Mr Justice Douglas was a 'substantial question.' He went on: 'We think the question is not substantial. We think further proceedings to litigate it are unwarranted.' Thus by a vote of six to three the stay was vacated on the ground that the Atomic Energy Act of 1946 did not supersede the earlier Espionage Act and furthermore that the primary overt acts were committed in 1944 and 1945.*

In the House of Representatives a debate on a foreign aid bill was interrupted to announce the Supreme Court decision. The news was greeted by scattered applause and comment from two Southern Democrats. 'Praise God from whom all blessings flow and thanks to the Supreme Court,' commented Representative Frank L. Chelf from Kentucky, while Representative W. McD. Wheeler from Georgia, who had previously tried to impeach Mr Justice Douglas for 'high crimes and misdemeanours in office,' declared that he would still press for the Justice's impeachment and suggested that Douglas should be given a 'one-way' visa to Russia.

The Rosenbergs' last remaining hope was that the President would act favourably in their second clemency petition. However, shortly after 2.00 p.m. the White House press secretary told the waiting reporters: 'The President declines to intervene.'

It had been agreed at the morning cabinet that the President should issue a statement and this was done in the early afternoon. The statement read in part:

> I am not unmindful of the fact that this case has aroused grave misgivings both here and abroad in the minds of serious people, aside from the considerations of law. In this connection, I can only say that, by immeasurably increasing the chances of atomic war, the Rosenbergs may have condemned to death tens of millions of innocent people all over the world. The execution of two human beings is a grave matter. But even graver is the thought of the millions of dead whose deaths may be directly attributable to what these spies have done.
>
> When democracy's enemies have been judged guilty of a crime as horrible as that of which the Rosenbergs were convicted; when the legal processes of democracy have been marshalled to their maximum strength to protect the lives of convicted spies; when in their most solemn judgment the tribunals of the United States have adjudged them guilty and the sentence just, I will not intervene in this matter.

Manny Bloch strove to do his best until the last glimmer of hope for a reprieve had flickered out. He sent the President a telegram asking for a

---

* The majority Justices were Vinson, Clark, Jackson, Reed, Burton, and Minton. The dissenting minority were Douglas, Black and Frankfurter.

clemency hearing with him and his colleagues, pointing out that the Supreme Court had never 'reviewed' the case. He followed this up with a letter from Ethel Rosenberg which he delivered at the White House, and an extract from Justice Jackson's opinion, endorsed by the majority, which seemed to imply that the Court did not approve of the death penalty but in this case was powerless to revise the sentence. However, it is doubtful if these documents, with the exception of the letter, ever reached the President, as they were intercepted by his special counsel Bernard Shanley, who passed them on to the Justice Department. After he had been denied admission to the White House by the guard on duty and also permission to use the guard's telephone, Bloch returned to his hotel and frantically tried to get through to the President's office, only to be told that the White House switchboard was 'busy'.

Meanwhile in New York another of the defence lawyers asked Judge Kaufman to stay the executions because, if they were carried out at 11.00 p.m. they would occur during the Jewish Sabbath, which began at sunset. The judge refused, saying he had already spoken to the Attorney-General and had been assured that the executions would not take place on the Sabbath. In fact, the Attorney-General had already given directions to change the fatal hour to some time before sunset, due on that day at 8.31. The time had accordingly been changed to eight o'clock. Thus it would be the first time that anyone could remember an execution being carried out in daylight and it would also be the first time that a woman had been executed for a federal offence since Mrs Surratt had been put to death for her part in the assassination of President Lincoln. Meanwhile, the direct line connecting the prison with the Justice Department in Washington remained open in case either or both of the Rosenbergs should decide to 'talk.'

Soon after the US Marshal in charge of the executions had informed the Warden of the change of time, wooden barricades, manned by armed guards and state troopers, were hastily put up across all roads leading to Sing Sing. Meanwhile, the condemned couple were allowed to spend most of the afternoon together but they still had to converse through a mesh screen, although on this occasion it was placed at the entrance to Ethel's cell in the Women's Wing. By this time Manny Bloch should have had Julius's letter written the previous day. 'I have drawn up my last will and testament,' Julius wrote, 'so that there can be no question about the fact that I want you to handle all our affairs and be responsible for the children, as you have in fact been doing. Ethel completely concurs in this request and is in her hand attesting to it. Our children are the apple of our eye, our pride and most precious fortune. Love them with all your heart and always protect them in order that they may grow up to be normal healthy people. . . . *Never let them change the truth of our innocence.*'

While they were together Ethel also wrote to their lawyer enclosing a letter to be delivered to the children:

19 June 1953

Dearest Sweethearts, my most precious children,

Only this morning it looked like we might be together again after all. Now that this cannot be, I want so much for you to know all that I have come to know. Unfortunately I may write only a few simple words; the rest your own lives must teach you, even as mine taught me.

At first, of course, you will grieve bitterly for us, but you will not grieve alone. That is our consolation and it must eventually be yours.

Eventually, too, you must come to believe that life is worth the living. Be comforted that even now, with the end of ours slowly approaching, we know this with a conviction that defeats the executioner!

Your lives must teach you, too, that good cannot really flourish in the midst of evil; that freedom—and all the things that go to make up a truly satisfying and worthwhile life must sometimes be purchased very dearly. Be comforted, then, that we were serene and understood with the deepest kind of understanding, that civilization had not as yet progressed to the point where life did not have to be lost for the sake of life; and that we were comforted in the sure knowledge that others would carry on after us.

We wish we might have had the tremendous joy and gratification of living our lives out with you. Your Daddy, who is with me in these last momentous hours, sends his heart and all the love that is in it for his dearest boys. Always remember that we were innocent and could not wrong our conscience.

We press you close and kiss you with all our strength.
> Lovingly,
> Daddy and Mommy
> Julie, Ethel

P.S. to Manny—The Ten Commandments religious medal and chain —and my wedding ring—I wish you to present to our children as a token of our undying love.

At 7.20 p.m. the guards came for Julius and he bade farewell to his wife, by touching the tips of her fingers with his through the mesh screen. They were not permitted a final embrace. Julius was then taken to the special cell where the guards prepared him for electrocution, slitting one trouser leg and shaving the top of his head where the cathodes were to be affixed.

Meanwhile Ethel had just enough time to address a few lines of farewell to the faithful Manny Bloch:

Dearest person, you and M—* must see to my children. Tell him it was my last request of him. . . .

* The psychiatrist who had attended Ethel Rosenberg in prison.

All my heart I send to all who hold me dear—I am not alone—and I die 'with honour and with dignity'—knowing my husband and I must be vindicated by history. You will see to it that our names are kept unsullied by lies—as you did while we lived so whole heartedly, so unstintingly.

You did everything that could be done.

We are the first victims of American Fascism.

Love you, Ethel

Attached to this letter was a torn piece of paper on which she had scrawled a few more words, probably the last she ever wrote: 'I cry for myself as I lie dead—for shall they know all that burned my brain and breast. . . .'

At 7.32 p.m. the White House press secretary announced that the President had read the 'mercy' letter from Mrs Rosenberg, which her lawyer had left with the police guard at the entrance. The President was said to have felt that 'the letter added nothing to his opinion on the case, expressed earlier in the day.'

At precisely 8 o'clock Julius began the short walk along the corridor to the death chamber in Sing Sing prison. Ahead of him went a young rabbi intoning from the 23rd Psalm:

Yea, though I walk through the valley of the shadow of death, I will fear no evil; for thou art with me . . . Thou preparest a table before me in the presence of my enemies. . . . Thou anointest mine head with oil; my cup runneth over.

Julius knew that he was the first to go, since had it been otherwise Ethel would have passed his cell. The large death chamber was crowded when he entered, with more than forty reporters, prison officials and other witnesses, including the US Marshal standing by the wall ready to relay any last moment message on the open line to Washington.

It was 8.02 p.m. when they put Julius in the 'chair.' It took the guards less then a minute to strap him down, adjust the cathode to his leg and lower the helmet with another cathode to contact the shaven spot on his head. All the while he gazed calmly ahead with just the trace of a smile on his lips, and when a guard approached with the mask he gave no sign and did not utter a single word. When all was ready, the executioner, who was paid $15 for each electrocution, pressed the switch which sent a current of between 1800 and 2000 volts through Julius's body, the voltage being reduced to 500 after three or four seconds, raised again to high voltage and again lowered, the process taking about a minute before the contact was broken. Meanwhile a powerful stench of burning flesh, urine and defecation filled the room, and this had to be cleaned up with ammonia before the next victim was led in. At 8.06 p.m. Julius Rosenberg was officially pronounced dead. The body was then removed to an adjacent room for the customary autopsy.

A few minutes later the rabbi entered Ethel's cell with two matrons. 'Did it happen?' she asked.

'Yes, he is dead,' was the reply. She sat still, showing no emotion.

'Ethel,' the rabbi pleaded with her for the last time. 'For the sake of the children who need you, will you say something which can still save you? Must this tragedy be completed?'

'I have nothing to say,' said the condemned woman firmly. 'I am ready.' The matrons offered her their arms, but she passed them without a gesture and followed the rabbi into the corridor and past her husband's empty cell with its silent message. If the witnesses in the death chamber had any thoughts that the pull of her children would be so strong that she would recant at the last moment, they were disappointed. She smiled wistfully as they led her to the chair, a sort of Mona Lisa smile, one onlooker described it. Just before she reached the chair, she held out her hand to the prison matron who attended her. As the latter grasped it, the woman about to die drew the other close and kissed her lightly on the cheek. Like her husband she, too, uttered no word. Also she took longer to die. After the same amount of electricity had been passed through her body, the doctors in attendance approached with their stethoscopes and, according to one of the journalists present, were surprised to detect some signs of life. She was accordingly given two more currents of electricity which repeated 'the kind of a ghastly plume of smoke that ran from her head.' Finally, at 8.16 p.m., Ethel Rosenberg was likewise officially pronounced dead. As the *New York Times* reported, the Rosenbergs went to their deaths 'with a composure that astonished the witnesses.'

Three days after the execution, Mr Justice Felix Frankfurter made public his dissenting opinion in the Supreme Court, decrying the haste with which the final legal point had been disposed of. 'To be writing an opinion in a case affecting two lives after the curtain has been rung down upon them has the appearance of pathetic futility,' was his comment. 'But history also has its claims.'

[6]

The Rosenbergs' funeral was not free from discord, either domestic or public, as had marked their lives. The first part of the service took place in a funeral home in Brooklyn. Julius's mother and two sisters attended. But both the Greenglasses stayed away. Nor were the two Rosenberg boys present. Outside the home, a crowd of some thirty thousand milled around, some scuffles between opposing factions broke out, and the police had to intervene to restore order.

'I place the murder of the Rosenbergs at the door of President Eisenhower, Mr Brownell and J. Edgar Hoover,' said Emanuel Bloch, who delivered the principal address. Indeed he spoke under an obvious feeling of strong emotion, as he continued:

> They did not pull the switch, true, but they directed the one who did pull the switch. This was not the American tradition, not American justice and not American fair play. This was Nazism that killed the Rosenbergs and if we forget the lesson we will cringe, we'll live on our knees and we will be afraid. Insanity, irrationality, barbarism and murder seem to be a part of the feeling of those who rule us.

From Brooklyn two hearses and several hundred other private vehicles accompanied the remains to Wellwood Cemetery, Fine Lawn, near Farmingdale, Long Island. There they were interred. At the time of their deaths Julius was thirty-five and Ethel thirty-seven.

Less than eight months after the execution of the Rosenbergs and before his guardianship of the Rosenberg children Robert and Michael could be formalised, Emanuel Bloch died from a heart attack, aged fifty-two.

The children were eventually adopted by a family called Meeropol, Abel and his wife Anne, teachers in New York City, who had previously offered to provide a temporary home for them while their parents were in prison. Robert and Michael Rosenberg took the surname of their adoptive parents, although they continued to see and stay from time to time with their grandmother Mrs Sophie Rosenberg, Julius's mother. The two boys also became teachers, got married and settled in Springfield, Massachusetts, with their wives and children. As might be expected, both brothers have been associated with the National Committee to Reopen the Rosenberg Case, which was formed early in 1974 and organised a mass memorial meeting in the Carnegie Hall in New York on 19 June of the same year, being the twenty-fifth anniversary of the executions. All tickets were sold out and, in Robert Meeropol's words, 'the ardent enthusiasm of the audience indicated that we were doing the right thing.'

In this context Robert has also written with his brother in their book *We Are Your Sons* (1975):

> Reopening our parents' case does not constitute simply a personal or historical confrontation. Their legacy was the sure knowledge that we could only affirm our humanity by working with others to improve the quality of life. This wisdom provided our parents with the strength they needed to insist on the truth as they faced death, and this knowledge sustained us in overcoming the horrors of our childhood and building useful lives . . . So we reasoned that to reopen the case must shed light on and thus improve the current political situation of Americans. From past

mistakes we had learned that if we presume to institute basic changes in our government, we must unite with the people and illustrate for them the destructive nature of those who govern in their names. Obviously, Watergate is not an isolated instance of deception, it is a portrait of governmental abuse of power and manipulation of public opinion that owes much of its foundation to the showcase trials of the late 1940s and early 1950s—including the trial, conviction and execution of our parents.[14]

The subsequent history of the other characters in the Rosenberg trial may be briefly noted. David Greenglass was released in 1960, having served less than two-thirds of his fifteen-year sentence. After being reunited with his wife, he and she both changed their names and places of residence so as to preserve their anonymity. Eventually, after considerable negotiation with their lawyer John Rogge, they agreed to meet Stern and Radosh in Rogge's office. There they had a discussion lasting two and a half hours in the spring of 1979. Some of their admissions to Stern and Radosh have already been mentioned: they were incorporated in the article entitled 'The Hidden Rosenberg Case' by the journalist and the historian which appeared in *The New Republic* (23 June 1979).

Morton Sobell, after serving more than five years in the grim maximum security penitentiary on Alcatraz Island, was transferred to the more humane Atlanta penitentiary in Georgia. In 1961, a clemency plea to President John F. Kennedy was rejected, although it was signed by many prominent American citizens, including Harold Urey, Maxwell Geismar and the Rev. Martin Luther King. In 1962 Sobell became eligible for parole, but his application was likewise turned down. However, a few years later the Court of Appeals ruled that he had served enough of his sentence to be so released, and he was accordingly set at liberty conditionally. 'Congratulations,' Michael Meeropol telegraphed Sobell. 'Part of my parents is alive in you.' They eventually met in 1972. Meanwhile Sobell wrote an account of his experiences entitled *Doing Time* which appeared in 1974, and in which he proclaimed his belief in the Rosenbergs' innocence.

Harry Gold, who had been sentenced to a thirty-year term, was released on parole in 1965. He went back to Philadelphia, where he died on 28 August 1972, aged sixty. He is buried there beneath a grave headstone inscribed 'Beloved son and brother.' He had been awarded the Order of the Red Star by his Soviet masters for outstanding work on behalf of the USSR. One of the privileges to which this decoration entitled him was free bus rides in the city of Moscow. But, as J. Edgar Hoover put it, in complimenting the Bureau agents on tracking him down, it was a privilege which fate was never to allow him to enjoy.[15]

[7]

Many thinking Americans and others in recent years would seem to have an uneasy conscience over the execution of the Rosenbergs, just as an earlier generation between the wars did over the case of Sacco and Vanzetti who were fated to wait for six years, three years more than the Rosenbergs, before they too were eventually put to death, likewise protesting their innocence to the last. Opinions remain sharply divided as to the guilt of the parties in each case. But regardless of their innocence or guilt, they should all certainly have been reprieved, at least on humanitarian grounds. Only if the Rosenbergs had confessed to having spied for the Russians in the atomic fields, would their lives have been spared, and this, as we have seen, they steadfastly refused to do.

Occurring as the Rosenberg trial did during the Korean war and at a time of national hysteria against Communism sedulously propagated by the notorious Senator McCarthy and his henchmen, one of whom was a prosecutor in the trial, the scales of justice were weighted against Julius and Ethel Rosenberg from the outset. The Government's case against them was based almost exclusively on the testimony of admitted accomplices, there was the unedifying spectacle of a brother giving evidence against his sister, and the trial judge blamed the Rosenbergs for American deaths in the Korean war, an exordium endorsed by President Eisenhower who rejected the defendants' petition for clemency despite the fact that the imposition of the death sentence for espionage in peace time was wholly unprecedented in American criminal jurisprudence.

During the years following the Rosenbergs' deaths, their case has repeatedly formed the subject of newspaper and magazine articles, books, and plays and television 'documentaries.' With the exception of the work of Sol Stern and Ronald Radosh, already referred to, all these publications appeared before the passing of the Freedom of Information Act and the consequent release by the FBI of over 150,000 documents for research relating to the case. Hitherto the most detailed and thorough examination of the case in book form has come from Walter and Miriam Schneir in their *Invitation to an Inquest*, first published in 1965. Among other features, they were the first to make a complete examination of the photostat of Gold's hotel registration card in Albuquerque (3 June 1950) and to suggest that it might have been fabricated. Certainly the Government's return of the original card to the hotel in August 1951, where it was later destroyed, is difficult to explain. The Schneirs have also demonstrated beyond doubt that the testimony about the console table being used for photography with a hollowed-out portion for concealing microfilms was false.

In many of these publications Judge Kaufman and the FBI were singled out for attack, particularly by the Schneirs. Consequently, in 1957,

Attorney-General Brownell assigned a Justice Department official named Benjamin Pollack to make a secret study of the Rosenberg–Sobell case from the Government point of view. 'As you know,' Kaufman wrote to Brownell when he heard that this study had been commissioned, 'I have not uttered a word—as indeed I should not—in answer to these horribly concocted Communist charges concerning my conduct in the trial, although I must confess on occasions it was rather difficult to remain silent. Indeed I have observed that over the past year or so this propaganda has become intensified and it has been a frustrating experience to feel that no one was making a reply to these accusations hurled at American justice and that we are contenting ourselves with the belief that decent people would not believe them.'

> It has, therefore, come as a great relief to me to know that you have undertaken the difficult task of exposing these accusations . . . I hasten to commend you for undertaking this task, but I should have known that in doing so you were merely exhibiting those characteristics for which you have always been known—contempt for falsehood and a reverence for the truth.[16]

Pollack's study, which Kaufman described as 'a very thorough and scholarly job,' hardly fitted this description, since it only devoted three out of one hundred and seventy pages to the defendants' case. Nor, for some unexplained reason, was it released until 1973.

Judge Kaufman was also concerned about a play entitled *The United States vs Julius and Ethel Rosenberg* which was first produced in Cleveland, Ohio, where it ran for twelve weeks in 1969 before being transferred to Broadway in a rewritten version called *Inquest*. What particularly upset the judge was that the *New York Times* reviewed it on two successive Sundays. However, a judicial colleague, Judge Simon Rifkind defended him in a letter to this journal in which he paid a warm tribute to his fellow judge, emphasising Judge Kaufman's 'extremely fair handling of the Rosenberg case.' Judge Rifkind declared:

> The facts do not support the unwarranted aspersions by these critics on American justice as it was displayed in the Rosenberg case . . .
>
> I should hate to believe [the reviewer] Mr Novick's statement that it is part of the received tradition of liberals that the Rosenbergs were innocent. It would not do credit to their intelligence or judgment. Memory fades as the years roll by, but I am prepared to challenge the assertion that liberals generally held so misguided a view.

The result was that Judge Kaufman became the recipient of numerous anonymous communications. One of them, typed in red on a card and accompanied by a programme of *Inquest*, read: 'You are a fine Jew . . . I hope you and your family can sleep nights . . . May "God" have mercy on your lousy soul.'

The judge continued to be the object of popular animosity, especially following the showing of the television documentary *The Unquiet Death of Ethel and Julius Rosenberg* throughout the United States, and also by the BBC in England, as has already been mentioned. Finally, after the formation of the National Committee to Reopen the Rosenberg Case the judge informed the FBI that he was 'so alarmed by the publicity received by the above Committee' that he asked the Government to provide him with an official escort for his personal protection when he had to make a public speech.

Until recently, both Rosenbergs have been generally regarded as either guilty or innocent, the former view being taken by Judge Kaufman, the trial judge, Judge Rifkind, Judge Irving Saypol, Walter Pollack of the FBI and others on the Government side; those who regarded them as innocent or their guilt as being not proven have included a considerable array of defenders in print such as Harold Urey, Professor Einstein, and those who have written what might be regarded as convincing briefs for the defence such as John Wexley (*The Judgment of Julius and Ethel Rosenberg*), Professor Malcolm Sharp (*Was Justice Done?*), Walter and Miriam Schneir (*Invitation to an Inquest*) and Alvin H. Goldstein (*The Unquiet Death of Julius and Ethel Rosenberg*), as well, of course, as the story of the Rosenberg children Robert and Michael Meeropol (*We Are Your Sons*). There are and have been, therefore, two strongly opposing camps. Now the journalist Sol Stern and historian Ronald Radosh have advanced a theory which can hardly be acceptable to either camp. In their view Julius Rosenberg did spy for the Russians, but his wife Ethel was deliberately 'framed' by the FBI with the object of being used as a lever to induce her husband to make a complete confession implicating other individuals in the existing Soviet spy ring. 'The indications are definite,' according to a Bureau report on the day of Julius Rosenberg's arrest, 'that he possesses the identity of a number of other individuals who have engaged in Soviet espionage.'

In particular there is the testimony of Jerry Tartakow, which has already been quoted. When it was first released by the FBI, the Meeropol brothers stressed that the FBI considered this witness 'unreliable.' That is quite true, since the Bureau at first did officially describe Tartakow as 'an informer of unknown reliability.' But it is only fair to point out that, after several months, the FBI agents changed their minds after they had checked some of Tartakow's information. However, it is for the reader to make up his or her mind as to Tartakow's credibility. Certainly Julius Rosenberg trusted him, and when Tartakow was released Julius arranged for him to work for Emanuel Bloch, and among other activities Tartakow used to drive Bloch and the Rosenberg children to visit their parents in Sing Sing.

The new evidence obtained from the FBI files has led Stern and Radosh, in their own words, 'to the inescapable conclusion that Julius Rosenberg was indeed at the hub of an espionage network that continued to operate until his arrest in 1950. But not Ethel.' They quote a thirteen-page memorandum dated 17 June 1953, two days before the Rosenbergs, execution, giving a list of questions which the FBI agents who arrived secretly at Sing Sing in the early hours of the following morning, were to put to Julius in the death house cell if he agreed to co-operate with the Government. There was only one question in the whole list which concerned Ethel. It was: 'Was your wife cognizant of your activities?'

According to Stern and Radosh, the 17 June memorandum, which they revealed for the first time in their article in the *New Republic* in 1979, was 'only one of several FBI documents demonstrating that Ethel Rosenberg was included in the indictment only as a hostage against her husband; that she was ultimately convicted on tainted evidence obtained at the eleventh hour [from the Greenglasses]. The purpose was to pressure her husband into revealing the details of his post-war espionage work.'

It is certainly a most plausible theory. But no final judgment can be made until the FBI releases the remaining documents on the case which they are still holding. When, if ever, that will be, is anyone's guess. But it is unlikely to happen so long as David and Ruth Greenglass are still alive.

Epilogue

Summing up, the most dangerous and damaging of the atom bomb spies was undoubtedly Klaus Fuchs, followed in a lesser degree by Allan Nunn May, and to some extent by Donald Maclean. As for Bruno Pontecorvo, although he defected to Russia with his family, there is no hard evidence that he ever worked on the bomb and, on his recent visit to Rome to attend a scientific conference by permission of his Soviet masters, he expressly denied it.

During his interrogation by the FBI agents, Clegg and Lamphere, in Wormwood Scrubs prison on 26 May 1950, Fuchs drew a detailed sketch of the A-bomb, which he assured his interrogators was similar to that which he had given, with explanatory notes, to his Soviet contact, 'Raymond' (Harry Gold), in June 1945. This was reproduced in a letter summarising what Fuchs had told the FBI, and was sent to the members of the Atomic Energy Commission on 18 July 1950. When Stern and Radosh showed Mr Philip Morrison, one of the top physicists in the Manhattan project, the sketch, released with other FBI papers, he remarked: 'This is the real thing.' By contrast, it will be recalled, David Greenglass did not produce his sketch for the Russians until September 1945, and, although it made an impression on the jury when he testified at the Rosenberg–Sobell trial, it was in fact a pretty crude effort and of little value. Nor was Fuchs's sketch produced by the prosecution, although Gold was a government witness and testified that Fuchs had given him information about the atomic bomb lens moulds with an accompanying drawing. However, whether Julius Rosenberg was or was not a Soviet spy, his brother-in-law's evidence sealed his fate, while his wife Ethel preferred to keep silent and go along with her husband.

Nobody knows how many atomic bombs are now in existence. It has been estimated, however, that by the year 2000 there will be over one million of them in one form or another throughout the world. 'I am glad that I am not a young man,' David Lilienthal, the first head of the US Atomic Energy Commission has stated, 'and I am deeply sorry for my grandchildren.'

When the first atom bomb was dropped on Hiroshima, on 6 August 1945, President Truman described it as 'the greatest thing in history.' It killed 78,150 human beings, as well as many others who died from the after-effects. On the same day, Winston Churchill had this to say: 'This revelation of the secrets of nature, long mercifully withheld from man, should arouse the most solemn reflections in the mind and conscience of every human being capable of comprehension. We must indeed pray that these awful agencies will be made to conduce to peace among nations, and instead of wreaking measureless havoc upon the entire globe, they may become a perennial fountain of world prosperity.'

Today, atom bomb spies operate little. The Communist bloc powers and the West are so aware of each other's scientific capabilities that what is known in espionage jargon as 'alternative means' is quite sufficient to keep track of most of what each side needs to know about its opponent's scientific capabilities; technical journals, diplomatic contacts, deductions from non-secret information, and technical devices ranging from satellites to 'bugs' are more than adequate.

Nevertheless, the stories of the atom bomb spies, the risks they took, and the penalties they suffered when they were caught, are worth reading and rereading. The atom bomb is still with us. Neutron bombs and death rays are in development. Espionage, and the atmosphere that produced it, is not solely a thing of the past.

And it should never be forgotten, too, how the chain reaction of atomic espionage discovery, starting with Nunn May and ending with the Rosenbergs, began with the defection of an obscure cypher clerk named Gouzenko. 'I am only a small but happy pebble on the democratic beach,' wrote Gouzenko afterwards, 'but no one appreciates more the wonders of democratic citizenship than I do . . . Yet few who own free citizenship as a birthright seem to appreciate it fully.'

Sources and Notes

The following abbreviations are used:

FBI = Archives of the Federal Bureau of Investigation, Department of Justice, Washington, D.C.
MKD = Diaries of W. L. Mackenzie King in the Canadian National Archives, Ottawa.
PRO = Public Record Office, Kew, London.
RRC = Report of the Royal Commission, 27 June 1946. Ottawa, 1946.

Chapter One *The Defector*

1 Igor Gouzenko, *This Was My Choice*, p. 208 ff. RRC pp. 11–29.
2 Gouzenko, p. 248.
3 Gouzenko, p. 302 ff. Montgomery Hyde, *The Quiet Canadian*, pp. 229–35.
4 MKD, 6 Sept. 45 (1092–93).
5 *id* (1094–95).
6 RRC, p. 642 ff.
7 Information supplied by Sir William Stephenson. *See also* Montgomery Hyde *op cit.*
8 MKD, 7 Sept. 45 (1096).
9 *id* (1095).
10 Malcolm MacDonald, *People and Places*, pp. 182–3.
11 MKD, 7 Sept. 45 (1095–96).
12 *id* (1097).
13 MacDonald, p. 183.
14 RRC, p. 227 ff.
15 MKD, 8 Sept. 45 (1099).
16 RRC, 453.
17 MKD, 8 Sept. 45 (1099).
18 RRC, p. 645.
19 MKD, 9 Sept. 45 (1100).
20 MacDonald, p. 195. Information supplied by Rt. Hon. M. MacDonald.
21 RRC, p. 452.
22 *id* p. 450.
23 MKD, 10 Sept. 45 (1102–3).
24 MacDonald, p. 196.
25 MKD, 10 Sept. 45 (1100–1).
26 RRC, p. 453.
27 MKD, 10 Sept. 45 (1102, 1104–5).
28 MacDonald, p. 198.
29 MKD, 23 Sept. 45 (1106).
30 Montgomery Hyde, p. 234. This version was given to me by Sir William Stephenson. On the other hand, Norman Robertson's biographer Professor J. L. Granatstein informs me that 'Corby' got its name from the fact that the growing files were kept in a Corby whisky case by Robertson's private secretary. Apparently Robertson did not drink whisky, but no doubt his guests did. Hence I prefer Stephenson's version.

31 MKD, 24 Sept. 45 (1108–9).
32 *id*, 26 Sept. 45 (1110).
33 *id*, 1 Oct. 45 (1112–19).
34 *id*, 7 Oct. 45 (1122).
35 *id*, 7 Oct. 45 (1122).
36 *id*, 8 Oct. 45 (1123–25).
37 *id*, 10 Oct. 45 (1128).
38 *id*, 21 Oct. 45 (1138).
39 *id*, 22 Oct. 45 (1142–3).
40 *id*, 23 Oct. 45 (1145).
41 *id*, 31 Oct. 45 (1150–1).
42 Francis Williams, *A Prime Minister Remembers*, p. 118.
43 RRC, pp. 638–42.
44 Gouzenko, pp. 320–1; Montgomery Hyde, p. 234.
45 Communicated by the Rt. Hon. M. MacDonald.
46 MKD, cited J. W. Pickersgill and D. F. Forster, *The Mackenzie King Record*, III, p. 134.
47 MKD, cited Pickersgill and Forster, III, p. 133.
48 *id*, p. 134.
49 *id*, pp. 136–7.
50 *id*, pp. 139–41.
51 *id*, p. 143.
52 *id*, p. 144.

Chapter Two   *The Royal Commission*

1 Richard Hirsch, *The Soviet Spies*, pp. 127–8.
1 Montgomery Hyde, *British Air Policy Between The Wars*, p. 471.
3 Churchill to Kingsley Wood PRO: Air 19/26. Churchill, *The Second World War*, I, pp. 301–2.
4 Churchill, III, 730; IV, 339–42. J. W. Wheeler-Bennett, *John Anderson Viscount Waverley*, p. 287 ff.
5 Bickham Sweet-Escott, *Baker Street Irregular*, p. 114. Churchill, IV, p. 844 and note. *See also* Knut Haukleid, *Skis against the Atom* (London, 1944), *passim*.
6 Information supplied by Sir William Stephenson.
7 Churchill, VI, p. 552–4.
8 James F. Byrnes, *Speaking Frankly*, p. 263.
9 MKD, cited Pickersgill and Forster, II, p. 147. Sentence at end of first paragraph added from Ms.
10 Alan Moorehead, *The Traitors*, pp. 36–39. Leonard Burt, *Commander Burt of Scotland Yard*, pp. 33–41.
11 MKD, cited Pickersgill and Forster, III, p. 149.
12 RRC, p. 693.
13 MKD, cited Pickersgill and Forster, III, p. 151.
14 Moorehead, p. 39.
15 *id*, p. 48.
16 *id*, pp. 43–47.
17 RRC, p. 123 ff.
18 *id*, pp. 447 ff.
19 *id*, p. 697.
20 *id*, p. 705.
21 MKD, cited Pickersgill and Forster, III, pp. 157–8.
22 RRC, pp. 255, 499–500.
23 *id*, p. 111 ff.
24 *id*, p. 375 ff, 481 ff.
25 *The Report of the Royal Commission appointed under Order in Council P.C. 411 of 5 February 1946 to investigate the facts relating to and the circumstances surrounding the communication by*

public officials and other persons in positions of trust of secret and confidential information to agents of a foreign power. Ottawa, 1946.

26 MKD, cited Pickersgill and Forster, p. 281.
27 RRC, pp. 11–14.
28 MKD, cited Pickersgill and Forster, IV, pp. 293.
29 RRC, p. 19 ff.
30 *id*, p. 648.
31 MKD, cited Pickersgill and Forster, III, pp. 282–3.
32 Gouzenko, p. 323. Private information.
33 Communicated by Richard Deacon.
34 Clutterbuck to Addison 22 August 1945. PRO: DO 35/1207/X/No 305.
35 Clutterbuck to Addison 22 November 1945. PRO: DO35/1207/K/No 3045.
36 MKD, cited Pickersgill and Forster, IV, p. 293.
37 Moorehead, p. 58 ff.
38 *id*, p. 86.
39 General Leslie Groves.
40 J. Edgar Hoover, 'The Crime of the Century,' *Reader's Digest* June 1951, pp. 113–48.
41 Moorehead, p. 98.
42 *id*, p. 105.

Chapter Three   *Klaus Fuchs and Bruno Pontecorvo*

1 Moorehead, *The Traitors*, pp. 106–13.
2 Margaret Gowing, *Independence and Deterrence. Britain and Atomic Energy*, II, p. 144.
3 Moorehead, p. 113.
4 FBI.
5 Moorehead, p. 117.
6 *id*, p. 119.
7 Kim Philby, *My Silent War*, p. 125.
8 Communicated by Sir Michael Perrin.
9 Moorehead, pp. 129–30.
10 *id*, pp. 132–41.
11 *id*, pp. 142–49.
12 Details of Fuchs's interrogation communicated by Sir Michael Perrin.
13 Moorehead, pp. 149–50. Burt, pp. 46–58.
14 Philby, pp. 125–6. Philby mistakenly refers to Lish Whitson as Lishman.
15 Moorehead, pp. 151–59.
16 *id*, p. 204.
17 FBI.
18 FBI: Report (53 pp) of Hugh Clegg and Robert Lamphere to Director, 4 June 1950. Interviews with Fuchs took place on May 20, 22, 23, 24, 25, 26, 27, 30, 31, June 1, 2. A shorter report (41 pp) was prepared by Joseph C. Welsh, an agent in the New York office.
19 Moorehead, pp. 166–67.
20 West, *The Meaning of Treason* (1965), p. 314.
21 Communicated by Sir Michael Perrin from Canadian Broadcasting Company's tape.
22 Francis Williams, pp. 118–19.
23 *The Times*, 2 Jan 1960.
24 The following account of Pontecorvo is largely based on an anonymous article ('*Il Dottore Jekyll e il "Tovarich" Maksimovic*') in the Italian magazine *Il Borghese*, 17 September 1978, pp. 157–64; also Moorehead, *op. cit*, pp. 170–200.
25 RRC, p. 118.

Chapter IV   On To The Rosenbergs

1 Walter Goodman, *The Committee*, p. 226 ff. *See also* Robert Carr, *The House Committee on Un-American Activities, passim.*
2 Goodman, p. 274.

3 *id*, pp. 279–81.
4 Walter and Miriam Schneir, *Invitation to an Inquest*, p. 90 ff.
5 *id*, p. 115.
6 *id*, p. 117.
7 FBI, Julius Rosenberg Papers, Section 5.
8 FBI, Memo of 21 June 1950.
9 *The New Republic*, 23 June 1979.
10 FBI, Report to Director from New York Office of Bureau.
11 *The New Republic*, 23 June 1979, p. 21.
12 Schneir, p. 119 ff. Wexley, Pilat, *passim*.
13 Pilat, *The Atom Spies*, p. 287. According to an FBI report dated 14 December 1951, Pilat, who also worked for the *New York Post*, informed the Bureau that he was going to write a book on 'various aspects of the so-called atom spies' and he asked the Bureau a number of relevant questions in his quest for information. However, the Bureau was uncommunicative and informed Pilat that it could not help, either approving or disapproving of his project. 'With regard to Julius Rosenberg, Pilat advised that Elizabeth Bentley had stated she had talked to Rosenberg on the telephone at Knickerbocker Village. Pilat wondered why the FBI didn't get to Rosenberg till 3 years later, as it seemed it would have been a simple matter for the Bureau to have merely gone to Knickerbocker Village and called all residents there to identify him.' FBI: Harry Gold file 31 serial 811.
14 FBI, Rosenberg file 2498–1.
15 FBI, Rosenberg file 17 serial 906.

Chapter Five *Were They Guilty?*

1 Schneir, p. 170 ff.
2 Pilat, pp. 290–91.
3 Rosenberg, *The Rosenberg Letters*, p. 21. Meeropol, *The Legacy of Ethel and Julius Rosenberg*, pp. 43–4. At Michael Meeropol's request I have taken the text of the so-called Death House letters from *The Legacy of Ethel and Julius Rosenberg* as being fuller and more accurate than that originally published in *The Rosenberg Letters*. Ethel and Julius Rosenberg agreed to the latter publication both to aid their cause and later to raise funds for their two children. The authenticity of the originals, consisting of nearly 400 letters and aggregating about 900 handwritten pages, has sometimes been doubted, but it is beyond dispute. The originals were formerly in the possession of the Rosenbergs' attorney Emanuel Bloch and later of his assistant Gloria Agrin: Schneir, p. 213. The suggestion that the Death House letters had been ghost-written was first publicly put forward by the journalist Leonard Lyons in his syndicated newspaper column. In fact, the *National Guardian*, which had published many of the letters, had taken them either from the originals supplied by Bloch, or from photostats of their handwriting: Belfrage and Aronson, *Something to Guard*, p. 174.
4 Belfrage and Aronson, p. 131 ff.
5 Schneir, pp. 177–8.
6 *id*, pp. 179, 228.
7 Meeropol, pp. 174–5.
8 Schneir, p. 193.
9 Rosenberg, pp. 152–65.
10 Schneir, p. 196 ff.
11 Sharp, *op cit.* p. 17.
12 Schneir, p. 212.
13 According to the *Washington Post*, during 1953 the White House received about 200,000 messages on the case—most of them urging clemency—with 21,500 telegrams alone arriving between June 16 and 21.
14 Meeropol, pp. 342–3.
15 Hoover, p. 148.
16 FBI, 15 October 1957. Published with other material from the FBI archives in *The Kaufman Papers* by the National Committee to Reopen the Rosenberg Case, New York, 1976.

Select Bibliography

Unpublished manuscript sources which have been used in the Canadian National Archives in Ottawa, the Federal Bureau of Investigation Papers in the Department of Justice, Washington, DC, and the Air Ministry and Commonwealth Office files in the Public Record Office in Kew, London, are noted above in the Sources and Notes.

The following printed sources have been consulted:

Belfrage, Cedric, and Aronson, James, *Something to Guard. The Stormy Life of the National Guardian 1948–1967*, Columbia University Press, 1978.

Biorkland, Elis, *International Atomic Policy 1945–55*, Allen & Unwin, 1956.

Blackett, P. M. S., *Military and Political Consequences of Atomic Energy*, Turnstile Press, 1948.

——*Atomic Weapons and East–West Relations*, Cambridge University Press, 1956.

Boyle, Andrew, *The Climate of Treason*, Hutchinson, 1979.

Bulloch, John, *Akin to Treason*, Arthur Barker, 1956.

Burt, Leonard, *Commander Burt of Scotland Yard*, Heinemann, 1959.

Carr, Robert K, *The House Committee on Un-American Activities*, Cornell University Press, 1952.

Clark, Ronald W., *The Birth of the Bomb*, Phoenix House, 1961.

Compton, A. H., *Atomic Quest*, Oxford University Press, 1956.

Cookridge, E. H., *Soviet Spy Net*, Frederick Muller, 1955.

Deacon, Richard, *A History of the Russian Secret Service*, Frederick Muller, 1972.

——*The British Connection. Russia's Manipulation of British Individuals and Institutions*, Hamish Hamilton, 1979.

Fineberg, S. A., *The Rosenberg Case: Fact and Fiction*, Oceana Publications, 1953.

Goldstein, Alvin H,., *The Unquiet Death of Julius and Ethel Rosenberg*, Lawrence Hill, 1975.

Goodman, Walter, *The Committee. The House Committee on Un-American Activities*, Secker & Warburg, 1968.

Gouzenko, Igor, *This Was My Choice*, Eyre & Spottiswoode, 1948.

Gowing, Margaret, *Britain and Atomic Energy 1939–1945*, Macmillan, 1964.

——*Independence and Deterrence. Britain and Atomic Energy 1945–1952*, 2 vols., Macmillan, 1974.

Groves, Leslie A., *Now It Can Be Told, The Story of the Manhattan Project*, André Deutsch, 1963.

Hirsch, Richard, *The Soviet Spies. The Story of Russian Espionage in North America*, Nicholas Kaye, 1948.

Hoover, J. Edgar, 'The Crime of the Century. The Case of the A-Bomb Spies', *Reader's Digest*, New York and London, June 1951.

Hyde, H. Montgomery, *The Quiet Canadian. The Secret Service Story of Sir William Stephenson*. London: Hamish Hamilton, 1962. Published in the US as *Room 3603*, Farrar, Straus, 1963.

Jordan, George Racey, and Stokes, Richard L., *From Major Jordan's Diaries*, Harcourt, Brace, 1952.

MacDonald, Malcolm, *People and Places. Random Reminiscences*, Collins, 1969.

Martin, David C., *Wilderness of Mirrors*, New York: Harper & Row, 1980.

Medvedev, Zhores, *Soviet Science*, Oxford University Press, 1979.

Meeropol, Robert and Michael, *We Are Your Sons. The Legacy of Ethel and Julius Rosenberg*, Houghton Mifflin, 1975.

Modelski, George A., *Atomic Energy in the Communist Bloc*, Melbourne University Press, 1959.

Moorehead, Alan, *The Traitors. The Double Life of Fuchs, Pontecovco and Nunn May*, Hamish Hamilton, 1952.

Newman, Bernard. *The Red Spider's Web. The Story of Russian Spying in Canada*, Latimer House, 1947.

Philby, Kim, *My Silent War*, MacGibbon and Kee, 1968.

Pickersgill, J. W. and Forster, D. F., *The Mackenzie King Record*. Vols III and IV, University of Toronto Press, 1970.

Pilat, Oliver, *The Atom Spies*, W. H. Allen, 1954.

Radosh. *See under* Stern.

Rosenberg, Julius and Ethel, *The Rosenberg Letters*, Denis Dobson, 1953.

Royal Commission. *Report of the Royal Commission appointed to Investigate the Facts relating to and the Circumstances Surrounding the Communication by Public Officials and other Persons in Positions of Trust of secret and confidential Information to Agents of a Foreign Power*. Ottawa: H. M. Controller of Stationery, 1946.

Schneir, Walter and Miriam, *Invitation to an Inquest*, W. H. Allen, 1966.

Sharp, Malcolm P., *Was Justice Done? The Rosenberg–Sobell Case*, New York, Monthly Review Press, 1956.

Stern, Sol, and Radosh, Ronald, *The Hidden Rosenberg Case* in *The New Republic*, New York, 23 June 1959.

Teller, Edward, and Brown, Allen, *The Legacy of Hiroshima*, Macmillan, 1962.

Truman, Harry S., *Year of Decision 1945*, Hodder & Stoughton, 1955.

——*Years of Trial and Hope 1946–1953*, Hodder & Stoughton, 1956.

West, Rebecca, *The Meaning of Treason*, Macmillan, 1949; Penguin Books, 1965.

Wexley, John, *The Judgment of Ethel and Julius Rosenberg*, New York: Cameron & Kahn, 1955. London: Sackville, 1956.

Williams, Francis, *A Prime Minister Remembers. The War and Post-War Memoirs of Earl Attlee*, Heinemann, 1961.

Index